Hideaways

Hideaways

Die schönsten Hotels und Destinationen der Welt

The World's most beautiful Hotels and Destinations

Band 7

Klocke Verlag

LEGENDEN DER LUXUSHOTELLERIE

Der siebte Bildband unserer beliebten HIDEAWAYS-Buchreihe versammelt wieder einen Reigen exklusiver Traumhotels wie Perlen auf einer Schnur. Unsere Weltreise für Genießer beginnt dieses Mal mit zwei absoluten Legenden der Luxushotellerie, mit dem Peninsula in Hongkong und dem Oriental in Bangkok. Seit seiner Eröffnung im Jahre 1928 genießt das Peninsula den Ruf, eine der allerersten Hoteladressen der Welt zu sein. Auf eine noch größere Tradition kann das Oriental in Bangkok zurückblicken, das im vergangenen Jahr seinen 125. Geburtstag feiern konnte und bereits mehr als ein Dutzend Mal zum besten Hotel der Welt gekürt wurde. Seit über einem Jahrhundert wählen es gekrönte Häupter, Staatsmänner und Würdenträger, Künstler und Prominente aus allen Bereichen als ihr Domizil in der thailändischen Metropole. Nach diesen beiden City-Refugien setzen wir unsere Reise zu den atemberaubenden Stränden der Seychellen, nach Mauritius und den Malediven fort. Eine außergewöhnliche Kollektion der feinsten Adressen Südafrikas zeigt Ihnen die ganze Vielseitigkeit dieses faszinierenden Landes. Geheimtipps in Griechenland, auf Sardinien und Mallorca stellen unter Beweis, dass man nicht immer in die Ferne schweifen muss, um das Besondere zu finden. Und auch in Deutschland und Österreich gibt es Juwelen der First-Class-Hotellerie, die durch stilvolle Architektur, verbindlichen Service und eine sprichwörtlich gute Küche jeden Aufenthalt zum Erlebnis machen. Ein Klassiker der Karibik, einer der schönsten nostalgischen Großsegler, der mit Top-Komfort und höchstem Luxus auf den sieben Weltmeeren unterwegs ist, sowie die exklusivsten Villen, die man auf Mustique mieten kann, machen dieses Buch wieder zu einer Pflichtlektüre für Connaisseure.

The seventh Hideaways coffee table book presents yet another selection of exclusive dream hotels like a string of pearls. Our world tour for the connoisseur begins in two absolute legends of luxury hotels – the Peninsula Hong Kong and the Oriental Bangkok. Ever since it opened in 1928, the Peninsula has enjoyed the reputation of being one of the world's most exclusive hotels. The Oriental Bangkok can look back on an even longer tradition and last year celebrated its 125th anniversary. It has been voted the best hotel in the world over a dozen times. For over a century crowned heads, statesmen and dignitaries, artists and VIPs from every sphere have chosen to reside at the hotel when they are staying in the Thai capital. Following these great city hideaways, we resume our journey and move on to the breathtaking beaches of the Seychelles, Mauritius and the Maldives. An exceptional choice of the very finest addresses in South Africa open up the whole wealth and diversity of this fascinating country. Our secret tips in Greece, Sardinia and Majorca illustrate that one does always not have to travel to far distant lands to find that very special Something. There are gems to be found in Germany and Austria too, first class luxury hotels whose architectural style, obliging service and superb cuisine make every stay an experience. A classic of the Caribbean, one of the most beautiful and nostalgic ships sailing the Seven Seas, which is equipped with the ultimate in comfort and the highest level of luxury, and the most exclusive villas for rent on Mustique make this volume once again obligatory reading for connoisseurs.

Thomas und Martina Klocke
HERAUSGEBER / PUBLISHER

Hideaways
Die schönsten Hotels und Destinationen der Welt
Band 7

Klocke Verlag GmbH
Höfeweg 40, 33619 Bielefeld, Telefon: 05 21 / 9 11 11-0, Telefax: 05 21 / 9 11 11 12
Internet: www.klocke-verlag.de, E-Mail: info@klocke-verlag.de
1. Auflage 2003

Nachdruck, auch auszugsweise, nur mit Genehmigung des Verlages.
Alle Rechte vorbehalten, insbesondere die der Übersetzung, Vervielfältigung,
Übertragung durch Bild- oder Tonträger, Mikroverfilmungen oder Übernahme in Datensysteme.

Fotos:
Ydo Sol, Klaus Lorke, Jürgen Gutowski, Martina Gutowski, Ulrich Helweg, Freddy Peterburs,
Stefan Fister, Christian Prager

Texte:
Thomas Klocke, Günter Ned, Jürgen Gutowski, Gundula Luig, Sabine Herder, Bernd Teichgräber

Grafische Gestaltung:
Sabina Winkelnkemper, Thomas Kacza, Sabine Flöter, Gábor Wallrabenstein

Lithographie:
Klocke Medienservice: Holger Schönfeld, Werner Busch

Produktion: Claudia Schwarz, Nicole Leermakers

Vertrieb: Stephan Klocke

Druck:
Oldenbourg Buchmanufaktur GmbH, Mannheim

Printed in Germany

ISBN-Nr. 3-934 170-24-2

Inhalt

China / Hongkong

12

The Peninsula Hong Kong

Thailand

24

The Oriental Bangkok

Seychellen

34

Banyan Tree

44

Sainte Anne Resort

Malediven

54

Soneva Gili

62

Rangali Island

Mauritius

70

The Oberoi, Mauritius

Südafrika

80

Kurland Country Hotel

88

The Collection by Liz McGrath

Dubai

98

One&Only Royal Mirage

Thailand

106

The Royal Coco Palm

Griechenland

114

Elounda Mare Hotel

122

Porto Elounda de Luxe

130

Mykonos Blu

ITALIEN

138

Hotel Romazzino

SPANIEN

148

Son Net

DEUTSCHLAND

156

Burg Schlitz

166

Fährhaus Munkmarsch

ÖSTERREICH

176

Thurnhers Alpenhof

184

Schloss Seefels

BARBADOS

192

Sandy Lane

MUSTIQUE

200

Mustique Villen

KREUZFAHRTEN

208

Sea Cloud

INDONESIEN

216

Pita Maha

THE PENINSULA HONGKONG

THE GRAND OLD LADY OF HONG KONG

Durch seine kultivierte Gastfreundschaft, seinen Charme und unvergleichlichen Service genießt das Peninsula seit seiner Eröffnung im Jahre 1928 weltweit den Ruf einer Hotellegende. 1994 erhielt die Grand Old Lady für eine Investitionssumme von 120 Millionen US-Dollar einen 30 Etagen hohen, architektonisch außergewöhnlichen Turm, der eine harmonische Symbiose zwischen Tradition und Moderne herstellt. Durch seine prädestinierte Lage in Kowloon liegt den Gästen der neuen Harbour View Suiten das faszinierende Lichtermeer der Skyline von Central zu Füßen. Die Peninsula Suite gehört zu den spektakulärsten in Hongkong und den luxuriösesten weltweit.

Ever since it opened in 1928 the Peninsula, a hotel legend, has earnt a reputation for charm, incomparable service, and sophisticated hospitality. In 1994 a tower 30 storeys high was added to the Grand Old Lady at a cost of 120 million US dollars. Remarkable in its architecture, the tower is an harmonious symbiosis between tradition and modernity. Owing to its location in Kowloon, guests in the new Harbour View Suites have at their feet the fascinating expanse of lights that forms the skyline of Central. The Peninsula Suite is without doubt one of the most spectacular suites in Hong Kong and one of the most luxurious in the world.

Text: Thomas Klocke · Fotos: Klaus Lorke

*Stilvoller Empfang:
Welcome to the Peninsula!*
**Stylish reception –
welcome to the Peninsula!**

Following the official ceremony on the 30 June 1997 marking the departure of Chris Patten, the last Governor of Hong Kong, after ninety-nine years of British rule, the Crown Colony was formally handed back to the President of China, Jiang Zemin. Many thought this would spell the end of the prosperous city in the South China Sea. In 1841 during the first Opium War between Britain and China, Hong Kong was seized by Captain Charles Elliott RN. After further clashes the Kowloon Peninsula and Stonecutter's Island were finally ceded to the British. The legendary 99-year lease was agreed in 1898 to secure the water supply. Many assumed that the handover would result in huge changes, but it appears they have not been quite so radical as expected. Obviously pillar-boxes are no longer red and English is in decline, but by and large the city of Hong Kong has retained its old fascination.

Whereas in the old days approaching Hong Kong by air to land on the narrowest of landing strips in the centre of town always used to be hazardous, bringing even the most experienced pilot out in a cold sweat, the new Chep Lap Kok Airport is up-to-date in every respect. To get to the Peninsula Hotel you can choose between a five-minute flight by helicopter which lands directly on the roof of the hotel, or take your place on a Connolly leather seat in one of the many classic brewster green Rolls-Royce Silver Spur IIIs from the car pool. How wonderful to take a refreshing cloth out of the ice box then be able to stretch your legs in the electronically adjustable seat. Welcome to Hong Kong, an arrival could not be more stylish.

The Peninsula is located in Tsim Sha Sui, the heart of the business, shopping and entertainment district on the Kowloon Peninsula. The underground Mass Transit Railway is only a minute away, and the journey to Central, the business quarter on Hong Kong Island, only takes ten minutes. If you can spare the time and want to view the skyline, take the Star Ferry which is used daily by many Hong Kong Chinese. Its jetty is also very close, only two minutes away from the hotel.

The Peninsula's new tower extension has not only doubled the room capacity but also created new suites with spectacular views of the harbour and city. Additional new facilities at this legendary hotel include a swimming pool

Nachdem am 30. Juni 1997 in einer feierlichen Zeremonie der letzte Gouverneur Chris Patten nach 99-jähriger britischer Herrschaft die Kronkolonie an den chinesischen Staatspräsidenten Jiang Zemin zurückgab, mutmaßten viele Zeitgenossen, dass hiermit die Blütezeit der prosperierenden Metropole am Südchinesischen Meer ebenfalls beendet würde. 1841 hatten die Engländer während des ersten Opiumkrieges zwischen China und Großbritannien durch Marinekapitän Charles Elliot Besitz von Hong Kong Island ergriffen. Nach weiteren Auseinandersetzungen wurden schließlich die Halbinsel Kowloon und Stonecutter's Island an Großbritannien abgetreten. Um die Wasserversorgung zu sichern, schloss man 1898 den legendären 99-Jahre-Pachtvertrag. Hatten viele gemutmaßt, dass es nach dem *Hand-over* zu massiven Veränderungen kommen würde, muss man heute feststellen, dass diese gar nicht so rigoros waren. Sicherlich sind die Briefkästen nicht mehr rot lackiert und die englische Sprache ist rückläufig, aber im Großen und Ganzen ist Hongkong die faszinierende Metropole geblieben, die sie immer war.

War der Anflug früher auf Hongkong mitten durch die Stadt auf die äußerst knapp bemessene Landebahn, die selbst den erfahrendsten Piloten feuchte Hände bereitete, mehr als abenteuerlich, so präsentiert sich der neue Flughafen Chek Lap Kok in allen Belangen modern und zeitgemäß. Um zum Peninsula Hotel zu gelangen, wählt man entweder den fünfminütigen Flug per Helikopter, der direkt auf dem Dach des Hotels landet, oder man nimmt im connollyledergepolsterten Fond eines der zahlreichen Rolls-Royce Silver Spurs III Platz, die im klassischen „Brewster Green" lackiert sind. Erst einmal ein kühlendes Erfrischungstuch aus dem Eisfach nehmen, die Beine im elektronisch verstellbaren Sitz strecken – *welcome to Hong Kong!* Stilvoller kann eine Ankunft nicht sein.

Das Peninsula liegt im Herzen des Geschäfts-, Shopping- und Unterhaltungsbezirkes Tsimshatsui auf der Halbinsel Kowloon. Die Untergrundbahn Mass Transit Railway ist zu Fuß in einer Minute zu erreichen, keine zehn Minuten dauert die Fahrt nach Central, dem Businessviertel auf Hongkong Island. Wer ein wenig mehr Zeit hat und gleichzeitig Ausblicke auf die Skyline genießen will, der wählt The Star Ferry, die auch von vielen Hongkong-Chinesen ganz alltäglich benutzte Fähre, deren Anleger sich ebenfalls nur zwei Minuten vom Peninsula

entfernt befindet. Der neue Turmanbau des Peninsula verdoppelte nicht nur die Zimmerkapazität, sondern schuf vor allem neue Suiten mit spektakulärem Hafen- und Stadtblick und ergänzte die Hotellegende um Einrichtungen wie einen Swimmingpool mit Sonnenterrasse, das Peninsula Spa, Business-Center, Bankett- und Konferenzräume und – *on the top*, in der 28. und 29. Etage, mit weitem Blick über Hongkong – das von dem französischen Designerstar Philippe Starck eingerichtete Restaurant Felix. Dieses aus Holz, Metall und Glas gestaltete einmalige Ambiente bringt eine neue, avantgardistische Dimension in das traditionsreiche Peninsula, das in diesem seinen 75. Geburtstag feiert.

Britische Wohnkultur mit modernster Hightech

Home away from home, anders kann man die insgesamt 246 Zimmer und 54 Suiten nicht bezeichnen. 141 Superior-, Deluxe- und Harbour-View-Räume, die berühmte Marco-Polo-Suite, 26 Grand-Deluxe- und Junior-Suiten liegen im Hauptgebäude. Dass die Zimmer über jeglichen modernen Komfort verfügen, braucht eigentlich nicht extra erwähnt zu werden. Hier jedoch einige zusätzliche Schmankerln: jeder Gast erhält während seines Aufenthaltes persönliche Fax-Durchwahlnummern, unter jedem Telefon befindet sich eine elektronische Weltzeituhr, die die Uhrzeit der wichtigsten Metropolen anzeigt, insgesamt gewährleisten drei ISDN-Telefone im Zimmer und zwei im Bad ständige Erreichbarkeit. Neben der Tür liest man von einer Digitalanzeige die aktuelle Außentemperatur und Luftfeuchtigkeit ab (die in den Sommermonaten schon einmal auf 90 Prozent Luftfeuchtigkeit vorbereitet), die Stromspannung ist umschaltbar, Vorhänge, TV, Radio, Klimaanlage sind alle durch integrierte Fernsteuerung in der Bettkonsole zu bedienen; hier befindet sich auch der Service-Rufknopf, falls man sich die gesamten technischen Kabinettstückchen doch lieber noch einmal erklären lassen möchte. Der neue Turm beherbergt 105 Kowloon View und Deluxe Harbour View Rooms, 26 Executive-, Deluxe- und Grand Deluxe Harbour View Suiten sowie die Duplex Peninsula Suite, die aus schwindelnder Höhe im 25. und 26. Stockwerk atemberaubende Aussichten bietet. Waren die Suiten im Hauptgebäude aufgrund ihrer luxuriösen Interieurs schon immer legendär, so offeriert das Peninsula seinen Suitengästen im Turm jetzt with a sun terrace, the Peninsula Spa, the business centre, banqueting and conference rooms and, right at the top on the 28th and 29th floor overlooking Hong Kong, the Felix Restaurant designed and furnished by the famous French designer, Philippe Starck. Its unique ambience created from wood, metal, and glass introduces a new avant-garde dimension to the Peninsula. This hotel so rich in tradition, celebrates its 75th anniversary this year.

British life style with the latest hi-tech

A home from home, there is no other way of describing the 246 rooms and 54 suites. 141 Superior, Deluxe and Harbour View rooms, the famous Marco Polo Suite and 26 Grand Deluxe and Junior Suites are housed in the main building. It goes without saying that the rooms have every conceivable luxury, but they do have an additional facility worth mentioning. Every guest is allotted personal direct fax numbers, and beneath each telephone is an electronic world clock showing the times in the most important cities of the world. The guest can therefore be contacted at all times on the three phones in the rooms and the two extensions in the bathroom. Beside the door is a digital display indicating the temperature and humidity outside which in the summer months often rises to 90 %. The voltage is convertible and curtains, TV, radio and air-conditioning can all be individually controlled from a bedside console which also has the room service button, in case one needs to have the whole technical paraphernalia explained once more.

The new tower houses 105 Kowloon View and Deluxe Harbour View rooms, 26 Executive, Deluxe, Grand Deluxe and Harbour View Suites, plus the Duplex Peninsula Suite which, at the giddy height of the 25th and 26th floor, affords breathtaking views. Whereas the suites in the main building became legendary for their luxurious interiors, the Peninsula tower now provides its suite guests with an additional perspective – that of the birds of the air. The Deluxe and Grand Deluxe suites have magnificent views both from the living room and from the bathroom. The suites occupy both corners of the tower and have floor to ceiling picture windows on two sides, so guests have a beautiful scene spread out below them - the ocean of lights of Kowloon and Hong Kong Kong Island.

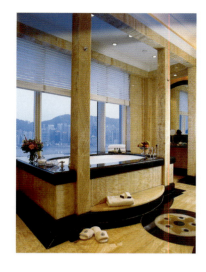

Seidentapeten und chinesische Antiquitäten setzen die Akzente.
Silk wallpaper and Chinese antiques set the tone.

Die Fernbedienung auf der Bettkonsole regelt alle wichtigen Funktionen.
The remote control console beside the bed regulates all important functions.

The Peninsula Suite is without doubt one on the most spectacular suites in Hong Kong and one of the most luxurious in the world. The floor area of 4,058 sq. ft is divided up into a bedroom with an adjacent bathroom and fully equipped gym, private study, a cosy dining area, a fully equipped kitchen, a large living room, a formal dining room and a conference room with video-conferencing facilities. Obviously it has an entrance hall and an area for security and the (24-hour) butler service. The huge floor to ceiling picture windows and the balcony overlook unforgettable views of Victoria Harbour and Hong Kong Island. The Venetian stucco work on the walls of the living room and bathroom, the silk wallpaper in the bedroom, the Chinese antiques and works of art and the deep pile carpets into which one sinks are the ultimate in luxury. You have your own steam bath in the shower, and the television in front of the bath and the mini-TV beside the shaving mirror provide information junkies with all they need.

Yet, who would want to watch telly here when one can never get enough of the view of the incredible skyline. There is a grand piano to provide live piano accompaniment during dinner, and through the enormous Bausch & Lomb telescope you can make discoveries of your own. A Rolls-Royce plus chauffeur is on permanent standby, and a separate lift connects the suite directly with the helicopter lounge and the Felix Restaurant. On request the Peninsula Suite can be converted into a two-bedroom suite or one with up to seven bedrooms by utilizing the adjacent room on the same floor. Finally it is worth mentioning that the security measures of the Peninsula comply with the stringent conditions of the American CIA and the British MI5.

Dining Experiences: From abalones and fusion cuisine to Kobe beef

The gastronomic range on offer at the Peninsula is as varied as the scope of its accommodation. All in all, there are seven different annexes which fulfil every desire of the globetrotter and the pampered bon vivant. The above-mentioned restaurant, the ultra-trendy Felix designed by Philippe Starck, is the hip place to be. The ultimate embodiment of contemporary

zusätzliche Perspektiven, und zwar Vogelperspektiven: Die Deluxe und Grand Deluxe Harbour View Suiten zum Beispiel erlauben grandiose Ausblicke sowohl aus dem Wohn- als auch aus dem Badezimmer. Die Suiten liegen in beiden Ecken des Turms und haben an zwei Seiten „Glaswände" vom Boden bis zur Decke. Die ganze Schönheit des Lichtermeeres von Kowloon, von Hongkong Island liegt den Gästen sprichwörtlich zu Füßen.

Die Peninsula Suite gehört zweifellos zu den spektakulärsten Suiten in Hongkong und den luxuriösesten weltweit. Auf einer opulenten Wohnfläche von 370 Quadratmetern verteilen sich ein Schlafzimmer mit angrenzendem Bad und voll ausgestattetem Fitnessraum, ein privates Arbeitszimmer, ein intimes Esszimmer, eine komplett eingerichtete Küche, ein großzügiges Wohnzimmer, ein formeller Dining Room und

ein Konferenzzimmer mit Videokonferenz-Facilities. Eine private Eingangshalle und eine Station für Sicherheits- und (24-Stunden-)Butler-Service sind ebenfalls obligatorisch. Riesige vom Boden bis zur Decke reichende Glasfenster und der Balkon erlauben unvergessliche Aussichten auf Victoria Harbour und Hongkong Island. Wände in *stucco veneziano* in den Wohnräumen und im Bad, Seidentapeten in den Schlafzimmern, chinesische Antiquitäten und Kunstgegenstände sowie Teppiche, in denen man zentimetertief einsinkt, setzen absolute Maßstäbe. Ein eigenes Dampfbad in der Dusche, Fernseher vor der Badewanne und Mini-TV neben dem Rasierspiegel lassen auch für Informations-Junkies keine Wünsche unerfüllt; doch wer sieht hier schon fern, wenn der Ausblick auf die unglaubliche Skyline einen Blick bietet, von dem man nie genug bekommen kann. Ein Flügel ermöglicht Live-Piano-Musik zum Dinner und durch das riesige Bausch-&-Lomb-Fernrohr wird man so manche Entdeckung machen können. Ein Rolls-Royce mit Chauffeur steht permanent *stand by*, ein separater Aufzug verbindet die Suite direkt mit der Helikopterlounge und dem Felix. Auf Wunsch kann die Peninsula Suite in eine Zwei-Schlafzimmer-Suite umgewandelt werden oder auf maximal sieben Schlafzimmer (durch angrenzende Räume auf der Etage) erweitert werden. Bleibt als Letztes zu ergänzen, dass die Sicherheitsvorkehrungen der Peninsula Suite den strengen Bestimmungen des amerikanischen CIA und des britischen MI5 genügen.

Dining Experiences: von Abalones über Fusion Cuisine bis zu Kobe-Beef

Ebenso vielseitig wie das Angebot an Zimmern und Suiten präsentiert sich auch das gastronomische Angebot im Peninsula. Insgesamt sieben verschiedene Dependancen lassen auch für weit gereiste und verwöhnte Gourmets keine Wünsche offen. Das bereits erwähnte, von Philippe Starck designte Felix ist absolut hip und trendy, die zeitgemäße Verkörperung einer prätentiösen Gastronomie mit verschiedenen Bereichen, die mit unterschiedlichen Materialien akzentuiert wurden. Vor dem Hintergrund des überdimensionalen Counters mit seiner erleuchteten Alabasteroberfläche, die durch Lichtspiele subtile Wellenbewegungen assoziiert, befinden sich das große Restaurant, das kleinere Balcony, die Wine Bar, die American Bar, eine kleine Disco und ein Private Room für maximal elf Person. Überall setzte Philippe Starck seine Akzente, sogar auf den Tischen, die reich mit Kristallgläsern und -schüsseln und originellen Salz- und Pfefferstreuern dekoriert sind. Und manchmal sitzt man auch auf dem Star-Designer: die Bezüge der Stühle sind mit Portraits von Philippe Starck und seinen Freunden bedruckt. Das Design hört jedoch im Restaurant nicht auf: Im Herren WC sind kleine, frei stehende Urinale vor einem riesigen bodentiefen Fenster angebracht ... *a lifetime experience!*

Küchenchefin Dee Ann Tsurumaki aus Hawaii ist ein Original. Sie liebt eine Fusion

design, the restaurant serves an unpretentious cuisine and has various areas whose difference is accentuated by differing materials. Beyond the huge bar which has an illuminated alabaster surface upon which subtle waves are created by a play of light, is the large restaurant, the smaller Balcony, the Wine Bar, the American Bar, a small disco, and a private room which can accommodate a maximum of eleven people. Philippe Starck has left his mark everywhere, even on the tables which are lavishly set with crystal glasses and bowls, and original salt and pepper pots. Sometimes one actually sits on the star interior designer himself. The upholstery design features portraits of Philippe Starck and his friends, but the design doesn't end in the restaurant. In the men's toilets tiny separate urinals have been set before a giant window reaching down to the floor – a once in a lifetime experience!
The female chef, Dee Ann Tsurumaki from Hawaii, is a real character. She loves fusion cuisine and has an instinctive feeling for blending ideas from east and west, often using Polynesian and Hawaiian ingredients in a creative way. Her Hawaiian Opakapaka carpaccio is an experience in itself. She enhances the fish with sesame oil, garlic soya and aromatic lomi tomatoes. The seared big-eye tuna in a sesame pepper crust is equally sensational served raw with a Pinot Noir sauce, so are the

Atemberaubend: der Blick von den Harbour View Suiten auf die Skyline von Hongkong.
Breathtaking: the view of the skyline from the Harbour View Suites.

Gaddi's Küchenchef Philip Sedgewich führt eines der besten Restaurants Asiens.
Gaddi's chef, Philip Sedgewich, runs one of the best restaurants in Asia.

Premium-Abalones gehören zu den teuersten Delikatessen der Welt, im Spring Moon kostet eine Portion bis zu 1 000,– Euro.
Premium abalones are among the costliest delicacies in the world. A portion in the Spring Moon costs Euro 1,000.-.

teriyaki grilled giant prawns served with a vinaigrette made of three kinds of pepper sauces. In contrast Gaddi's, the elegant gourmet restaurant on the first floor, serves a classic French cuisine. It is one of the best addresses in the whole of Asia. Sumptuously comfortable it has velvet upholstered armchairs, Bergére chairs, a collection of antique chests and hand-woven Chinese carpets all of which surround a priceless object, the Ming Dynasty Coromandel Screen, which is displayed in the centre of the restaurant and of which there are only two examples in the world. Priceless crystal chandeliers and porcelain tableware specially designed for the Peninsula by Bernadaud of Limoges, create a genteel and refined atmosphere. Distinguished private dinners take place in a separate dining room with its own lounge. Its Chinese décor creates a distinctive ambience. Since the end of 1999, the kitchen staff have been under the direction of Philip Sedgewich, an Englishman who has worked alongside Anton Mosimann, Alain Ducasse and Hans Haas in Munich. His cuisine is based on classic French cooking to which he adds further finesse with his sensitive, creative touch. Since all products have to be flown in dining at Gadd's has its price. A St Pierre with a Venus mussel ragout, green asparagus, Italian cherry tomatoes and Garganelli seaweed costs about 60 Euro. For a six course meal you will have to shell out 135 Euro. The wine list includes all the great wines from Bordeaux, and Burgundy and 35 champagnes. The Verandah Restaurant where breakfast, lunch and dinner are served is a mirror image of the original neo-classical architecture of the hotel of 1928. Pastel shades, pecan nut wood and stone floors, colonial style rattan furni

Cuisine, mixt mit großem Fingerspitzengefühl Ideen aus Ost und West und würzt sie oftmals mit kreativen polynesischen und hawaiischen Ingredienzen. Ein Erlebnis ist das Hawaiian Opakapaka Carpaccio. Den Fisch aus ihrer Heimat verfeinert sie mit Sesamöl, Garlic Soy und aromatischen Lomi-Tomaten. Ebenso sensationell der Seared Big Eye Tuna, eingehüllt in eine Sesam-Pfefferkruste, roh serviert mit einer Pinot-Noir-Sauce, oder die Teriyaki-grilled Giant Prawns mit einer Vinaigrette aus drei verschiedenen Pfeffersaucen.

Klassisch französisch wird dagegen im Gaddi's gekocht, dem eleganten Gourmetrestaurant in der ersten Etage, das zu den besten Adressen in ganz Asien gehört. Verschwenderisch komfortabel, mit Samt bezogene Sessel und Bergére-Stühle, eine Sammlung antiker Truhen, handgewebte chinesische Teppiche umgeben das in der Mitte des Restaurants platzierte Prunkstück, den „Coromandel-Paravent" aus der Ming-Dynastie, von dem es weltweit nur noch zwei Exemplare gibt. Wertvolle Kristallüster und das eigens für das Peninsula entworfene Tafelporzellan von Bernadaud aus Limoges vermitteln eine Atmosphäre höchster Eleganz. Im separaten, privaten Dining Room mit eigener Lounge finden Einladungen auf höchstem Niveau statt. Chinesisch inspiriertes Interieur sorgt hier für das erlesene Ambiente. Seit Ende 1999 steht die Küche unter der Leitung des 33-jährigen Engländers Philip Sedgewich, der bereits bei Anton Mosimann, Alain Ducasse und Hans Haas im Münchner Tantris am Herd stand. Seine Küche baut auf klassischer französischer Kochkunst auf, die er mit gefühlvoller Kreativität verfeinert. Dadurch, dass alle Produkte eingeflogen werden müssen, hat das Dinner im Gaddi's auch seinen Preis: ein St. Pierre mit Venusmuschelragout, grünem Spargel, italienischen Kirschtomaten und Garganelli-Meeresalgen kostet knappe 60 Euro, für ein 6-Gang-Menü muss man 135 Euro berappen. Die Weinkarte listet alle großen Gewächse aus Bordeaux und Burgund auf, allein das Angebot an Champagner umfasst 35 Positionen.

Spiegelbild der neoklassizistischen Originalarchitektur des Hotels von 1928 ist das Restaurant The Verandah, in dem Frühstück, Lunch und Dinner serviert werden. Sanfte Farbtöne, Pecan-Nusshölz- und Steinböden, Rattanmöbel im Kolonialstil, Deckenventilatoren und Palmen lassen das Gefühl tropischer Lebensfreude aufkommen. Die Küche kombiniert klassische „hausgemachte Spezialitäten" mit einer kalorienreduzierten Cuisine. Gesunde, leichte Zubereitungen, eine Riesenauswahl an Salaten, Pasta und vegetarische Gerichte bestimmen die Speisenkarte. Im krassen Gegensatz zu dem kalorienbewussten Angebot der Vorspeisen und Hauptgerichte steht die Dessertkarte, die eine Vielzahl von Soufflés und als Höhepunkt „Chocomania", eine Fülle schokoladiger Desserts, offeriert.

Wie in jedem Grandhotel in internationalen Metropolen ist die Lobby kommunikativer Treffpunkt für Gäste aus aller Welt. Seit über 70 Jahren ist The Lobby im Peninsula magischer Anziehungspunkt für ein kosmopolitisches Publikum, hier genießt man den Kontrast von Weitläufigkeit und Intimität in einem luxuriösen Rahmen. Leichte Mahlzeiten und Snacks werden ebenso gereicht wie der traditionelle Afternoon Tea mit klassischer Begleitmusik. Seit kurzem gibt es jetzt eine eigene „Peninsula

Classic Tea Collection". Fünf verschiedene Sorten indischen Tees – Earl Grey, Darjeeling, Peninsula Afternoon Tea, Peninsula Breakfast Tea und der exklusive Peninsula Tea – sind die neueste kulinarische Innovation des Hauses. Die Tees repräsentieren dabei höchste Qualität: während gängige Tees zerriebene Teeblätter aufweisen, bestehen die Peninsula-Teesorten aus ganzen Blättern. Lediglich zwei Prozent der feinsten Blättchen eines Teestrauches finden für die Peninsula-Tea-Collection Verwendung.

Im chinesischen Restaurant Spring Moon macht man eine Zeitreise: das Art-déco-Ambiente vermittelt das Flair der 30er Jahre, so muss das Peninsula zur Zeit seiner Eröffnung ausgesehen haben. Eine Kollektion historischer Teekännchen hinter der Theke zitiert die außergewöhnliche chinesische Teekultur, im Spring Moon werden 25 verschiedene Teesorten offeriert, die von speziell ausgebildeten *tea masters* als Begleitung zum Essen zelebriert werden. Die Küche kredenzt mittags Dim Sums, das sind kleine, im Dampf gegarte würzige und süße Häppchen. Abends wird's hier schon etwas abenteuerlicher, da konzentriert sich das Angebot auf kantonesische Spezialitäten, wobei Haifischflossensuppe, *Bird's Nest* (gekochte Schwalbennester) und *Abalones* vielleicht nicht jedermanns Sache sind. Die authentische chinesische Küche bevorzugt viele Gerichte nicht unbedingt wegen des Geschmacks, sondern vor allem aufgrund der gesundheitsfördernden und oftmals auch aphrodisischen Wirkung. Die größte Köstlichkeit sind dabei die *Abalones*, eine Art Muscheln, die bis zu fünfzehn Jahre alt werden können und vor der japanischen Küste in reinstem Wasser leben. Zur Konservierung werden sie getrocknet, die eigentliche Zubereitung dauert dann zehn Tage. Vor dem Verzehr werden sie mehrere Tage eingeweicht, drei bis vier Tage köcheln sie vor sich, dann werden sie abschließend mit Gemüse, Fisch oder Hühnchen gedünstet oder gekocht. Je älter eine *Abalone*, um so wertvoller ist sie, wobei es ganz wichtig ist, dass der äußere Muskelkranz beim Fangen unbeschädigt bleibt, da sich hier die meisten Vitamine und Nährstoffe befinden. Eine solche Premium-*Abalone* kostet im Spring Moon 7.500 HK$ – Sie haben richtig gerechnet: 1 000 Euro.

Im Imasa, dem wunderschön ausgestatteten japanischen Restaurant, stillt man seinen Appetit mit kunstvoll zubereiteten Sushi und Sashimi, Maki Mono und Hand Roll. Hat sich bei uns das „Essen vom heißen Stein" als Party-Gag nicht richtig durchgesetzt, sind die Zubereitungen vom *Ishiyaki Stone Grill* im

ture, ceiling fans and palms stir yearnings for life in the tropics. The cuisine is a combination of classic house specialities with a low calorie cuisine. The menu is dominated by light healthy dishes which include an enormous selection of salads, pasta and vegetarian food. In stark contrast to the reduced calorie starters and main courses, the dessert menu lists numerous soufflés and has a superb "Chocomania" section featuring a whole host of chocolatey desserts.

As in every Grand Hotel in cosmopolitan cities, the lobby is a meeting place and centre of communication for guests from all over the world. For more than seventy years the lobby of the Peninsula has exerted a magical attraction for its sophisticated clientèle. It is a place where you can enjoy space and intimacy at once in a luxurious environment. Light meals and snacks are available, and traditional afternoon tea is served to the strains of classical music. Recently the "Peninsula Classic Tea Collection" was introduced. This latest culinary innovation comprises five different sorts of Indian tea – Earl Grey, Darjeeling, Peninsula Afternoon Tea, Peninsula Breakfast Tea and the exclusive Peninsula Tea, all of them top quality. While teas for wider consumption are broken, the Peninsula teas are whole leaves. Only the finest smaller leaves of a tea bush are used for the Peninsula Tea Collection.

The Chinese Spring Moon restaurant is a journey back in time. Its art déco ambience conveys the atmosphere of the 1930s – the Peninsula must have looked just like this when it first opened. A collection of historic antique tea pots behind the bar testify to the restaurant's amazing tea culture – the Spring Moon offers 25 different kinds of tea which is brewed by specially trained tea masters and served with the meal. At midday dim sum (small savoury and sweet steamed dumplings) are served. In the evening it gets more exciting when the kitchen concentrates on Cantonese specialities, though shark fin soup, birds' nests (boiled swallows nests) and abalones may not be to everybody's taste.

Authentic Chinese cuisine is not exclusively based on taste but also on dishes which are good for your health and food which is effective as an aphrodisiac. The greatest delicacy of all however are abalones, a kind of mussel which can be up to fifteen years old and are found in the purest water off the Japanese coast. They are preserved by drying, and the preparation process takes about ten days. Before they are consumed they are left to soak for several days, simmered for three or four days, then finally they are steamed or boiled with vegetables, fish or young chicken. The older the abalone the greater its value, though it is most important that its outer muscular case is undamaged when caught, because it contains most of the vitamins and nutrients. A prime abalone cost 7,500 HK$ – your calculations are correct, 1,000.– Euro. At the Imasa, the wonderfully furnished Japanese restaurant, one can satisfy one's appetite with creatively prepared sushi and sashimi, maki mono and hand rolls. Even if back home eating from a hot stone hasn't really caught on as the latest party gimmick, the food

Das von Philippe Starck designte „Felix" ist eines der außergewöhnlichsten Restaurants der Welt. Bei der Reservierung unbedingt auf „Harbour View Seating" bestehen.
The "Felix" designed by Philippe Starck is one of the most unusual restaurants in the world. When booking insist on a harbour view.

Authentische japanische Küche wird im „Imasa" serviert.
Authentic Japanese cuisine is served in the "Imasa".

Tempel der Schönheit: die Beautyfarm.
Temple of beauty: the Beauty Farm.

*Seit zwanzig Jahren immer
für die Gäste da: Chef
Concierge Michael Wilson.*
Head concierge, Michael Wilson, has
been assisting guests for twenty years.

produced on the Ishiyaki Stone Grill is a particular speciality. One has the choice of seafood, vegetable or beef, and this means yet another Asian speciality because you have the choice between US prime beef and Kobe beef. Kobe cattle (called after the town of the same name) are fattened in a most unusual way. They are fed only on cereals, root vegetables and potatoes. In addition the animals receive a daily ration of beer which increases their appetite – and probably makes them happy, even if their happiness only lasts for 20 months. The cattle are also massaged every day causing a very thin layer of fat to form which creates an even marble effect throughout the meat. Inevitably, this degree of care and attention is reflected in the price. A portion of Kobe beef in the Imasa costs 100.– Euro. The Chesa is reminiscent of the Swiss homeland of General Manager Peter C. Borer. In the cosy and homely atmosphere of a typical alpine guesthouse, one can savour regional Swiss specialities ranging from Zurich "Geschnetzeltes" (meat cut up into strips and stewed to produce a thick sauce) to fondue. Peter Borer has been managing the Peninsula since 1994 and was behind the building of the tower extension. What is more, he has been Group Manager Asia from 2002, and is now in charge of the interests of the noted Peninsula Hotel Group.

The Spa – Wellness above the roofs of Hong Kong

Anyone wishing to relax after indulging in the hotel's gastronomic portfolio, or after a taxing business meeting or shopping trip, can take the lift up to the eighth floor to the Peninsula Spa. Occupying an area of 17,222 square feet this health, fitness and beauty centre is unparalleled. Its pool area which has Roman-style columns, friezes and stucco work is magnificent. A large sliding glass front shields those inside from cooler air, so it can be used throughout the year. The water in the 20-yard pool is kept at an agreeable temperature of 26–29 °C. Additional attractions go are the waterfall dropping into the pool and three whirlpools. On the floor below is the sun deck where guests get the feeling they are on a huge ocean liner about to enter Victoria Harbour. High grade teak, comfortable loungers and deck chairs set the tone. You can also have a light lunch here, or enjoy delicious reduced salt and low calorie snacks, herbal teas, freshly squeezed orange juice and afternoon tea. For the more energetic there is a gym with the very latest computerized fitness equipment. Under the guidance of experienced personal trainers, the body power machines and stamina-building equipment such as cycles, rowing machines, steppers and treadmills, generate renewed dynamism and fitness. There is also cardio-equipment to gently exercise the heart at the right pulse rate. The Beauty Centre provides beauty treatment, skin analysis (skin care, cleansing, facial massage and lymph drainage), full body peeling, masks and cellulite removal, all using Clarins products.

From t'ai chi and feng shui to Breakfast at Tiffany

If guests wish to learn more about Chinese traditions and customs, they can attend workshops in Chinese Medicine, Cantonese cuisine or the traditional way of brewing tea at the Peninsula Academy. Participants are escorted through Hong Kong, giving them an opportunity to experience Hong Kong not as a tourist but as an insider. The courses concentrate on certain aspects, so that during this four-day cultural experience one gets to know the city's colourful markets where fresh ingredients are bought for the typical wok

Imasa eine besondere Spezialität. Man wählt unter Seafood, Gemüse oder Beef. Und hier taucht eine weitere asiatische Spezialität auf, denn bei allen Rindfleischgerichten kann man wählen zwischen *US Prime* und *Kobe Beef*. Kobe-Rinder werden in der gleichnamigen japanischen Stadt auf eine außergewöhnliche und sehr seltene Weise gemästet. Ihr Naturkraftfutter besteht nur aus Getreide, Futterrüben und Kartoffeln. Zudem erhalten die Rinder eine tägliche Ration Bier – das erhöht den Appetit – und macht wahrscheinlich glücklich, auch wenn das Glück insgesamt nur zwanzig Monate dauert. Außerdem werden die Rinder täglich von Hand massiert, wodurch sich auf dem Muskelfleisch eine sehr dünne Fettauflage bildet und das Fleisch mit einer feinen, gleichmäßigen Marmorierung durchzogen wird. So viel Fürsorge schlägt sich natürlich auch im Preis nieder, die Portion *Kobe Beef* im Imasa kostet 100,– Euro.

Die Chesa ist eine Reminiszenz an die Heimat des Schweizer General Managers Peter C. Borer. In der gemütlichen und heimeligen Atmosphäre eines typischen Alpengasthauses lässt man sich hier regionale schweizerische Spezialitäten vom Zürcher Geschnetzelten bis zum Fondue munden. Peter C. Borer leitet das Peninsula seit 1994, auch der Turmanbau stand unter seiner Verantwortung. Seit 2002 ist er zusätzlich als Group General Manager Asia auch für die Belange der renommierten Peninsula Hotel Group zuständig.

The Spa – Wellness über den Dächern von Hongkong

Wer nach dem Genuss des gastronomischen Portfolios, nach anstrengenden Business-Meetings oder Shopping-Bummeln Entspannung sucht, der nimmt den Fahrstuhl in die achte Etage. Auf über 1 600 qm Fläche präsentiert sich hier das Peninsula Spa mit einem Gesundheits-, Fitness- und Schönheitscenter, das seinesgleichen sucht. Mit Säulen, Friesen und Stukkaturen im klassisch-römischen Stil wurde der Poolbereich prachtvoll gestaltet. Eine bewegliche große Glasfront schirmt geschlossen kühlere Luft ab und erlaubt so eine ganzjährige Nutzung. Das Wasser im 18 Meter langen Becken misst angenehme 26–29° Celsius, ein in das Becken führender Wasserfall und zwei Whirlpools sind zusätzliche Attraktionen. Eine Etage tiefer befindet sich das Sundeck, auf dem die Gäste das Gefühl haben, auf einem überdimensionalen Oceanliner in den Victoria Harbour einzulaufen: edles Teakholz, komfortable Liegen und Deckchairs bestimmen das Ambiente. Leichte Lunchgerichte, köstliche salz- und kalorienarme Snacks, Kräutertees, frisch gepresste Säfte und auch Afternoon-Tea können hier genossen werden. Für Aktive stehen im Gym modernste, computergesteuerte Fitness- und Kraftmaschinen zur Verfügung, Ausdauergeräte wie Fahrräder, Ruder- und Steptrainer und Laufbänder sowie Geräte für ein schonendes Herz-Kreislauf Training im richtigen Pulsfrequenzbereich, generieren unter Anleitung erfahrener Personal-Trainer neue Dynamik und Fitness. Im Beauty-Center stehen Anwendungen wie Schönheitsbehandlungen mit Hauttypanalyse (Pflege, Reinigung, Gesichtsmassage oder Lympdrainage), Büstenbehandlung, Ganzkörperpeelings, Masken, Anti-Cellulite-Behandlungen, alles mit Clarins-Produkten, auf dem Programm.

Von Tai Chi und Feng Shui bis zum Frühstück bei Tiffany

Ob chinesische Kräutermedizin, kantonesische Küche oder traditionelle Teezubereitung – in der *Peninsula Akademie* können sich die Gäste bei exklusiven Workshops weiterbilden und die fernöstlichen Geheimnisse der chinesischen Sitten und Bräuche kennen lernen. Die Teilnehmer werden von Kennern durch Hongkong geführt – so erlebt man die faszinierende chinesische Metropole nicht als Tourist, sondern als Insider. Die Kurse setzen verschiedene Schwerpunkte, beim viertägigen *Chinese Cultural Experience* lernt man die bunten Märkte der Stadt kennen, aus dem frischen Einkauf werden im Anschluss an die Exkursion gemeinsam mit den Peninsula-Küchenchefs die typischen Wok-Gerichte in der Hotelküche zubereitet. *Tai Chi*, die uralte Kampfkunst, die heute als Meditation für Körper und Geist trainiert wird, gehört ebenso zum Programm wie die traditionelle Art der Teezubereitung, die Grundlagen der Kräutermedizin oder *Feng Shui*, die Philosophie chinesischer Baukunst. Das Peninsula *Lifestyle Experience* widmet sich ganz den Themen Exklusivität, Komfort und Service. Die Gäste werden mit dem Rolls-Royce vom Flughafen abgeholt und mit der Limousine zum Shopping in den besten Geschäften chauffiert. Der Abend endet mit einem festlichen Dinner im Felix, der nächste Tag beginnt mit einem Louis-Vuitton-Frühstück im spektakulären China Clipper. Ein Gourmet-Menü im Gaddi's und der Besuch des spektakulären Weinkellers sind weitere Highlights. Fazit: Das Peninsula Hongkong gehört zu den raren Perlen der internationalen Luxushotellerie, in denen ein Aufenthalt für jeden anspruchsvollen Weltenbummler zu einem der absoluten *musts* zählt. Nicht nur eine faszinierende Hardware macht hier den Aufenthalt zu einem unvergesslichen Erlebnis, auch der einzigartige Servcie, für den die Peninsula Hotels weltweit berühmt sind, die Verbindlichkeit eines jeden Mitarbeiters, der einem jeden Wunsch von den Augen abzulesen scheint, setzt Maßstäbe.

dishes cooked at the end of the excursion back at the hotel together with the Peninsula chef. The ancient Chinese martial art of t'ai chi, practised today as meditation for body and mind, is included on the programme alongside traditional tea making, the fundamentals of herbal medicine, feng shui and the philosophy of Chinese architecture. The Peninsula Lifestyle Experience is one of total exclusivity, luxury and service. Guests are collected from the airport by a Rolls-Royce and driven in a limousine to go shopping in the best shops. The evening closes with a festive dinner at the Felix and the following day begins with a Louis Vuitton Breakfast in the famous China Clipper. Further highlights are a gourmet meal at Gaddi's and a visit to the spectacular wine cellar. To sum up, the Peninsula Hong Kong is one of the rare gems amongst international luxury hotels, and staying there is an absolute must for the sophisticated globetrotter. Not only does the remarkable building make the stay an unforgettable experience, the incredible service for which Peninsula hotels are renowned worldwide, and the courtesy of every member of staff who literally read your wishes from your eyes set standards indeed.

Ein Erlebnis: die Anreise mit dem Helikopter.
Arriving by helicopter is a real experience.

Mit den exklusiven Fernrohren von Bausch & Lomb kann man ausgiebig den Hafen beobachten.
One can observe the harbour through the exclusive Bausch & Lomb telescopes.

Im Gegensatz zum Haupteingang des Oriental vermittelt der Eingang zur „Author's Residence" Romantik und Nostalgie.
In contrast to the main entrance of the Oriental, the entrance to the "Author's Residence" has an air of romance and nostalgia.

THE ORIENTAL BANGKOK

THE LIVING LEGEND

Dieses Hotel ist eine Legende, aber wie es schon der Prägedruck auf dem Briefpapier dokumentiert, eine „lebendige Legende". Im vergangenen Jahr feierte das Oriental seinen 125. Geburtstag. Seit über einem Jahrhundert wählen es gekrönte Häupter, Staatsmänner, Würdenträger, Künstler und Prominente aus allen Bereichen als ihr Domizil in der thailändischen Metropole. Von den knapp 400 Zimmern sind 35 Suiten, über die man ein eigenes Magazin herausgeben könnte, wenn man über das Thema „Suite Dreams" schreibt. Die außergewöhnlichsten befinden sich in der „Author's Residence" und wurden berühmten Schriftstellern gewidmet, die hier gewohnt haben und sich hier zu einigen ihrer bekanntesten Werke inspirieren ließen.

This hotel is a legend, and judging by the embossed letter paper it is a living legend. Last year, the Oriental celebrated its 125th anniversary. For over a century, crowned heads, statesmen, dignitaries, artists and VIPs from all spheres of life have been choosing it as their preferred residence in the Thai capital. The accommodation of almost 400 rooms includes 35 suites about which an exclusive magazine could be produced if one wanted to focus on "suite dreams". The most remarkable ones are in the "Author's Residence", and are dedicated to famous writers who have spent time here, and been inspired to write some of their best-known works.

Fotos: Klaus Lorke · Text: Thomas Klocke

Oben: Die James Michener Suite spiegelt mit ihrem eleganten Interieur auch die literarischen Werke des Autors wider, der viele Jahre Südostasien, den Mittleren Osten und den pazifischen Raum bereist hat.
Above: The elegant décor of the James Michener Suite reflects the literary works of an author who spent many years travelling around South-East Asia, the Middle East and the Pacific region.

Herzlicher Empfang in der Lobby. Mitte: Die Lobby der „Author's Residence" verzaubert mit dem inspirierenden Charme der Kolonialzeit. Hier wird nachmittags der Afternoon Tea zelebriert.
A warm welcome in the lobby. Centre: The lobby of the Author's Residence, has the inspiring charm of the colonial era, and is where afternoon tea is served each day.

The Oriental is the most famous and possibly the most highly rated hotel in the world. In fact, the much respected hit list of the American business magazine, the "Institutional Investor", has voted it "Best Hotel in the World" fifteen times. The phenomenon of this flagship of the Mandarin Oriental Hotels only sinks in at second glance, because the actual building is not unduly impressive. The architecture of this many-storey hotel is notably unspectacular, and also its location right beside the Chayo Praya river on which the threatening, long river express boats plough their noisy way through the water like tuned racing gondolas, is not exactly a feast for the eyes. Reception on arrival is very friendly and obliging, and check-in formalities can be completed in your room, albeit in the meantime this has become common practice in many hotels. After taking an initial turn around premises, passing a huge swimming pool where you really can indulge your yen to swim, and going through the exotic garden and the lobby of the "Author's Residence", we decide to visit the Spa to relax after the long flight. The hotel's own river shuttle boat takes us over to the opposite side of the river where the wellness zone, the Thai Cooking School and the Sala Rim Naam Thai restaurant are located. At the Spa we are instantly greeted with a beaming smile and addressed by our names, then we are led into one of the spa's suites. Although we have long been occupying ourselves with the subject of wellbeing, and have already seen a very great deal, this private temple to body and mind exceeds everything we have experienced so far. While the Spa Manager explains the place which will be our surroundings for the next three and half hours – showing us the pleasant jacuzzi surrounded by black granite, and familiarizing us with the Finnish sauna and the steam bath – we are discreetly served a fragrant lemon grass tea. The treatment begins in half an hour so we can enjoy the ambience in peace - the soothing warmth given off by the teak walls, the agreeable aroma of scented candles, the relaxing music and the delicious tea. Both our massage therapists greet us by name and explain "The Revitalizer" programme we have chosen. It comprises papaya body cleansing treatment, a massage with essential oils, a facial and a foot massage. After we have selected our personal fragrance from a variety of aromatic oils, we sink into a blissful world of wellbeing, a degree of relaxation never pre-

Das Oriental ist das bekannteste Hotel und wohl auch am meisten ausgezeichnete Hotel der Welt, allein in der viel beachteten Hitliste des amerikanischen Business-Magazins „Institutional Investor" wurde es mehr als fünfzehnmal zum „Best Hotel of the World" gewählt. Das Phänomen des Flaggschiffs der Mandarin Oriental Hotels erschließt sich erst auf den zweiten Blick, denn die „Hardware" ist nicht sonderlich beeindruckend. Die Architektur der vielgeschossigen Gebäude ist äußerst unspektakulär und die direkte Lage am Chao Praya River, auf denen die dröhnenden Longtailboote wie getunte Renngondolas ihre lauten Bahnen ziehen, auch nicht gerade eine Augenweide. Der Empfang in der Lobby ist sehr freundlich und verbindlich, die Check-in-Formalitäten erfolgen bequem auf dem Zimmer, aber das wird mittlerweile in vielen Luxushotels praktiziert. Nach

einem ersten Rundgang vorbei am riesigen Swimmingpool, in dem man die Lust am Schwimmen wirklich voll auskosten kann, durch den exotischen Garten und die Lobby der „Author's Residence", entschließen wir uns zu einem Besuch im Spa, um nach dem langen Flug zu entspannen. Das hoteleigene Shuttleboot bringt uns auf die gegenüberliegende Seite des Flusses, wo sich der Wellnessbereich, die Thai Cooking School und das thailändische Restaurant Sala Rim Naam befinden.

Im Spa werden wir mit einem strahlenden Lächeln sofort mit Namen begrüßt und in eine der Oriental Spa Suiten geführt. Obwohl wir uns schon lange mit dem Thema Wellness beschäftigen und schon viel gesehen haben, übertrifft dieser private Tempel für Körper und Seele alles bisher Erlebte. Während uns die Spa-Managerin unser Reich für die nächsten dreieinhalb Stunden erklärt, uns den wohltemperierten viously experienced which we never want to end.

The Oriental has been managed for thirty-five years by Kurt Wachtveitl. We meet for a delicious lunch of dim sum at the China House so that he can relate the whole story of the legendary suites. Since we were last together at the HIDEAWAYS party in Berlin, "Mr. Kurt" as he is respectfully called by his 1,100 strong staff, has changed. He now sports a beard which immediately reminds one of Sean Connery. This charismatic hotelier is as much of a legend as the hotel he has successfully managed for the last thirty-five years, making him the longest serving luxury hotel Manager in the world.

With bright eyes and an infectious laugh he tells us of the spirit behind the history of the Oriental. In 1886 two Danish captains built a small guesthouse on the banks of the Chao Praya river near the French Embassy. Only a year later, a young naval officer boarded here while waiting for the first ship he was to command. Years later this man was a renowned literary figure, his name was Joseph Conrad, and with him began the tradition of writers who would stay at the Oriental to write some of their most famous works. In 1884 this fine residence was purchased by a Danish merchant who complete rebuilt it. The Russian Crown Prince stayed here as did Fabergé, the jeweller. Foreign correspondents and authors such as Somerset Maugham, Noel Coward and Graham Greene, always preferred to stay at the Oriental. Following its occupation during the Second World War by Japanese troops and later on by the Americans, ultimately Jim Thompson, the silk magnate, resurrected the hotel and it flourished anew.

The names of the VIPs who have stayed go on for pages, and read like a Who's Who of the international aristocracy – from Queen Margaret of Denmark and King Gustav of Sweden to the Monegasque Royal Family. Elizabeth Taylor, Henry Kissinger, Roger Moore, Boris Becker, Michael Jackson, Richard Nixon, the list is endless. It would probably be easier to list those who had not already stayed at the hotel. Johannes Rau, President of the Federal Republic of Germany, also stayed here for a week at the end of his visit to the 2002 World Cup in Japan and Korea.

Asked about the most memorable moment of his career, Wachtveitl tells of a visit he made to Hong Kong in 1981 where he learnt that the Oriental has been voted "The World's Best Hotel" by a renowned American business magazine. "When I got back, nearly all the staff were gathered in the lobby, and they'd prepared a welcome for me fit for an Army General returning from a victorious campaign. The most fantastic thing about the Thai people is that they can celebrate such an occasion and enjoy themselves, yet the next day switch back to being conscientious and ambitious about defending such success." The team has achieved this – from 1981 to 1990 the Oriental headed the list of the very best hotels, and has since been honoured with a whole array of outstanding international accolades and awards.

After lunch we go over to the "Author's Residence", a small, tranquil wing of the original hotel. Compared with the modern "River Wing" which has almost 400 rooms, and the "Garden Wing", it looks like a refuge from a past era. In the lobby one immediately has the feeling of being transported back into colonial times. You can tarry a while in a comfortable rattan armchair sensing the inspirational atmosphere, and in the afternoon, enjoy a traditional high tea which is still celebrated to

Links: Entspannen und genießen – das nostalgische Bad der James Michener Suite.
Left: Relax and enjoy – the nostalgic bathroom of the James Michener Suite.

Der „Trophy Room": hier sind die unzähligen Awards des Oriental ausgestellt. Im Anschluss liegt die Library, die u. a. mit den Werken berühmter Schriftsteller bestückt ist.
The Trophy Room: on display are the Oriental's numerous awards. Adjacent to it is the library, well stocked with works of well-known authors and others.

Der Boot-Shuttle bringt die Gäste auf die andere Seite des Chao Praya Rivers zum Oriental-Spa.
The boat shuttle crosses Chao Praya River taking guests over to the Oriental Spa on the other side.

Oben: Der Living Room der stilvollen Oriental Suite. Rechts: Ebenso eine Legende wie das Hotel: Seit 35 Jahren leitet Kurt Wachtveitl das Oriental.

**Above: The living room of the stylish Oriental Suite.
Right: Kurt Wachtveitl, as much of a legend as the hotel itself.
He has been managing the Oriental for 35 years.**

Im großzügigen Bad der Oriental Suite wird man von luxuriöser Ambiance umschmeichelt.

In the spacious bathroom of the Oriental Suite one is enfolded by a luxurious ambience.

perfection here. Next to the lobby is the "Trophy Room" where all the awards - of which all the staff are very proud - are exhibited and which provide the motivation for the continued high standard of service. The secret behind the success of the hotel's incomparable service is undoubtedly the fact that nearly two thirds of the staff have worked at the Oriental for over 15 years (!) – quite remarkable, like so much in this hotel. When Kurt Wachtveitl takes us to the suites, we discover a small plastic stick leaning upright against the door. Wachtveitl immediately explains: "The staff can tell from the little stick whether or not the guest is already in the room, even when there is no 'do not disturb notice on the door'. This way we can avoid disturbing the guest. In the new rooms on the River Wing there are the latest infra-red sensors which serve the same purpose."

We go first into the Somerset Maugham Suite. The author first stayed at the Oriental in 1923 when he was recovering from a bout of malaria. Hand-carved four posters and a bold colour combination predominates - green carpet and purple upholstery, the writer's favourite colours – reflecting the grandeur of the Kingdom of Thailand. The bathroom has an original free-standing bath with old English taps which, while conveying a certain nostalgia, lacks nothing by way of the very latest mod cons. Opposite, the Noel Coward Suite is identically furnished to the Somerset Maugham Suite, but in strong blue and green tones which remind one of the glorious colours of a peacock.

In contrast to the romance and nostalgia of the first two, the James Michener Suite is the epitome of modern elegance. The exquisite purple silk canopy above the bed, the light walls and the clean lines of the furniture reflect the literary works of James Michener whose years of travelling took him through South East Asia, the Middle East, America and the Pacific region, where he wrote his best-known works, "Hawai" and "Caravans". All his life he was interested in the work of young Asian writers, so it was for Kurt Wachtveitl a great pleasure in 1981 to secure the author as a speaker at the annual S.E.A. Write Awards, which is under the patronage of Queen Sirikit and is co-

Jacuzzi zeigt, der mit elegantem schwarzen Granit eingefasst ist, uns mit der Finnischen Sauna und dem Dampfbad vertraut macht, wird diskret ein duftender Zitronengrastee mit Lavendelhonig serviert. Die Behandlung fängt erst in einer halben Stunde an, so dass wir in Ruhe das Ambiente genießen können: die warme und beruhigende Ausstrahlung der Teakholzwände, das angenehme Aroma der Duftkerzen und die entspannende Musik, dazu entspannt der köstliche Tee. Auch unsere beiden Massage-Therapeutinnen begrüßen uns mit Namen, sie erklären uns das Programm, das beim ausgewählten „The Revitaliser" aus einer Papaya-Körperreinigung, einer Essential-Oil-Massage, einer Gesichtsbehandlung und einer Fußmassage besteht. Nachdem wir unseren persönlichen Duft unter den verschiedenen Aromaölen ausgewählt haben versinken wir in eine Wonne des Wohlgefühls, einer noch nie erlebten Entspannung, von der man sich nur wünscht, sie möge niemals enden.

Das Oriental wird seit fünfunddreißig Jahren von dem Deutschen Kurt Wachtveitl geleitet. Wir treffen uns zum Lunch im China House, um bei einem köstlichen Dim-Sum-Menü von ihm aus erster Hand etwas über die Geschichte und die legendären Suiten zu erfahren. Seit unserem letzten Treffen auf der HIDEAWAYS-Party in Berlin hat sich „Mr. Kurt", wie er von seinen über 1 100 Mitarbeitern respektvoll genannt wird, optisch verändert, ein gepflegter Vollbart lässt spontan Assoziationen mit Sean Connery aufkommen. Der charismatische

Hotelier ist ebenso eine Legende wie das Hotel, das er seit nunmehr 35 Jahren so erfolgreich leitet – er ist weltweit der dienstältestete Manager eines Luxushotels.

Mit leuchtenden Augen und ansteckendem Lachen erzählt er uns mit Verve die Geschichte des Oriental: 1876 errichteten zwei dänische Kapitäne an den Ufern des Chao Praya Rivers eine kleine Pension in der Nähe der französischen Botschaft. Bereits ein Jahr später stieg hier ein junger Marineoffizier ab, der auf das erste Schiff wartete, das er als Kapitän befehligen sollte. Jahre später wurde dieser Mann in der Literatur weltbekannt, sein Name war Joseph Conrad und mit ihm wurde die Tradition der Schriftsteller eingeleitet, die im Oriental wohnten und hier einige ihrer berühmtesten Werke verfassten. 1884 wurde die feine Herberge von einem dänischen Kaufmann erworben, der es völlig neu umbauen ließ. Der russische Kronprinz wohnte hier ebenso wie der Juwelier Carl Fabergè; Auslandskorrespondenten und Autoren wie W. Somerset Maugham, Noel Coward und Graham Greene machten das Oriental zu ihrem bevorzugten Domizil. Nach der Besetzung durch japanische und amerikanische Truppen im Zweiten Weltkrieg brachte der spätere Seidenkönig Jim Thompson das Haus wieder zu neuer Blüte. Die Namen der prominenten Gäste, die seitdem im Oriental gewohnt haben, ist seitenlang und liest sich anfangs wie ein Gotha des internationalen Hochadels, angefangen von Königin Margarethe von Dänemark über König Carl Gustaf von Schweden bis zur monegassischen Fürstenfamilie. Elizabeth Taylor, Henry Kissinger, Roger Moore, Boris Becker, Michael Jackson, Richard Nixon, die Liste ließe sich endlos fortsetzen und wahrscheinlich wäre es einfacher, die Prominenten aufzuzählen, die noch nicht das Glück hatten, hier zu nächtigen. Auch Bundespräsident Johannes Rau nutzte im Anschluss seines Besuches der Fußballweltmeisterschaft in Japan und Korea seine Asienreise zu einem einwöchigen Urlaub im Oriental. Nach seinem bewegendsten Moment in seiner Karriere gefragt, erzählt uns Kurt Wachtveitl von einem Besuch in Hongkong im Jahre 1981, wo er erfuhr, dass das Oriental von dem renommierten amerikanischen Business-Magazin zum erstenmal zum „The World's Best Hotel" gewählt wurde: „Bei meiner Rückkehr nach Bangkok hatten sich fast alle Mitarbeiter in der Lobby versammelt und bereiteten mir einen Empfang wie einem Feldherrn, der nach einem erfolgreichen Siegeszug heimkehrt. Das Phantastische an den Thailändern ist die Fähigkeit, so ein Ereignis zu feiern und zu genießen und gleichzeitig am nächsten Tag auf das Pflichtbewusstsein und den Ehrgeiz umzuschalten, den man benötigt, um solch einen Erfolg zu verteidigen." Dies gelang dem Team bravourös, allein von 1981 bis 1990 war das Oriental stets die Nummer eins der Bestenliste, begleitet von einer Vielzahl von weiteren internationalen Ehrungen und Auszeichnungen, die einmalig sind. Nach dem Lunch gehen wir in die „Author's Residence", den kleinen, beschaulichen Flügel des ur-sponsored by the Oriental.

The fourth suite in the Author's Residence has been named after Joseph Conrad who, as already mentioned, came to the Oriental in 1887 to assume his first command as a naval officer, a story he tells in his novel "The Shadow Line". A four-poster with heavy silk fabric in muted colours lends a cosmopolitan elegance to the whole interior. The modern cabinets with all the latest technology lack for nothing. The Bose hi-fi equipment plus CD-player, two telephone lines, continuous Internet access, a fax machine and the console beside the bed for the lights, air-conditioning and service are standard in all the accommodation.
It would be beyond the scope of this piece to include all the other suites, such as the Barbara Cartland Suite which is all in pink, and the Captain Anderson Suite with its maritime décor, which was named after a founder of the East Asiatic Company who was also one of the former owners of the Oriental. We shall therefore focus on the finest suite of all, the Oriental Suite.
Occupying almost 3,230 sq. ft.,

Bei seinem ersten Besuch im Oriental erholte sich Somerset Maugham von einer Malariainfektion. Später konnte er die Aufenthalte in der nach ihm benannten Suite sicherlich mehr genießen.
On his first visit to the Oriental, Somerset Maugham was struck down with malaria. Later on, he would have enjoyed his stay in the suite named after him much more.

Das Gourmetrestaurant Le Normandie ist eine der besten Feinschmeckeradressen in ganz Asien.
The Le Normandie Restaurant is one of the best gourmet restaurants in the whole of Asia.

the suite has a stylish elegance created by wood panelling, ceiling frescoes, a lavishly equipped bathroom and a separate dining room where one dines in style in highly sophisticated surroundings. Those who prefer to dine elsewhere, not in the privacy of their own suite, have at their disposal an incomparable choice of cuisine. On the top floor of the Garden Wing is The Normandie restaurant which serves great haute cuisine par excellence and, in addition, affords a fantastic view over the River Chao Praya. One can indulge one's taste buds with tuna steak tartare marinated in three different mustard varieties, steamed sea bream with a Chablis-Sevruga caviar sauce, and loup de mer with a salt crust. Lord Jim's fish restaurant serves all the treasures of Neptune's kingdom. Midday opulent buffets are set out and in the evening it has a creative à la carte menu. A paradise is laid out for buffet buffs each evening on the Riverside Terrace. A buffet of this nature – over a hundred different dishes ranging from the finest meat to the freshest seafood as well as a veritable orgy of desserts – must surely be unique worldwide. During the winter months, as well as the Riverside Terrace there is also the open-air Ciao restaurant where you can still your appetite with excellent Italian cuisine and home-made pasta. The place for lunch is the China House which serves typical dim sum variations and Cantonese dishes in the evening. Those who prefer authentic Thai cooking cross the river by boat to the Rim Naam Terrace. Every evening, the restaurant of the same name serves a four-course Thai menu while you observe the beauty and grace of native Thai dancers, male and female, performing traditional Thai dancing. Those keen on Thai food, which is a remarkable harmony between hot chillies and many other spices with a bal-

sprünglichen Hotels, der neben dem modernen, fast vierhundert Zimmer beherbergenden „River Wing" und dem „Garden Wing" wie ein Refugium aus vergangener Zeit wirkt. In der Lobby fühlt man sich denn auch spontan in die Zeit des Kolonialstils versetzt, hier nimmt man auf bequemen Rattansesseln Platz, verweilt ein wenig, um die inspirierende Atmosphäre zu genießen, oder genießt nachmittags den traditionellen High Tea, der hier in Vollendung zelebriert wird.

Neben der Lobby befindet sich der „Trophy Room", wo alle Auszeichnungen präsentiert werden, auf die alle Mitarbeiter sehr stolz sind und die sie zu ständiger Höchstleistung motivieren. Ein Geheimnis für den Erfolg, für den unvergleichlichen Service ist sicherlich die Tatsache, dass fast zwei Drittel der Mitarbeiter länger als 15 Jahre (!) im Oriental arbeiten – wie so vieles einzigartig an diesem Haus. Als uns Kurt Wachtveitl zu den Suiten führt, entdecken wir vor der ersten Tür auf dem Boden ein kleines Plastikstäbchen, das senkrecht gegen die Tür gelehnt ist. Wachtveitl erklärt sofort dieses kleine Geheimnis: „Durch das Stäbchen sieht unser Service stets, ob der Gast im Zimmer ist oder nicht. Auch wenn kein Do-not-disturb-Schild vor der Tür hängt, können wir so jegliche Störung vermeiden. In den neuen Räumen im River Wing haben alle Zimmer modernste Infrarotsensoren, die dem gleichen Zweck dienen." Wir betreten zuerst die Somerset Maugham Suite. Der Autor wohnte erstmalig 1923 im Oriental, als er sich hier von einer Malariainfektion erholte. Handgeschnitzte Himmelbetten und eine mutige Farbkomposition mit grünem Teppichboden und lilafarbenen Polsterbezügen – den Lieblingsfarben des Schriftstellers – setzen die

Akzente und spiegeln die Pracht und den Glanz des Königreiches Thailand wider. Das Badezimmer mit seiner originellen frei stehenden Badewanne und den alten englischen Armaturen dokumentiert einerseits Nostalgie, lässt aber andererseits keinen modernen Komfort vermissen. Vis-à-vis liegt die Noel Coward Suite, die über identisches Mobiliar wie die Somerset Maugham Suite verfügt, jedoch in kräftigen Blau- und Grüntönen eingerichtet wurde und an das prachtvolle Farbspiel eines Pfaues erinnert. Die James Michener Suite verkörpert im Gegensatz zu den beiden ersten statt Romantik und Nostalgie moderne Eleganz. Der edle purpurne Seidenbaldachin über dem Bett, die hellen Wände und das geradlinige Mobiliar spiegeln auch die literarischen Werke von James Michener wider, der viele Jahre Südostasien, den Mittleren Osten, Amerika und den pazifischen Raum bereist hat, wo seine berühmtesten Werke *Hawaii* und *Caravans* entstanden. Er hat sich Zeit seines Lebens für die Arbeit junger asiatischer Schriftsteller interessiert und es war Kurt Wachtveitl eine große Freude, den renommierten Autor 1981 als Laudator für die jährlich ausgeschriebenen S.E.A. Write Awards zu gewinnen, der unter der Schirmherrschaft von Königin Sirikit stand und von dem Oriental als Co-Sponsor unterstützt wird. Die vierte Suite in der Author's Residence wurde nach Joseph Conrad benannt, der wie eingangs erwähnt 1887 ins Oriental kam, um sein erstes Kommando als Marinekapitän anzutreten. Diese Geschichte erzählt er in seiner Novelle *The Shadow Line*.

Ein Himmelbett mit schweren Seidenstoffen in gedeckten Farben vermittelt hier wie das gesamte Interieur weltläufige Eleganz. An modernsten technischen Kabinettstückchen fehlt in allen Suiten natürlich nichts, die

Bose-Hi-Fi-Anlage mit CD-Spieler, zwei Telefonleitungen, ständiger Internet-Zugang, Steuerpulte für Licht, Klimaanlage und Service neben dem Bett und Telefax mit persönlicher Nummer sind überall obligatorisch. Alle weiteren Suiten, wie die ganz in Rosa gehaltene Barbara Cartland Suite oder die im maritimen Flair gestaltete Captain Anderson Suite, einer der ehemaligen Besitzer des Orientals und Gründer der East Asiatic Company, aufzuzählen, würde den Rahmen sprengen, so widmen wir uns nur noch dem Suiten-Highlight, der Oriental Suite. Auf mehr als 300 Quadratmetern genießt man hier stilvolle Eleganz, die geprägt wird von wertvollen Holzverkleidungen, Deckenmalereien, einem verschwenderisch gestalteten Badezimmer und einem separaten Dining Room, in dem man umgeben von höchster Tischkultur speisen kann.

Wer dies nicht in der privaten Atmosphäre seiner Suite zelebrieren möchte, dem steht ein unvergleichliches gastronomisches Angebot zur Verfügung. In der obersten Etage des Garden Wings wird im Restaurant The Normandie, einer der besten Adressen Asiens für klassische französische Küche, wahrlich eine Grande Cuisine par excellence aufgetischt, und das mit einer faszinierenden Aussicht auf den Chao Praya River. Hier verwöhnt man seinen Gaumen mit Köstlichkeiten wie Tatar vom Thunfisch mariniert in drei verschiedenen Senfsorten, gedämpfter Seebrasse in Chablis- und Sevruga-Kaviar-Sauce oder einem Loup de mer, zubereitet in der Salzkruste. Im Fischrestaurant Lord Jim's werden alle Schätze aus Neptuns Reich serviert, mittags mit opulenten Buffets, abends in kreativen A-la-carte-Zubereitungen. Das Paradies für Buffet-Liebhaber wird jeden Abend auf der Riverside Terrace präsentiert: mehr als einhundert verschiedene Gerichte, vom feinsten Fleisch bis zu frischestem Seafood, und eine wahre Orgie an Desserts dürfte in dieser Form ebenfalls weltweit einmalig sein. In den Wintermonaten befindet sich neben der Riverside Terrace das Open-Air-Restaurant Ciao, wo eine exzellente italienische Küche mit hausgemachter Pasta den Appetit stillt. The China House ist zum Lunch die Adresse für typische Dim-Sum-Variationen, abends wird hier klassisch kantonesisch gekocht. Wer eine authentische thailändische Küche bevorzugt, lässt sich mit dem Boot übersetzen und nimmt auf der Terrace Rim Naam Platz. Im gleichnamigen Restaurant wird drinnen allabendlich ein thailändisches Vier-Gang-Menü mit einer folkloristischen Tanzdarbietung angeboten, bei der man die Schönheit und Grazie der thailändischen Tänzerinnen und Tänzer erleben kann. Wer der thailändischen Küche verfällt, dieser einzigartigen Harmonie zwischen der Schärfe des Chilis und vieler anderer Gewürze und der ausgleichenden Süße zum Beispiel der Kokosnussmilch, der kann sich gleich am nächsten Tag in der Thai Cooking School anmelden, wo er in die Geheimnisse der asiatischen Kochkunst eingewiesen wird. Die Hilfestellung in der Speisekarte bezüglich der Schärfe mit einer Chili-Schote für mild, zwei für scharf und drei Schoten für sehr scharf sollte man übrigens durchaus ernst nehmen! Auf alle Gäste, denen dieses Angebot noch nicht ausreicht, wartet die Oriental Queen, eine romantische Barke, die zum Dinner Cruise auf dem Fluss der Könige unter zumeist sternenklarem Himmel kreuzt. Nach dem Dinner sollte man nicht den Besuch der legendären Bamboo Bar versäumen, die im behaglichen Kolonialstil zu Live-Jazz einlädt und schon mehrfach zum „World's Best Jazz & Blues Venue" gekürt wurde. Kurt Wachtveitl, der übrigens mit dem Bundesverdienstkreuz, mit dem Orden des Weißen Elefanten, der höchsten Auszeichnung Thailands, und „Thailand's Royal Decoration Fourth Class" für seine kulturellen Verdienste geehrt wurde, verdeutlicht mit einer letzten Anekdote das Servicegeheimnis jedes Mitarbeiters, die sich geradezu einen Sport daraus machen, ihre Gäste zu kennen: „Als ich einmal mit dem Fahrstuhl nach oben fahren wollte, kam noch ein Gast hinein. Da ich die Etage für ihn drücken wollte, fragte ich ihn, in welchem Stock er wohnen würde. Der Gast anwortete schmunzelnd: Sie sind wirklich der Einzige hier im Hotel, der nicht weiß, in welchem Zimmer ich wohne."

anccing element of sweetness, coconut milk for instance, can sign up the next day for a course at he Thai Cooking School. The key used on the menu, chilli symbols indicating the degree of hot spiciness of a dish i.e. one chilli = mild, two chillies = hot, and three chillies very hot, should be taken very seriously! Awaiting guests for whom all this is still not enough, and who prefer to go on a "Dinner Cruise", is the "Oriental Queen", a romantic barque which cruises the river of the kings beneath the star-studded heavens. After dinner, don't miss a visit to the legendary Bamboo Bar, where live jazz is played. Kurt Wachtveitl who, incidentally, has been decorated with the gong of Order of the Federal Republic of Germany, the Order of the White Elephant (Thailand's highest decoration) and Thailand's "Royal Decoration Fourth Class" for his cultural contribution, tells one more story to illustrate the dedication of his staff to individual customer service. "I was once going up in the lift and a guest got in with me. I wanted to press the button for him, so I asked him which floor he was on. The guest answered, 'you really must be the only person in this hotel who doesn't know which room I'm in' ".

Thailand
Bangkok

Honeymooner's Paradise

BANYAN TREE SEYCHELLES

Die 115 Inseln der Seychellen verteilen sich auf rund 400 Quadratkilometer in der Weite des Indischen Ozeans. Für viele sind sie der Inbegriff romantischer Urlaubsträume und nicht umsonst heiß geliebt bei Hochzeitsreisenden. Rund um die weitläufige Intendance-Bucht auf der Hauptinsel Mahé findet junge wie reife Liebe ein Paradies für sinnliches Erleben: das neue Banyan Tree Seychelles.

The 115 islands of the Seychelles are scattered across the length and breadth of roughly 154 square miles of the Indian Ocean. For many they are the epitome of romantic holiday dreams, so it is not without reason that they are so loved by honeymoon couples. Around the broad Intendance Bay on the main island of Mahé, young love and old find a paradise for sensuous experience – the new Banyan Tree Seychelles.

Text: Gundula Luig · Fotos: Stefan Fister/Banyan Tree

Luxuriöse Logis: eine Beachfront-Villa mit privatem Pool und umzäuntem Gartengrundstück.
Luxurious accommodation: a Beachfront Villa has its own private pool and fenced garden.

Kolonialstil in Verbindung mit luftiger Transparenz zeichnet das gelungene Ambiente der Lobby aus.
The colonial style of the lobby and its airy transparency create its special ambience.

Kaum zu sehen in der üppigen Vegetation: die Hillside-Villen.
The Hillside Villas are scarcely visible between the thick vegetation.

Der Garten meiner Beachvilla ist in ein zauberhaftes Mondlicht getaucht. Terrasse, Massage-Pavillon und Pool sind sanft beleuchtet. Die Luft streicht warm über meine Haut, unaufhörlich und beruhigend monoton rollt die Brandung des Indischen Ozeans an den weißen Sandstrand der weit geschwungenen Intendance-Bucht. Ein Blütenteppich aus Bougainvillea und Frangipani scheint auf den Teakholzplanken der Terrasse zu schweben, leitet mich sicher zum blubbernd sprudelnden Outdoor-Jacuzzi in einer geschützten Ecke des Tropengartens. Flackernde Kerzen säumen den

The garden of my Beach Villa is bathed in the magical light of the moon. The terrace, the massage pavilion and the pool are illuminated by the soft light. The air gently caresses my skin and waves break continuously and reassuringly on to the white sandy beach of the sweeping curve of Intendance Bay. A flowery carpet of bougainvillaea and frangipani seems to be floating on the teak planks of the terrace leading me to a bubbling outdoor Jacuzzi in a sheltered corner of the tropical garden. Flickering candles line the edge, and over it tower banana palms and a spreading type of rubber tree. My villa too is lit by the romantic light of numerous candles, and the bed is artistically decorated with hundreds of flower petals in the centre of a heart shape. A joss stick fills the air with an aphrodisiac fragrance, and a bottle of wine waits to have its cork removed. "Intimate Moments" is the package deal for lovers,

Edle Interieurs, natürliche Materialien und inseltypische Kunst schaffen eine Atmosphäre zum Wohlfühlen.
Superb interiors, natural materials and ethnic art work create a feel-good atmosphere.

Die Dusche ist gleichzeitig eine entspannende Dampfsauna mit freiem Gartenblick.
The shower also serves as a relaxing steam sauna with a view of the garden.

Auch vom Bad hat man Zugang zum Tropengarten.
The tropical garden can also be accessed from the bathroom.

Rand, überragt von Bananenpalmen und einer breit ausladenden Gummibaumart. Auch meine Villa wird innen romantisch vom Schein zahlreicher Kerzen illuminiert, das Bett kunstvoll geschmückt mit Hunderten Blütenblättern, in der Mitte ein stilisiertes Herz. Ein Räucherstäbchen verströmt aphrodisierenden Duft, eine Flasche Wein wartet darauf, entkorkt zu werden. „Intimate Moments" – das besondere Arrangement für Liebende, perfekt inszeniert vom Banyan Tree Seychelles.

Wie seine Schwesterhotels in Phuket, auf den Malediven und in Bintan verwöhnt das erst im Februar 2002 eröffnete Nobelresort an der Südwestküste Mahés mit einem exklusiven Privatvillen-Konzept. Meine Beachfront-Pool-Villa ist ein Traum. 251 Quadratmeter Luxus im Tropenparadies. Weiße Villenarchitektur im viktorianischen Stil – eine Hommage an die koloniale Vergangenheit der Inselgruppe – mit Holzschindeldach und raumhohen Glasfronten für permanenten Sichtkontakt mit der üppigen Flora des gepflegten Gartens. Cremefarbene Fliesen und Sandstein setzen die überdachte Terrasse in einen harmonischen Kontrast zum Königsblau des vorgelagerten Pools. Ein Sonnendeck mit zwei Teakliegen verlangt geradezu nach Mußestunden. Und für Spa-Anwendungen in

Nicht nur Honeymoon-Paare sind begeistert von den „Intimate Moments" im privaten Jacuzzi.
Not only honeymoon couples are keen on "intimate moments" in their own private Jacuzzi.

*Hoch über der Brandung „schwebend":
der Jacuzzi der Hillside-Villa „Frégat".
"Floating" high above the surf – the Jacuzzi of
"Frégat", one of the Hillside Villas.*

Herzlich willkommen! Der Empfang des Banyan Tree Spas.
Welcome. The reception area of the Banyan Tree Spa.

Eins mit der Natur: einer von acht bemerkenswert luxuriösen Massage-Pavillons.
One with nature – one of the eight outstanding massage pavilions.

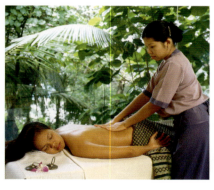

Der thailändische Massage-Pavillon bildet die Stirnseite des großzügigen Privatpools.
The Thai massage pavilion forms the end wall of the large private pool.

Spa-Therapeutin Nok gibt eine unglaublich entspannende „Essence of Earth"-Massage.
Spa therapist Nok giving an incredibly relaxing "Essence of Earth" massage.

staged to perfection by the Banyan Tree Seychelles. Like its sister hotels in Phuket, the Maldives and Bintan, this luxury resort of exclusive private villas only opened in February 2002, pampers its guests on the southwest coast of Mahé. My own Beachfront Pool Villa is a dream in a tropical paradise with 2,700 square feet of space. The white villas built in Victorian style as a reminder of the islands' colonial past, have a wood shingle roof and ceiling-high glass frontage, so that you always have the luxuriant flowers of the beautifully tended garden in view. The cream-

absoluter Privatsphäre steht mir ein eigener thailändischer Massage-Pavillon zur Verfügung. Großzügig und elegant präsentieren sich die Interieurs der Villa: Kingsize-Bett, weiße Chaiselongue im Glaserker, an den Wänden traditionelle, inseltypische Kunst. Symmetrie bestimmt das Design. Eine frei stehende Wand trennt Wohn- und Schlaftrakt optisch vom Bad- und Relaxbereich. Transparenz und die allgegenwärtige Verbindung zur Natur lassen nach kurzer Gewöhnung ein unbeschreibliches Gefühl von Freiheit aufkommen. Einfach toll, durch die deckenhohe Glaswand der Dampfsauna (die gleichzeitig auch als Dusche dient) in den von außen uneinsehbaren Garten zu schauen. Zu den Wohlfühlfaktoren dieser stimmungsvollen Logis gehören auch eine individuell regelbare Aircondition, Deckenventilator, Minibar und Kaffeekocher sowie Unterhaltungsmedien wie Sat-TV, DVD-Player und CD-Spieler. Wer eine der wunderbaren Hillside-Pool-Villen bewohnt (sie sind quadratmetermäßig etwas kleiner, aber nicht minder komfortabel), schaut wie aus einem Adlerhorst über die schwarzen

Granitklippen hinaus aufs Meer. Besonders die Villa 209 mit dem schönen Namen „Frégat" kann an Ambiance und Privatsphäre kaum überboten werden.

Rund 30 Minuten Autofahrt ist die Intendance-Bucht vom internationalen Airport und nur eine dreiviertel Stunde von der beschaulichen Hauptstadt Victoria entfernt. Doch wer in die Welt des Banyan Tree Seychelles eintaucht, lässt vom ersten Augenblick an alles andere hinter sich. Wenn es einen Ort gibt, um Frieden mit sich selbst zu finden, um Körper und Geist wieder in Harmonie zu vereinen, dann diesen. In der Ruhe und Weitläufigkeit dieses geradezu ätherischen Resorts beginnt die Seele ganz von selber zu baumeln. Eine nachhaltige Unterstützung findet der Gast im grandiosen Banyan Tree Spa – es ist Zuflucht für die Sinne, ein Hort des unbeschreiblichen Wohlgefühls, des Eintauchens in sich selbst, der tiefen Entspannung. Spa-Managerin Oijai Nawathammapon und ihre zwölf diplomierten thailändischen Therapeutinnen sind Meisterinnen im „Vertreiben" von jeglichen Anspannungen. Sie wissen genau,

Wem der eigene Pool nicht ausreicht, wechselt in den Masterpool mit Traummaßen.
If your own pool isn't big enough, you can use the much larger master pool.

coloured tiles and sandstone of the covered terrace create an harmonious contrast to the royal blue of the pool. The sundeck with two teak loungers is an open invitation to let go and relax. Spa facilities are available in one's very own Thai massage pavilion. The villa is spacious and the décor elegant. There is a king-size bed, a white chaise longue standing in a glass bay, and on the walls are local art works typical of the island. The design is characterised by its symmetry. A partition divides the living and sleeping areas from the bathroom and relaxation area. After a short while, the transparency of the place and its ever-present link with nature evoke an indescribable feeling of freedom. It's simply fantastic to be able to look straight into a private garden – concealed from public view – through the ceiling-high glass wall of the steam sauna (which also serves as a shower). Other feel-good factors of this idyllic, atmospheric villa are the adjustable air-con, ceiling fan, minibar and coffee machine as well as the entertainment hi-tech such as SAT TV, DVD-player and CD player. Guests in the wonderful Pool Villas (slighter smaller floor area but no less luxurious) live as if in an eagle's nest perched on

Exotischer Hochgenuss aus der Thai-Küche: gebratene Jacobsmuscheln und Hummerkrabben mit Aioli und grünem Chili.
Exotic delights of Thai cuisine: fried scallops and king prawns with aioli and green chillies.

Guter Geschmack ist sein Metier: der australische Küchenchef Nicholas Easton.
Good taste is his metier – Nicholas Easton, the Australian chef.

Private Dining im romantischen Rahmen.
Private dining in a romantic setting.

Exquisite Thai-Cuisine wird im eleganten Gourmetrestaurant „Saffron" serviert.
Exquisite Thai cuisine is served in the elegant "Saffron" gourmet restaurant.

the black granite cliffs overlooking the sea. Especially Villa 209 with the lovely name "Frégat" has an ambience and privacy which can be scarcely matched. Intendance Bay is roughly a half-hour drive from the international airport, and only three-quarters of an hour from Victoria, the quiet capital. Yet, from the moment they arrive, guests staying at the Banyan Tree Seychelles leave everything else behind. If there is a place where body and soul can be reunited in harmony, it is here. In the tranquillity and space of this virtually ethereal resort, the soul begins to let go of its own volition. Support of a lasting kind can be sought in the grandiose Banyan Tree Spa. Oijai Nawathammapon and her twelve qualified Thai therapists are experts in driving out all manner of tension and stress. They know exactly which massage to apply for which situation, and use west-

welche Massage in welcher Lebenslage die richtige ist, leisten mit westlichen wie fernöstlichen Techniken wirksame „Streicheleinheiten" für Physis und Psyche. Das wunderbarste Erlebnis (und das am häufigsten nachgefragte) ist die „Royal Banyan Massage". Drei Stunden totales Relaxen, umgeben von der zauberhaften Ambiance eines nach drei Seiten zum Dschungel hin offenen, herrschaftlichen Massage-Pavillons. Leise Musik mischt sich mit dem vielstimmigen Gesang exotischer Vögel und dem immer währenden Rauschen des Ozeans. Das Zeremoniell beginnt mit der Wahl eines Lieblingsduftes, der dann dezent den Raum erfüllt, und einem erfrischenden Fußbad. Anschließend wird die Haut in der Dampfsauna für die Aufnahme der wertvollen Öle und Essenzen vorbereitet (alle auf natürlicher Basis und zum Teil aus frischen Ingredienzen direkt zubereitet). Ein Honig-Sesam-Körperpeeling danach glättet jeden Zentimeter Haut, macht sie schmuseweich und samtzart. Die nachfolgende „Essence of Earth Massage" mit aromatischen Ölen sorgt für ein absolutes Maß an Tiefenentspannung, bringt sanft die Körperenergien wieder in Fluss und stärkt gleichzeitig das Immunsystem. Von der Kopf- bis zur Fußreflexzonenmassage erlebt man bei diesem einzigartigen Wellness-Programm das ganze Können der thailändischen Massage- und Entspannungskunst. Hinterher fühlt man sich wie neu geboren. Paare können die Anwendungen auf Wunsch gemeinsam

genießen. Das vielseitige Massagetherapie-Programm wird mit einem entsprechend hochkarätigen Beautyangebot, einem Spa-Shop sowie einem Fitness-Center komplettiert.

Liebe geht durch den Magen, heißt es so schön. Und weil die vielen verliebten Honeymooner gelegentlich auch mal was essen müssen, kommt die Küche leicht und angenehm aromatisch daher. Im reizenden Restaurant „Saffron" lässt die Gourmetzunge sich von original thailändischer Kochkunst bezaubern. Phantastisch das im Bananenblatt gegrillte Fischfilet mit Chili und Tamarindensauce oder die köstliche Hühnersuppe mit frischer Kokosmilch und Zitronengras. Das Zitronengras wird im eigenen Kräutergarten des Resorts angebaut (als frisch aufgebrühter Tee wirkt es übrigens sehr aufmunternd und belebend). Unschlagbar auch die à la minute zubereiteten Thai-Curries wie Ente mit rotem Curry oder das grüne Rinder-Curry mit Aubergine und süßem Basilikum. Kein Wunder, dass das „Saffron" für seine anspruchsvolle Cuisine schon mit einem Award ausgezeichnet wurde. Einen unglaublichen Panoramablick, verbunden mit internationaler und asiatischer Kochkunst vereint das Ganztagesrestaurant „Au Jardin d'Epices". Unter der Ägide von Executive Chef Nicholas Easton wird dort von Pasta über fangfrischen Fisch bis zu gebratenem Thai-Reis mit Gemüse und Hühnchen eine leichte, anspruchsvolle Bistroküche aufgetischt.

ern and far-eastern techniques to administer "tender loving care" for body and soul. The most wonderful (and most frequently requested) experience is the Royal Banyan Massage. Three whole hours of total relaxation surrounded by the enchanting ambience of a majestic massive pavilion open on three side to the jungle. Soothing music mingles with the polyphony of exotic songbirds and the perpetual sound of the ocean.

The ceremony begins with choosing a favourite fragrance which then gently pervades the room, after this one has a refreshing footbath. Finally the skin is softened up in the steam sauna before the application of precious oils and essences, some of which are prepared on the spot with fresh natural ingredients. The honey-sesame body peeling smoothes every inch of the skin making it soft and velvety. The ensuing "Essence of Earth Massage" using aromatic oils brings about total deep relaxation and stimulates the body's energy while at the same time strengthening the immune system. This unique wellness programme includes the whole gamut of Thai massage and relaxation techniques from head to foot reflex zone. Afterwards one feels new-born. Couples can enjoy the treatment together. The varied programme of massage therapy is matched by equally high-quality beauty treatment, a spa shop and a fitness centre.

It is said that love goes through the stomach, and because the many adoring honeymoon couples have to eat now and again, the cuisine is light and aromatic. In the lovely "Saffron" restaurant, bon vivants can delight in original Thai cooking. The grilled fish filets with chilli and tamarind sauce wrapped in banana leaves is simply fantastic, so is the delicious chicken soup. The lemon grass is grown in the resort's own herb garden (it lifts the spirit and is very stimulating when prepared as an herbal tea). The quick-fix Thai curries such as duck with a red curry, and the green beef curry with aubergine and sweet basil are unbeatable. The "Au Jardin d'Epices" restaurant which is open all day combines an incredible panoramic view with the international cuisine and Asian cooking. Under the direction of Chief Executive Nicholas Easton, a sophisticated menu of light bistro food is served ranging from pasta and freshly-caught fish, to fried Thai rice with pullet and vegetables.

Von einer leichten Brise erfrischt, genießt man den Blick von der Bar „La Varangue" hinaus aufs Meer.
Admiring the ocean view from the "La Varangue" Bar, refreshed by a light breeze.

Das neue Juwel auf den Seychellen

SAINTE ANNE RESORT

The new gem in the Seychelles

Das Hotel Royal Palm, das Dinarobin Golf & Spa, das Paradis Golf & Fishing Club und das Shandrani sind nur einige der Top-Hotels, die die einheimische Hotelgruppe Beachcomber seit vielen Jahren auf Mauritius sehr erfolgreich unter den besten Adressen der Insel etabliert hat. Ende des vergangenen Jahres folgte das erste Hotelprojekt auf den Seychellen, das Sainte Anne Resort. Eine Viertelstunde von der Hauptinsel Mahé entfernt, entstand auf einem kleinen Eiland im National Marine Park ein weiteres Hideaway für höchste Ansprüche.

The Royal Palm Hotel, the Dinarobin Golf & Spa, the Paradise Golf & Fishing Club, and the Shandrani are just some of the top hotels which the local Beachcomber Hotel Group has succesfully established on Mauritius over many years, and which count among the best addresses of the island. At the end of last year, the group embarked on its first hotel project in the Seychelles, the Sainte Anne Resort. On a small island in the National Marine Park only fifteen minutes away from the main island of Mahé, is a further hideaway which comes up to the highest standards.

Text & Fotos: Jürgen Gutowski

Der traumhafte Strandabschnitt der Royal Villa.
The Royal Villa's beautiful strip of beach.

Exklusive Interieurs empfangen die Gäste der Royal Villa.
Guests at the Royal Villa are surrounded by exclusive interiors.

The plane comes to a halt right in front of the coconut palms. The international airport on the Seychelles is bathed in the tropical light of a Monday morning in the middle of the Indian Ocean, not far from the equator. Steaming air and jungle smells stream into the cabin. The temperature is already 30 °C. early in the morning, as it is every day and always has been, unchanged for millions of years. It's a day like any other yet here everything is different. The takamaka trees register the colours of every season at once, iridescent Spring green beside the golden colours of autumn foliage. Brilliant red flame trees with bright red sparrows fluttering around in its branches stand beside bare latex trees completely stripped of leaves with frigate birds, rare visitors from the north, observing from their boughs. At the open air passport control the officer stamps a coco-de-mer in my passport, and a few minutes later I am sitting in a taxi taking me to the nearby private jetty of the St Anne Resort close to the harbour in Victoria which, with only 16,000 inhabitants, is the smallest capital in the world. Water and cool flannels are handed out at the jetty and someone takes my luggage, which I find later on sorted out in my room. The crossing takes less than fifteen minutes. St Anne, a small island after which the latest addition to the Mauritian Beachcomber hotel group has been named, is in the National Marine Park east of Mahé. The red-tiled roofs of the Sainte Anne Resort shimmer from a distance through the palms fringing the beach. Behind it are hills densely covered with impenetrable jungle interspersed with the granite rocks common to the Seychelles, and which enclose the ends of "Saint Anne's" three beaches. Guests are received at an open-air reception area covered by a Japanese-style roof. The restaurants, the Clarins-Spa and the bar are also out in the open, hardly surprising in a tropical climate all the year round. I register my details with a fruit cocktail in hand, then

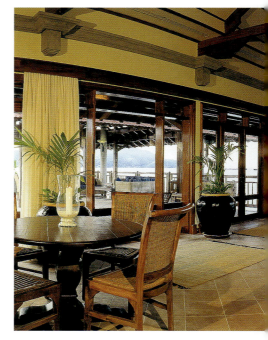

Die Maschine kommt direkt vor den Kokospalmen zum Stehen, der Internationale Airport der Seychellen liegt in der tropischen Beschaulichkeit eines Montagmorgens mitten im Indischen Ozean, nicht weit vom Äquator. Dampfend heiß strömt Dschungelluft und -duft in die Kabine, 30 Grad schon am frühen Morgen. Wie an jedem Morgen, an jedem Tag rund ums Jahr, seit Jahrmillionen unverändert. Ein Tag wie jeder andere; doch alles ist anders hier. Auf den Takamakabäumen finden alle Jahreszeiten gleichzeitig statt, Frühlingsgrün leuchtet neben goldenem Herbstlaub. Knallrote Flammenbäume, durch deren Blätter genauso rote Spatzen toben, neben völlig entblätterten Latexbäumen, auf deren knorrigen Ästen weiße Fregattevögel die seltsamen Ankömmlinge aus dem Norden observieren. Durch die Open-air-Passkontrolle, der Beamte stempelt eine *coco-de-mer* in mei-

Ein uneinsehbarer Pool gewährleistet den Gästen der Royal Villa ultimative Privatsphäre.
The pool which is hidden from view ensure complete privacy for Royal Villa guests.

am driven by one of the staff along good island roads to my little terrace villa on the west beach of the resort. Humming up hill and down dale we drive by two floodlit tennis courts, cross an artificial brook, and park the Smart car in a correspondingly tiny parking space on the "road". I go into my "Villa Providence" one of the 79 standard rooms which on closer inspection turns out to be spacious enough. The accommodation (approx. 540 square feet) is divided into zones for living, sleeping and bathing. It has showers inside and out, and a "gazebo" – an open-air pavilion - adds a further 322 square feet to the living area. A small private garden lends the accommodation a real sense of space. Standing in the middle of the room on the warm terracotta tiles covering the floor from the terrace to the bathroom, I survey the scene. There is a large double bed on which are bright scatter cushions and a bolster large enough for two. On either side of the bed at the head end are swivel

Selbst die Standardzimmer verfügen über eine Wohnfläche von 50 qm sowie einen 30 qm großen Open-air-Pavillon.

Even the standard rooms have an area of over 538 sq. feet, and a 322-foot open-air pavilion.

Seychellen-Idylle pur: rundgewaschene Felsen und menschenleere Strände.

Seychelles idyll: rocks rounded by waves and deserted beaches.

lamps on stands which resemble organ pipes, and hanging on the wall is a work of art, a wooden palm leaf displayed behind glass. The chair beside the desk and the armchairs are of a pale rattan and have cushions matching the ones on the bed. In my room is a chest with a bowl of fruit on it, and the minibar in the corner is stocked with local "Seybrew" and soft drinks. I also have a TV with 12 international channels, adjustable air-conditioning, a kettle and instant tea and coffee, room service is available from morning to night. The room has more than is promised by other five-star hotels in the Seychelles.

The light and airy bathroom shows how Beachcomber professionals have learnt from the mistakes of their Seychelles competitors. They have thought of absolutely everything. There are two wash-basins, a real walk-in wardrobe, plenty of hangers, a safe (super-fluous really, considering the

nen Pass, die einzige Abbildung eines weiblichen Hinterteils in meinem Ausweis, und wenige Minuten später sitze ich bereits im Taxi zur nahe gelegenen Privat Jetty des Sainte Anne Resorts nahe dem Hafen von Victoria, der mit 16 000 Einwohnern kleinsten Hauptstadt der Welt. In der überdachten Anlegestelle werden Wasser und kühle Tücher gereicht, jemand nimmt sich des Gepäcks an, das ich später wohl sortiert in meinem Zimmer wiederfinden werde. Nicht mal eine Viertelstunde dauert die Überfahrt nach Ste. Anne, der kleinen Insel im National Marine Park östlich von Mahé, nach der soeben das jüngste Kind der mauritianischen Hotelgruppe Beachcomber benannt wurde. Die

roten Ziegeldächer des Sainte Anne Resorts schimmern schon von Ferne durch die Palmen am Strand. Dahinter erheben sich dicht bewachsene Hügel, undurchdringlicher Urwald, durchbrochen von den für die Seychellen so typischen Granitfelsen, die auch die drei Strände der „Heiligen Anna" an ihren Enden einfassen.

Das Kinderspiel „Fang' den Hut" kommt mir in den Sinn: Die Rezeption mit ihrem japanisch anmutenden Vierfachdach, open air wie die Restaurants, das Clarins-Spa und die Bar, empfangen die Gäste hell und klar, kein Wunder bei unaufhörlichem Tropenwetter rund ums Jahr. Bei einem erfrischenden Fruchtcocktail erledige ich die Formalitäten, und danach fährt ein motorisierter guter Geist mich über befestigte Inselsträßchen zu meiner Villa am westlichen Strand des Resorts. Vorbei an zwei Flutlichttennisplätzen surren wir über Berg und Tal, überqueren einen künstlich angelegten Bach und parken das „smarte" Fahrzeug in einem passend winzigen Carport an der „Straße". Ich betrete meine „Villa Providence", eins von 79 Standardzimmern, das sich jedoch bei näherem Hinschauen als echte Raumgröße erweist: 50 qm Wohn-, Schlaf- und Badefläche mit Innen- und Außenduschen, dazu der „Gazebo", ein nochmals knapp 30 qm umfassender, möblierter Open-air-Pavillon, und ein kleiner privater Garten daneben, der meinem Gesamtgrundstück wahre Größe verleiht. Auf warmen Terrakottafliesen, die den Boden von der Terrasse bis zum Bad bedecken, stehe ich in der Mitte des Zimmers und schaue mich um: Ein großes Doppelbett, auf dem bunte Zierkissen und eine pärchenfähige Nackenrolle ruhen, links und rechts am Kopfende schwenkbare Nachtlämpchen an orgelpfeifenähnlichen Haltern, an der Wand ein glasgeschütztes Palmenblatt, ein Kunstwerk ganz aus Holz. Schreibtischstuhl und Sessel aus hellem Rattan mit Kissen passend zu denen auf dem Bett. Eine Truhe mit einem Früchteteller, in der Ecke eine Minibar mit ein-

Auch in den Villen „Belle Vue" und „Villa Providence" braucht man auf keinen Luxus zu verzichten.
Guests in the "Belle Vue" and "Villa Providence" villas are also fully provided for.

heimischem „Seybrew" und Softdrinks, TV mit 12 internationalen Programmen, eine regelbare Air-Con, Wasserkocher samt Instantkaffee und Tee, Room Service von früh morgens bis kurz vor Mitternacht – der Raum hält mehr als andere Seychellen-Hotels im Fünf-Sterne-Bereich verspricht! Und auch nebenan im lichtdurchfluteten Bad haben die Profis von Beachcomber aus den Fehlern der Seychellen-Konkurrenz gelernt und an alles gedacht: Es gibt zwei Waschbecken, einen wirklich begehbaren Kleiderschrank, wirklich ausreichend Kleiderbügel, einen – bei exklusiver Insellage eigentlich überflüssigen – Safe, ein Bügeleisenbrett, separates WC, Innen- und Außenduschen und vieles mehr, was Sinn und Laune macht.

Am menschenleeren Strand, unter gewaltigen Takamakabäumen hindurch, an uralten Flaschenhalspalmen vorbei, wandere ich den rund einen Kilometer langen Weststrand hinauf. In der Ferne ragen die bewaldeten Höhen der Nachbarinsel Mahé in den tropischen Himmel, Frachtschiffe landen gemächlich im nahen Hafen von Victoria an, über dem lächelnden Spätnachmittag kreisen fliegende Hunde auf der Suche nach ihrer vegetarischen Nachspeise. Dort, wo der Strand zu Ende ist, wo riesige Granitblöcke grau und gewaltig wie Elefantenrücken das Gestade begrenzen, entdecke ich das kulinarischste Baumhaus, das je ein Architekt zwischen Baumkronen, Felsen und Strand „gestelzt" hat. Ein paar Treppen hinauf, durch das Spalier zweier Pälmchen, die jedem Gast sanft die Schultern streicheln, und ich befinde mich im „Mont Fleuri", das kulinarische Reich von Chef Fabio di Poli, der hier Abend für Abend die lukullischen Sensationen seiner italienischen Heimat inszeniert. Unter den vier spitzen Strohdächern, umfächelt von milden Meeresbrisen und italienischen und französischen Chansons, genieße ich in diesem romantischen Baumhaus später köstlichstes Risotto, ein Glas perlenden Chardonnay aus Südafrika, und ich lasse mich ausnahmsweise überreden zu einer echten „Cohiba Exquisito" direkt aus Havanna. Mont Fleuri – bei der „Heiligen Anna", Grund genug für einen Besuch der Insel!

Ein hübscher Spaziergang oder der kostenlose Shuttle führen zum zweiten Restaurant von Sainte Anne: Neben dem geschwungenen Pool, gegenüber der Bar, nicht weit vom wunderbar weißen Sandstrand, den man hier großzügig erweitert hat, finde ich mich im „L'Abondance", dem exquisiten Spezialitätenrestaurant, wo Chef Marcel Driesen aus

exclusive island location), a separate toilet, inside and outside showers, and much else to keep you happy.

I take a stroll along the deserted 2/3-mile long western beach, walking beneath massive takamaka trees and past ancient bottleneck palms. In the distance the wooded heights of the neighbouring island of Mahé rise up into the tropical sky. Freighters berth in leisurely fashion in the nearby Victoria harbour, and in the sunny late afternoon large Batman-like bats circle in search of their vegetarian dessert.

At the end of the beach bordered by giant grey granite blocks, I come across a culinary tree house which at some point an architect built on stilts between the treetops, the rocks and the beach. Going up a couple of steps and through a little trellis of palm fronds which brush my shoulder, I find myself inside "Mont Fleuri", the culinary realm of the chef

Im Spa-Pool kann man genüsslich die Seele baumeln lassen.
One really let go in the Spa pool.

Fabio di Poli, who at dinner time serves up the sensational creations of his home country, Italy. Ensconced beneath the tree house's four pointed roofs and fanned by mild sea breezes, I enjoy a delicious risotto washed down with a pearly glass of South African Chardonnay to the sound of Italian and French chansons. I am even persuaded to have a genuine Chiba Exquisit direct from Havanna. Mont Fleuri is reason enough to visit the island of Saint Anne. A pleasant walk leads to the second restaurant – or you can go by the free shuttle. L'Abondance is an exquisite restaurant beside a curved pool opposite a bar, and not far from the wonderfully white beach which has been considerably extended. As well as Creole chicken curry, the Dutch chef Marcel Driesen also cooks at least 20 fresh fish dishes and Arab food, including lamb and grilled veal ribs with spring onions and shiitake mushrooms. His incredible chicken roulades served with teriyaki sauce are

Holland neben kreolischem Hühner-Curry mindestens zwanzig frische Fischgerichte, außerdem arabische Lammfleischkreationen, gegrillte Kalbsrippe mit Frühlingszwiebeln und Shiitakepilzen oder die unerhört leckeren Chicken-Rouladen mit Teriyaki-Soße reicht. Das Ganze bei klassischen Klängen und Kerzenschein, ganz nach Wunsch zwischen mächtigen steinernen Säulen unterm roten Dach oder unterm Sternenhimmel und grünen Palmen. Ich will die „Heilige Anna" nicht schon wieder bemühen, aber auch hier muss die Lieblingsheilige des Genussmenschen Martin Luther unsichtbar die Hand der sieben Köche führen!

Nur ein paar Minuten spaziere ich vom L'Abondance einen kleinen, privaten Hügel hinauf. Normalerweise haben hier nur die Gäste der „Royal Villa" Zutritt (oder „Zufahrt" im privaten E-Mobil, das im Tagespreis von 3500 bis knapp 6000 Euro bereits enthalten ist). In diesem von Türmchen besetzten Tropenschlösschen erfüllt sich jeder Traum: Auf rund 500 qm Wohn-, Schlaf-, Feier-, Bade-

Feine Küche mit Panoramablick: das Restaurant „Mont Fleuri".
Fine cuisine with a panoramic view: the "Mont Fleuri" restaurant.

und Aussichtsfläche legt Beachcomber dem distinguierten Reisenden das bislang ultimativste Ferienwohnerlebnis der Seychellen zu Füßen. Drei fulminante Spitzdach-Schlafzimmer, wo man unter handgeschnitzten Holzkonstruktionen nächtigt, sind ausgestattet mit privatem Balkon oder Terrasse, alle mit riesigem eigenen Bad mit 180-Grad-Panoramafenster und Whirlpool – drei Wohnungen in einer verteilen sich über die verschiedenen Ebenen des Domizils. An den Wänden schillern die tropischen Gemälde des berühmtesten Malers der Seychellen, Michael Adams. Die Kleiderschränke sind angesichts ihrer Geräumigkeit eher schon befahrbar als begehbar, der Pool in Form einer überdimensionalen Vogelschwinge lädt draußen auf zwei Etagen zum Bade, dazwischen ergießt sich zwischen gewaltigen Granitblöcken ein Wasserfall von einem Becken ins andere. Das Zentrum der „Royal Villa" ist das rund 100 qm große Wohnzimmer, wo man neben Zimmerpalmen in wuchtigen Töpfen und meterhohen griechischen Vasen in schwarz-blauen, wuchtigen, rückenrunden Sofas und Sesseln ruht. DVD, Flat Screen und mehr sind obligatorisch, aber Naturfernsehen pur bieten die 15 Meter umlaufenden Panoramafenster vom Boden bis zur Decke. Der Blick streift über den gleichzeitig offenen und überdachten Außenpavillon, über den bereits erwähnten – von außen uneinsehbaren – Pool samt Sonnenliegen hinüber nach Mahé und weiter zum Strand und auf die grünen Höhen und weiter in die Weiten des Indischen Ozeans. Und ganz weit draußen, in den segelnden Wolken, da wo Horizont und Himmel sich berühren, da lächelt Sainte Anne gütig auf den staunenden Journalisten. Doch nein, das ist nur des Autors Poesie.

delicious, and all this can be enjoyed to the strains of classical music and candlelight. You can either sit between large stone pillars beneath a red ceiling or under the stars and the green palms. Saint Anne must be guiding the hands of the cooks here.
Later on, I take a walk up the little private hill only a few minutes from L'Abondance. Normally only guests staying at the "Royal Villa" have access either on foot (or by the private Emobile included in the daily rates from 3,500 – about 6,000 Euro). In allowing for 5,400 square feet of space divided into areas for living, sleeping, bathing and viewing, Beachcomber has provided its distinguished visitors with the very ultimate in top holiday accommodation in the Seychelles. Each of the three wonderfully spacious bedrooms where you sleep beneath a hand-carved wooden construction has a balcony or terrace, each with an enormous bath, a picture window and a whirlpool. Three apartments rolled into one are spread across the various levels of the residence. Hanging on the walls are brightly coloured paintings of tropical themes by Michael Adams, the most famous artist in the Seychelles. The wardrobes are so large that they qualify as "drive-in" rather than "walk-in". Outside, a pool on two levels in the shape of a bird's wing is a tempting prospect. In between two giant granite blocks is a waterfall with water gushing from one basin to another. The centre of the Royal Villa is a living area covering roughly 1,080 square metres of floor space. One relaxes on massive blue-black rounded sofas and armchairs surrounded by house palms in massive pots and tall Grecian urns. It goes without saying that there is DVD and a flat screen, but you have live TV on your own doorstep, the encircling floor-to-ceiling picture window. I gaze past the covered, open-sided pavilion and the private pool and sunbeds hidden from view, taking in the scene. Beyond it is Mahé and the beach, and beyond that the green hills and a vast expanse of the Indian Ocean. Even farther out, where clouds are sailing by and heaven touches the earth at the horizon, Sainte Anne is smiling down on this amazed travel writer – if I may be allowed a little poetic licence.

Küchenchef des Spezialitätenrestaurants L'Abondance: Marcel Driesen.

Marcel Driesen – Chef of the L'Abondance speciality restaurant.

Die Hüter von Eden *The Guardians of Eden*

SONEVA GILI

Text: Jürgen Gutowski, Fotos: Jürgen & Martina Gutowski

Die Hüter von Eden *The Guardians of Eden*

Alle 44 Suiten auf dem kleinen Eiland Lankanfushi werden ausschließlich von Water Villas beherbergt.
All 44 suites on the little island of Lankanfushi are in the Water Villas.

The night flight to Male ends with a magnificent finale. Mother Nature has prepared our reception – a dazzling watercolour and a kaleidoscope of peacock feathers scattered below in the warmest sea in the world. As our plane descends oval lagoons - stretches of turquoise and light blue water hemmed in by the white rim of a protective reef - shimmer, and in the centre of each is lush green foliage. The scene expands as our jet descends. Even Male's airport is a separate island, one of 1,200 which constitute the Republic of

Der Nachtflug nach Male endet in einem prachtvollen Finale: Zum Empfang präsentiert Mutter Natur ein vielfarbiges Gemälde aus gleißenden Wasserfarben und einem Kaleidoskop aus Pfauenaugen, verstreut dort unten im wärmsten Meer der Welt. Während die Maschine tiefer sinkt, schillern die ovalen Lagunen, die runden Flachgewässer in Türkis und Hellblau, an den Rändern durch ein schützendes Riff weiß eingefasst, in der Mitte grün bewachsen, immer größer werdend herauf zum landenden Jet. Selbst der Flughafen von Male ist eine Insel für sich, eine von mehr als 1200, die die Islamische Republik Malediven bilden.

Am Zoll und an den Passkontrollen arbeitet man zügig, und so sitze ich bereits nach wenigen Minuten im Speed-Boot nach Lankanfushi. Ein Butler reicht schon an Bord kühle Tücher und Drinks und packt im Gegenzug meine Schuhe ein, irgendwann nächste Woche wird er sie mir wieder aushändigen. Schnell wird klar: Dress Code und Vorschriften sind Fehlanzeige im Soneva Gili Resort auf dem nur 600 mal 200 Meter kleinen Eiland im maledivischen Nord-Atoll, das wir schon nach einer guten Viertelstunde Bootsfahrt erreichen.

Barfuß betrete ich die hölzernen Planken, aus dem hier die Inselträume sind. Wie die Finger einer Hand ragen diese „Jetties" an drei Stellen der Koralleninsel jeweils ein paar hundert Meter weit in die türkisfarbenen Fluten. Alle 44 Suiten und Residenzen von Soneva Gili – ohne Beispiel auf den Malediven – sind „Water Villas": auf Stelzen in die hellblaue Lagune gesetzt wie Hütchen in einem überdimensionalen Monopolyspiel. Die Schlossallee sozusagen bilden die sieben Crusoe-Residenzen, doch hier versagt das Monopolybild, denn diese Villas erreicht man weder über einen Holzsteg noch mittels einer Straße, sondern nur mit dem eigenen Paddelboot oder mit dem *Dhoni*, einer kleinen überdachten Fähre, die zu jeder Tages- und Nachtzeit bereit steht, die beneidenswerten Robinson Crusoes zum Restaurant oder zur Tauchschule, zum

Maldives. Customs' officers work fast so after only a few minutes I am sitting in a speed boat to Lankanfushi. Without delay a butler hands out cold flannels and drinks, and in return takes my shoes and packs them. They will be handed back to me sometime next week. I get the message - dress code, rules and regulations are simply dispensed with at the Soneva Gili Resort, a tiny island of only 30 acres in the north atoll of the Maldives. We arrive just over 15 minutes later. I step barefoot on to the wooden planks which form island dreams. Each of the three jetties is a couple of hundred yards long and reaches out from the coral island into the turquoise water like the fingers of a hand. All of the 44 suites and residences of Soneva Gili are Water Villas perched on stilts standing in the light blue lagoon, like little huts on a huge Monopoly board. They are without parallel in the whole of the Maldives. For instance, the seven Crusoe Residences are on Park Lane, but here the Monopoly metaphor ends because they can't be reached either via a wooden walkway or by way of a street. They can only be accessed by paddleboat, or by "dhoni", a small covered ferry which is available at any time of the day or night to ferry the enviable Robinson Crusoes to the restaurant, the diving school, a neighbour or into the sunset! Yet only rarely do guests take advantage of this service because the temptation never to leave one's watery castle until the end of one's days is too great - and this doesn't only apply to the Robinsons but to all the overwater residents of Soneva Gili. Every single villa causes the long-haul traveller to gasp as he steps into his private refuge. The two-storey wooden house is at once the perfect example of environmentally-friendly architecture and a shelter of uncompromising luxury, evidence indeed within an area of 1,615 square feet that a moderate

Die Crusoe-Residenzen erreicht man nur mit dem eigenen Paddelboot oder einem kleinen Dhoni.

The Crusoe residences can only be reached with your own paddle boat or by the small dhoni.

HIDEAWAYS 57

Das Wohnzimmer der 150 qm großen Residenzen ist mehr als großzügig geschnitten. The living room in the residences, which are 1,615 square feet in area, is large.

level of tourism and a holiday in the land of Cockaigne need not be a contradiction in terms. All the roofs and floors, walls and furniture, curtains and mattresses, lamp shades, fruit bowls, toiletries, door stoppers and glass building blocks are made from ecologically-sound materials. The water and sparkling wine glasses are recycled, the teak comes from a plantation, all the colours applied are non-toxic, the candles, the ropes - everything is locally produced. The staff conduct themselves in hotel text book fashion - 160 assistants cater for the needs of 90 guests at most with total commitment and great charm. The result is a standard of service which has no parallel, and not only in the Maldives. However, let's return to the suites. In the middle of the ground, or rather the water floor, there is a large open roofed-over lounge with large wooden board games ranging from backgammon to chess. The space has several niches in which are bright mattresses and cushions, and a fan spins above a chest of drawers which has a well-stocked minibar. Beside it are steps which lead down to the cantilever sun deck and the water. On the left is the air-conditioned bedroom which is dominated by a king-size bed with bed-clothes of finest linen and draped with a gauze mosquito net. The ceiling-high picture window and a further cosy corner padded with romantic cushions in bright, sunny colours afford uninterrupted ocean views. Those who are not content with such "tele"-views can open a little cupboard which contains a state-of-the-art flat-faced TV with international satellite programmes and a DVD-player. Even videos are available à la carte. It only takes minutes for room service to deliver "Goldfinger", "Evita", "Our man in Havana" or any other film on the 13-page list, as well as popcorn, home-made chocolate, or a glass of Sauterne with blue cheese. For

Nachbarn oder in den Sonnenuntergang zu chauffieren. Doch nur selten scheint jemand diesen Fährdienst in Anspruch zu nehmen, denn zu groß ist wohl die Verlockung, das eigene Wasserschloss nicht mehr zu verlassen

Naturerlebnis pur: eine Massage direkt am Sandstrand.
Pure bliss – massage on the beach.

bis zum Ende aller Tage. Und das ist verständlich nicht nur bei den Robinsons, sondern bei allen Over-Water-Residenten von Soneva Gili. Denn jede Villa verschlägt selbst dem weit gereisten Luxus-Traveller mit sofortiger Wirkung den Atem, wenn er sein privates Refugium betritt. Das doppelstöckige Holzhaus ist gleichzeitig ein Paradebeispiel ökologisch-organischer Architektur sowie Hort kompromisslosen Luxus'. Auf rund 150 Quadratmetern Wohnfläche wird bewiesen, dass sanfter Tourismus keineswegs im Gegensatz zu schlaraffenlandähnlichen Urlauben steht. Alle Dächer und Dielen, alle Wände und Möbel, sämtliche Vorhänge und Matratzen, Lampenschirme und Obstschalen, Toilettenartikel, Türstopper, Glasbausteine etc. sind aus umweltfreundlichen Materialien. Sekt- und Wassergläser wurden recycelt, das Teakholz stammt aus Plantagenzucht, alle verwendeten Farben sind ungiftig, die Kerzen, Seile – alles entstammt einheimischer Produktion. Das Personal präsentiert sich wie im Lehrbuch der Hotellerie: 160 Menschen kümmern sich hier voll wirklich freundlicher Hingabe um die höchstens 90 Gäste – das Ergebnis ist ein Service-Niveau, das nicht nur auf den Malediven seinesgleichen suchen dürfte! Doch zurück zu den Suiten: In der Mitte des Erd- oder besser Wassergeschosses findet sich eine große offene, wenngleich überdachte möblierte Lounge, hier laden große hölzerne Spiele zu Backgammon oder Schach, mehrere Nischen dieses „Zwischenraums" sind gepolstert mit freundlichen Matratzen und Kissen, über der Kommode, in der sich eine reich bestückte Minibar

befindet, dreht sich der Ventilator, daneben führt eine kleine Treppe zur Sonnenplattform hinunter zum Wasser. Zur Linken betritt man das klimatisierte Schlafzimmer, dominiert von einem hochwertigen Kingsize-Bett, das betucht ist mit feinstem Linnen und beschirmt mit heller Gaze in Form eines Moskitonetzes. Durch Panoramafenster vom Boden bis zur Decke und in einer weiteren romantischen Kissen-Kuschelnische in sonnigen Farben hat man freien Blick auf die Weiten des Ozeans – und wem soviel Fernsicht nicht reicht, der öffnet ein weiteres Schränkchen, in dem sich ein moderner Flachbildfernseher mit internationalen Satellitenprogrammen und ein DVD-Player befinden. Selbst die Videos werden à la carte gereicht, binnen Minuten liefert der Room Service „Goldfinger", „Evita", „Havanna" oder einen anderen Streifen aus der dreizehnseitigen Filmliste, dazu auf Wunsch frisches Popcorn, selbst gemachte Schokolade oder ein Glas Sauternes mit Blue Cheese. Wem der Sinn mehr nach Hörgenuss steht, hat die Wahl unter rund 300 CDs aus allen erdenklichen Musik-Genres. Nur den

those who prefer to listen rather than watch, there are around 300 CDs of all conceivable types of music. The only other sound you can hear is the ever-blowing warm wind on your private terrace, which is also furnished and partially roofed-over, and being concealed from view.
Each villa has two little flights of steps down to the fascinating underwater world of the Maldives. Snorkel fun is literally on your doorstep and is illuminated at night. Even in knee-deep water this side of the reef one encounters the spectacular life of this watery realm. Ray and all manner of brilliantly coloured fish and innumerable sea creatures dart around the bright coral formations in the crystal-clear waters. The highlights of Maldivian underwater world can also be experienced on day safaris to 20 different

Mit Früchten aromatisierte Bäder und Massagen versierter Therapeuten garantieren im Spa höchste Entspannung.
The fruit aroma baths and massage provided by the spa's experienced therapists enable you relax completely.

In dem Restaurant wird eine delikate mediterran-asiatische Küche serviert, bei der natürlich Fisch und viel frisches Obst die Hauptprodukte darstellen.

The restaurant serves a delicious Mediterranean-Asian cuisine with plenty of fish and fruit.

diving grounds in the north and south atoll, where reef fish such as sharks, barracudas, tuna fish and the famous mantas live side by side. A popular diving venue is the nearby "Manta Point", which has in the meantime gained a worldwide reputation for its huge manta population. An absolute must for all underwater photographers is the "Cleaner Station" where "underwater flyers" sometimes up to nearly 20 feet in width are relieved of their parasites one after another by patient couples of "worker fish". Skin divers descend to a depth of about 98 feet into the coral gardens to observe the rainbow coloured tropical fish which since 1995, just like mussels and coral, may no longer be caught. Back on land we drink beer from Bremen or Bangkok, fizzy beer from Munich or mineral water from Pellegrino. There aren't many hotel bars that can offer such a comprehensive choice of drinks. The straw-thatched Soneva Bar built on stilts standing in the still water looks like a wooden flying saucer hovering over the turquoise lagoon of Lankanfushi Island. Guests sit either at tables or, if they're so inclined, stretch out on a large turquoise mattress and cushions in one of the open air niches. Here a midday siesta isn't frowned upon but positively encouraged. Whether at the bar or in the restaurant on land,

ewigen warmen Wind hört man dagegen auf der privaten Dachterrasse; sie ist ebenfalls möbliert, zum Teil überdacht, auf jeden Fall uneinsehbar.

Zwei direkte Treppchen zur faszinierenden Unterwasserwelt der Malediven gibt es in jeder Villa, das Schnorchlerglück ist hier buchstäblich unmittelbar und nachts sogar beleuchtet. Schon im knietiefen Wasser diesseits des Riffs begegnet man den spektakulären Bewohnern dieser Gefilde: Rochen, Trompeten- und Schmetterlingsfische und unzählige weitere Meeresbewohner tummeln sich im kristallklaren Wasser um die bunten Korallenformationen. Die Highlights maledivischer Unterwasserwelt lassen sich etwas weiter entfernt am Hausriff oder auf einer der Tagessafaris zu 20 verschiedenen Tauchgebieten im Nord- und Süd-Male-Atoll erleben, wo sich Rifffische, Haie, Barrakudas, Thunfische und die berühmten Mantas ein Stelldichein geben. Ein begehrtes Tauchziel ist denn auch der nahe „Manta-Point", der wegen seiner ge-

waltigen Mantapopulation inzwischen weltweite Reputation genießt. Ein Muss für alle Unterwasserfotografen ist dabei die *Cleaner Station*, wo sich die bis zu sechs Meter Spannweite messenden „Unterwasserflieger" geduldig und der Reihe nach von paarweise „arbeitenden" Putzerfischen von ihren Parasiten befreien lassen. In bis zu 30 Meter tiefe Korallengärten steigen die Taucher und bestaunen die regenbogenfarbenen Tropenfische, die hier genauso wie Muscheln und Korallen seit 1995 nicht mehr gefangen bzw. entnommen werden dürfen.

Zurück an Land trinken wir ein Bier aus Bremen oder Bangkok, ein Weizen aus München oder ein Wasser aus Pellegrino: Nicht viele Hotelbars bieten einen solchen 360-Grad-Rundumblick an. Strohgedeckt und gleichfalls auf Stelzen ins flache Gewässer gebaut, gleicht die Soneva Bar einem hölzernen Ufo, schwebend über der türkisfarbenen Lagune von Lankanfushi Island. Hier sitzt man entweder an Tischen oder aber man streckt sich

nach Lust und Laune in eine der Open-Air-Nischen aus großen türkisgrünen Matratzen und Kissen, der Mittagsschlaf am Orte des Genusses ist hier nicht verpönt, sondern ausdrücklich erwünscht. Ob an der Bar oder im Restaurant an Land: Am zutreffendsten lässt sich die Küche von Soneva Gili beschreiben als „Mediterranean-Asian". Das umfangreiche A-la-carte-Menü reflektiert die Schätze des Meeres, jedes Mahl ist ein Treffen der frischesten Meeresfrüchte, das Fleisch wird importiert aus Australien und Kräuter und Gemüse stammen größtenteils aus dem eigenen gehegten und gepflegten Kräutergarten, dessen fruchtbarer Boden eigens aus Indien importiert wurde. Jeden Abend steht ein neues, leichtes Vier-Gänge-Menü auf der Karte, dazu vegetarische und Spa-Spezialitäten. Ich staune über die Fülle von Küche und Keller angesichts der Abgeschiedenheit dieser winzigen Sandbank, scheinbar verloren in den Weiten des Indischen Ozeans. Und dieses Staunen verstärkt sich noch beim Blick in den Weinkeller des Resorts, der angesichts von zwölf verschiedenen Champagnermarken und der edelsten Sorten aus Burgund, Trentino, Spanien, Österreich, Australien, Südafrika, Israel und Chile – um nur einige Anbaugebiete zu nennen – eigentlich wie ein Safe gesichert werden müsste. Dies ist jedoch genau wie bei den Unterkünften nicht notwendig, versichert amüsiert der Wein-Butler, Sicherheitsprobleme aller Art sind auf dieser Robinsoninsel unbekannt!

Jenseits des Sternezählens setzt man bei den Hotels aus der Six-Senses-Familie auf eine genussvolle Sinnlichkeit und erhabenen Luxus, wobei alles höchsten internationalen Standards entspricht und doch zusammengeht mit einem einfachen, natürlichen Feeling für lokales Design, original einheimische Architektur und unprätentiösen Service. Das Lebensgefühl und die Erfahrungen, die sich angesichts dieser „einfachen" Urlaubswerte einstellen, lassen sich umschreiben mit den Worten „aufatmen", „Zeit haben", „entspannen", „genussvolles Nichtstun" und „zu sich kommen". So besuchen denn die Gäste nicht eine von vielen austauschbaren Hotelinseln auf den Malediven, sondern sie sind zu Gast bei Soneva Gili oder dem Schwesterhotel Soneva Fushi, jenen unverwechselbaren Orten, an denen das Bewusstsein für Natur und Mensch an erster Stelle steht, nicht so sehr ein Produkt, sondern vielmehr eine Erfahrung – *Soneva is good for you.*

the cuisine can be described as Mediterranean-Asian. The large à la carte menu reflects the wealth of sea, and every meal is a combination of freshest sea food, meat imported from Australia, and herbs and vegetables most of which are grown in the resort's own carefully tended herb and vegetable garden for which fertile soil was imported from India. Every evening a light new four-course meal is on the menu, including vegetarian meals and special spa food. I am astounded at the abundance of food and drink despite the isolation of this tiny sandbank, seemingly lost in the vast expanse of the Indian Ocean. My amazement increases when I see the resort's wine cellar which should really be secured like a safe in view of the fact that it stores twelve different brands of the finest champagne, the best wines from Burgundy, Trentino, Spain, Austria, Australia, South Africa, Israel and Chile to mention but a few of the wine-growing regions. Amused, the wine butler assures us that such precautions are as unnecessary as they are with the accommodation units. Security problems of any nature are unknown on this castaway island. The Six Senses hotel group focuses on indulging the senses and creating sublime luxury at the highest international standard, yet manage to combine these aspects with a simple, natural sense for local design, original indigenous architecture and unpretentious service. The special feeling of being alive and one's experiences of these "simpler" values on holiday could be circumscribed as "breathing in", "taking time out" "releasing tension", "delicious idleness" and "self-discovery". People coming here are not just visiting one of the many interchangeable hotel islands in the Maldives. At Soneva Gili or at its sister hotel Soneva Fushi, guests are in unmistakable places where awareness of nature and of human beings are a top priority, places which are not a product but rather an experience of which one can be truly say, "Soneva is good for you".

Die türkisfarbene Lagune von Lankanfushi Island ist an Naturschönheit schwer zu überbieten.

The scenic beauty of Lankanfushi Island's turquoise lagoon would be hard to match.

ISLAND

Hilton präsentiert ultimatives Malediven-Resort
Hilton's ultimate Maldives Resort   Text & Fotos: Jürgen Gutowski / Hilton

The air taxi flies in a wide curve to land. As it banks the sun's rays pierce the porthole and sunlight moves through the cabin. It's hot in the little propeller-drive plane but the ventilators are doing their very best, as is the barefooted pilot who brings the plane with the floats safely down on to the turquoise waters. The seaplane becomes a boat, and a few minutes later we berth at the bridge which links Rangali Island with its somewhat larger sister island of Ranglifinolhu. The flight from Male has taken half an hour. Awaiting our arrival beneath a sunroof are members of staff with cool flannels and ice-cold fruit cocktails. I am welcome, no doubt about that.

I had already heard the rumour that the Hilton was planning something out of the ordinary for the Maldives, something this region of the world hasn't had until now. I hadn't quite believed it, and doubted it even as we approached, because from the air the two

Die sensationellen „Sunset Water Villas" überraschen mit dem eigenen Whirlpool auf der Terrasse über dem Ozean.

A surprising feature of the sensational Sunset Water Villas is the whirlpool on the terrace overlooking the ocean.

D as Air-Taxi setzt in weitem Bogen zur Landung an, durch die kleinen Bullaugen der zwanzigsitzigen Propellermaschine fällt ein Bündel aus Sonnenstrahlen und wandert einmal durch die Kabine. Es ist heiß im Miniflieger, doch der Ventilator tut sein Bestes. Wie die barfüßigen Piloten, die das Flugmaschinchen mit den Wasserkufen schließlich sicher auf die türkisfarbenen Fluten setzen. Das Flugzeug wird zum Boot, und wenige Minuten später legt es an der Brücke, die Rangali Island und die etwas größere Schwesterinsel Ranglifinolhu verbindet, nach dem halbstündigen Flug von Male an. Unter einem Sonnendach warten bereits die ersten guten Geister mit kühlen Tüchern und einem eisgekühlten Fruchtcocktail. Ich bin willkommen, keine Frage!

Ich hatte schon davon munkeln gehört, dass Hilton auf den Malediven etwas ganz Besonderes plant, etwas bisher nicht da Gewesenes in dieser Region der Welt, indes geglaubt hatte ich es nicht so recht. Selbst während des Anflugs nicht, denn aus der Luft sehen diese beiden kleinen Inseln genauso schillernd und verträumt-tropisch aus wie viele andere. Doch hier auf Rangali erlebe ich

mein „blaues Wunder", was nicht nur mit Badewasser, Pool oder Himmelszelt zu erklären ist. Noch habe ich die „Over Water Villas" und vor allem die „Sunset Water Villas" nicht gesehen, und so schlendere ich zunächst und wie so oft barfuß in die sandige Rezeption, die Formalitäten sind fix erledigt, und weiter geht's zu meiner Beach Villa. Versteckt unter Kokospalmen reihen sich hier 100 kleine Gästehäuschen, alle mehr als 70 Quadratmeter Wohnfläche bietend, alle gebührend Abstand haltend, einmal um die Insel. Alle gesegnet mit einer großen möblierten Veranda und Open-Air-Badezimmer, brei-

shimmering little islands still looked as dreamy as many others. Now I've arrived on Rangali I'm astounded, and it's not only to do with the water, the pool and the sky above ... and I haven't even seen the Water Villas and the Sunset Water Villas yet!
I stroll barefoot into reception and after the formalities have been speedily dealt with, I am taken to my Beach Bungalow.
Tucked away beneath coconut palms are about 100 little guest houses encircling the island, all of them over 750 square feet in area, and all with plenty of space between them. Each one has a large furnished verandah and an open air bathroom. Wide four posters strewn with flowers, fan, minibar, safe, CD player and adjustable air-conditioning cannot be taken for granted in the Maldives, even in top hotels.
An espresso machine which can also make tea or coffee is provided plus various granules, and there is

Spektakulär: Der Glasfußboden in den Sunset Water Villas bietet Durchblick und bringt die Bewohner des Meeres zum Greifen nah.

Spectacular: the glass floor in the Sunset Water Villas allows you to view the sea creatures below within touching distance.

Phantastische Erlebnisse für Body & Soul liefert das einzigartige Over Water Spa.

The incredible Over Water Spa provides fantastic experiences for body and soul.

fresh fruit and a bottle of sparkling wine in the fridge. I shed my travel gear, and after a shower in the open-air bathroom I go for a walk around the island which only takes ten minutes. One saunters on fine white sand in the shadow of the ubiquitous palms, or in the intense heat of a gigantic sun, which bleaches the sand white and keeps the water at a steady 30 ºC. throughout the year. I walk past the Sunset Grill, a romantic overwater restaurant and bar on stilts over 50 yards from the shore, and go by the water sports where beginners can learn water skiing and windsurfing before reaching the footbridge linking the two tropical islands. It is only a third of a mile long, so you can walk it. American guests like to go jogging, but I prefer the shady dhoni which pendulums between Rangali and Ranglifinolhu. Once on the boat I realize the water has an extraordinary quality, a luminosity sparkling like the eye of God reflecting the heavens, its radiance and colour releasing a rush of adrenalin. The dhoni captain smiles quietly. He knows how profoundly these elements affect the visitor. On Rangali I pass by the "Vilu Restaurant" idyllically situated

ten – mit bunten Blüten verzierten – Himmelbetten, Ventilator, Minibar, Safe, CD-Player und auch einer regelbaren Klimaanlage, die auf den Malediven selbst in Top-Hotels alles andere als selbstverständlich ist. Eine Espresso/Kaffee/Tee-Maschine mit mehreren Pulvern ganz nach Gusto steht ebenso bereit wie frische Früchte und eine Flasche Sekt im Kühler. Raus aus den Reiseklamotten, ich zisch' mir eine Dusche im Open-Air-Badezimmer, und dann mache ich eine kleine Inselwanderung. Sie dauert nur zehn Minuten, dann habe ich das Inselchen bereits umrundet. Auf weißem, feinen Sand bin ich gelaufen, wahlweise im Schatten allgegenwärtiger Palmen oder in der Hitze der gigantischen Sonne, die hier mit Milliarden Watt den Strand weißt und die Meeresfluten auf ganzjährig 30 Grad temperiert. Vorbei am Sunset Grill, einem romantischen Over-Water-Restaurant mit Bar, 50 Meter weit draußen auf Stelzen ins Meer gesetzt, vorbei auch an den Water-Sports, wo Newbies Wasserski und Windsurfen lernen, hin zur Brücke, die die beiden tropischen Eilande verbindet. Man kann den halben Kilometer zu Fuß gehen, man kann hier sogar in der Mittagssonne joggen, wie amerikanische Gäste es vormachen, aber ich bevorzuge das schattige Dohni, das permanent zwischen Rangali und Ranglifinolhu hin und her pendelt. Erst auf dem Boot wird mir klar, wie das Wasser hier beschaffen ist. Seine Leuchtkraft ist von betörender Intensität, wie das Auge Gottes gleißt und funkelt es in Himmels spiegelnder Kraft und in adrenalinfördernder farblicher Vielfalt. Der Dhoni-Käpitän lächelt mild, er weiß, dass diese Elemente so manchen Zugereisten aus den Latschen hauen. Auf Rangali passiere ich dann das idyllisch an der kristallklaren Lagune gelegene „Vilu Restaurant", wo ultimative euro-asiatische Schmauserlebnisse auf die Gäste warten, wie sich später herausstellen wird. Von hier sind es nur ein paar Schritte zum gleichnamigen Weinkeller, der mit 18 Grad Celsius absolut „coolste" Spot von Rangali, in dem Gruppen bis zu 12 Personen bei den besten Weinen der Welt und erlesenen Speisen zusammensitzen können.

Wieder „über Tage" angekommen, gehe ich zunächst über einen 40 Meter langen Steg hinüber zum Spa. Spas gibt es viele, mittlerweile auch hier auf den Malediven. Doch dies ist nicht irgendein Spa! Denn er wird betrieben von „Chiva-Som". Die traditionellen, uralten asiatischen Therapien und Massagen werden nun auch hier auf Rangali mit den

neuesten westlichen Techniken kombiniert, um Körper, Geist und Seele miteinander zu versöhnen. Die klassische Thaimassage, aber auch Stressreduktion, Tiefenentspannung, orientalische Fußrituale, Body Wraps und vieles mehr steht auf den Rezepten gegen Verspannung, Übergewicht und andere Folgen westlicher Lebensunart. Das Ganze in einem ruhigen Ambiente aus Holz und Glas, sights & sounds und aromatherapeutischer Düfte, die die vier Spa Villas durchwehen. Der Fußboden ist durchsichtig, so dass man die Massage gewissermaßen als über dem Aquarium schwebend erfährt, allerdings mit dem Unterschied, dass das Aquarium dort unten den natürlichen, freien Lebensraum der wohl faszinierendsten „Meeresfrüchte" darstellt, die man sich denken kann. Entspannung mit Durchblick! Ein Durchblick, der auch einigen Water Villas spendiert wurde. 50 dieser von Stelzen getragenen Megahütten, unterteilt in drei Kategorien, schweben über den Wassern der Lagune. Soeben erst fertig gestellt und schon auf dem Weg in die Bestenlisten der Welt sind die zwei „Sunset Water Villas" auf Rangali Island. Sie lassen die exklusive Kundschaft sowie die Konkurrenz nicht nur auf den Malediven aufhorchen. Denn was bis-

beside the crystal clear lagoon where, I am soon to discover, superb Euro-Asian cuisine awaits its guests. From here it is only a few steps to the wine cellar of the same name which is kept at a temperature of 18 °C, making it the coolest spot in Rangali. There is seating for groups of up to 12 people who will enjoy the best wines in the world and exquisite food.

I surface again and walk along the 131 foot-long jetty to the Spa. Spas proliferate nowadays, in the meantime in the Maldives too, but this is no ordinary spa. On Rangali ancient, traditional Asian therapies and massage are combined with the latest western techniques, to reconcile body, soul and mind. Classic Thai massage, stress reduction treatment, deep relaxation techniques, Oriental foot rituals, body wraps and much else are embraced to counter tension, obesity and other consequences of an unhealthy western life style. All treatment takes place within an ambience of wood and glass, surrounded by sights and sounds and the fragrances of aromatherapy pervading the ether of the four Spa Villas. The floor is transparent so that during massage one has

Weltklasse: Die 250 qm umfassenden „Sunset Water Villas" über der blauen Lagune bieten Spitzenhotels wie dem Burj Al Arab aufs Feinste Paroli.
World class: the Sunset Water Villas (2,690 sq. ft) above the blue lagoon vie with exclusive hotels such as the Burj Al Arab.

the sensation floating over an aquarium with the a difference, the aquarium beneath the treatment rooms looks on to the most fascinating "fruits de mer" imaginable, giving the living space another dimension. A floor with a view indeed! Some of the Water Villas share the view. Fifty of these mega-huts on stilts divided into three categories appear to hover above the water of the lagoon. The two Sunset Water Villas on Rangali Island were only recently completed, yet they are already on the way to being listed alongside the best in the world. VIP clients and the competition are taking note, because what has only been available until now at Frégate Island Private in the Seychelles and at the Burj Al Arab in Dubai has now been realized on two tiny islands of Rangali. The straw-roofed houses on stilts offer nearly 2,700 square feet of floor space above the turquoise waters well out to sea. The sea bed is visible through the glass floor of the living room, so you can gaze in wonder at ray, reef shark and all the other the multi-coloured creatures of the Indian Ocean and stay by day

Zauberhaft: Die romantische Blütendeko für Honeymoon-Paare lässt verliebte Herzen lodern.

Enchanting: the romantic flowery décor for honeymoon couples sets hearts ablaze.

lang exklusiven Hotels wie Frégate Island Private auf den Seychellen oder dem Burj Al Arab in Dubai vorbehalten war, wurde nun auch auf den beiden winzigen Inselchen von Rangali Wirklichkeit. Die strohgedeckten Stelzenhäuschen bieten nicht weniger als 250 Quadratmeter Wohnfläche weit draußen im türkisfarbenen Meer. Der Fußboden im Wohnbereich bietet Durchblick auf den Meeresboden, denn er ist aus Glas. Rochen, Riffhaie und vielfarbige Unterwasserbewohner des Indischen Ozeans lassen sich so bei Tag und Nacht trockenen Fußes und flutlichtunterstützt bewundern. Nebenan warten zwei fulminante Schlafzimmer, man hat die Wahl zwischen einem futuristisch anmutenden, kreisrunden Megabett mit einem Durchmesser

von 250 Zentimetern, das sich per drahtloser Fernbedienung um die eigene Achse bzw. vor den jeweils gewünschten Panoramaausblick dreht, und einem klassischen Doppelbett im zweiten Schlafzimmer, das „nur" Meeresblick bietet. Beide Lager sind eingehüllt in erlesene italienische Bettwäsche aus dem Hause „Frette", in beiden Badezimmern finden sich Pflegesets von Bvlgari, und überall in diesem sensationellen „Lebens(t)raum" ist man umgeben von der warmen Ausstrahlung neuseeländischen Redwood-Holzes. Von der riesigen Veranda, auf der selbstredend der eigene Whirlpool brodelt, hat man per Holztreppe einen privaten Zugang zu den koloriertesten Fluten der Welt. Im Preis von 2 500 US-Dollar pro Nacht ist ferner ein eigenes Speed Boat samt Chauffeur inkludiert sowie ein privater Butler, der in der Küche des Refugiums nach den Wünschen der Gäste kulinarische Gaumenfreuden zelebriert. Weitere „Kleinigkeiten" bilden mehrere 44-Zoll-Plasmabildschirme, DVD und Bose-Soundsysteme, zwei Bäder & Außenduschen, Air-Con, Bar und vieles me(e)hr. Und steht man abends draußen auf der umlaufenden Veranda vor dem Spektakel eines maledivischen Sonnenuntergangs, wie er hier inflationär und täglich neu aufscheint, dann beschleicht eine ganz konkrete Hoffnung das Bewusstsein: Alle Air-Taxis der Welt mögen über Nacht ausgemustert worden sein.

and by night when it is floodlit. Beside the living area are two large bedrooms. You can choose between a huge futuristic circular bed over 8 feet across which can be turned on its own axis by cordless remote control to face any panoramic view you prefer, or a classic double bed in the second bedroom which "only" has a sea view. Both beds have exclusive Italian "Frette" bedlinen, and in both bathrooms there are sets of Bvlgari toiletries. The New Zealand redwood lends a warmth to the whole of this sensational living space. The huge verandah on which you have your own private whirlpool also has wooden steps which lead down into the most colourful waters of the world. The price of US$ 2,500 per night includes your own speedboat and chauffeur, your own Butler and kitchen in your hideaway, who can conjure updishes of your choice. Other "little" amenities are the 43" plasma satellite TV, DVD, surround sound music system, two bathrooms and outside showers, air conditioning and much else. In the evening, standing on the verandah encircling the villa and admiring the spectacular Maldives sunset, a very real hope creeps into one's mind – that overnight all the air taxis in the world are taken out of service.

Ultimative euro-asiatische Schmauserlebnisse zelebrieren das „Vilu Restaurant", und sein Weinkeller, die sich idyllisch an die glasklare Lagune schmiegen.

The idyllic Vilu Restaurant and it's Wine Cellar beside the crystal clear lagoon serves the ultimate in Euro-Asian cuisine.

Asia meets Africa
THE OBEROI, MAURITIUS

Zu den jüngsten Projekten der renommierten Oberoi-Hotelgruppe gehört das im November 2001 eröffnete Oberoi, Mauritius. Eine Perle an den Gestaden des Indischen Ozeans, eingebettet in die idyllische Küstenlandschaft der Baie aux Tortues an der Nordwestküste der Insel.

One of the most recent projects of the renowned Oberoi hotel group was opened in Mauritius in November 2001. It is a gem beside a beach in the Indian Ocean, set in the idyllic coastal region of the Baie aux Tortues on the island's north-western coast.

Text: Gundula Luig · Fotos: Stefan Fister

Auf acht Hektar traumhaft modellierte Gartenlandschaft verteilt sich dieses zauberhafte neue Oberoi Resort.
The new Oberoi Resort is set in 20 acres of its own beautifully tended grounds.

Feine Stoffe und natürliche Materialien zeichnen das Interieur jeder Luxusvilla aus.
The décor of each villa features quality fabrics and natural materials.

Wie sagte Malcolm de Chazal, der berühmte mauritianische Maler und Poet, so treffend: „Es scheint, als hätte ein Riese Mauritius modelliert und bemalt ..." Die Insel, die zu den Maskarenen gehört und flächenmäßig die Größe von München kaum übersteigt, fasziniert mit einer Fülle von unterschiedlichsten Landschaften. Über und unter Wasser. Was an Land als imposante Gebirgsformation, bizarres Hochland oder raumgreifende Ebene mit unendlich scheinenden Zuckerrohrfeldern auf knapp 1 900 qkm so abwechslungsreich das Herz erfreut, setzt sich im wärmsten Ozean der Erde als geradezu paradiesischer Unterwassergarten fort. Kein Wunder, dass sich Mauritius zu einem der bevorzugtesten Ziele für Individualreisende aus aller Welt entwickelt hat. Nicht zuletzt wegen des rund ums Jahr angenehmen Klimas, das je nach Saison im Durchschnitt mit Temperaturen zwischen 18 und 30 °C verwöhnt.

Nur zwanzig Minuten von der belebten Inselhauptstadt Port Louis entfernt (abends sieht man die unzähligen Lichter am Horizont flackern) schmiegt sich das neue Oberoi, Mauritius in den von Menschenhand sensibel und spannungsreich gestalteten Küstenabschnitt der Baie aux Tortues. Ein Großteil der beim Bau in der Erde gefundenen Steine fand in natürlichen Mauern und Abgrenzungen wieder Verwendung. Auch im markanten, zwölf Meter hohen Aquädukt, der wie ein stummer Zeuge vergangener Tage den Eingangsbereich des Resorts bewacht. Damit zollt der renommierte thailändische Architekt Lek Bunnag, der für das außergewöhnliche Hotelprojekt verantwortlich zeichnet, der mauritianischen Kultur seinen Tribut. Denn seit der Kolonialzeit nutzt man bis heute solche Aquädukte für die Bewässerung der Zuckerrohrplantagen. Im Oberoi speist der Aquädukt einen idyllischen Naturteich, in dem sich farbenfroh Massen von verfressenen Koi tummeln und abends ein betörendes Froschkonzert unterhält. Rechts neben diesem zentralen Punkt der Anlage gruppieren sich die Gemeinschaftsgebäude im Halbkreis: Hauptrestaurant, Bar, Teepavillon, Shop, Tagungsräume sowie Rezeption. Architektonisch dominieren hier die afrikanischen Elemente in Form von offener Bauweise und mit Zuckerrohrschilf gedeckten, hohen und spitz zulaufenden Dächern. Andererseits trifft der Gast in der gesamten, rund acht Hektar umfassenden Hotelanlage überall auf die asiatischen Wurzeln des Oberoi. Steinskulpturen fernöstlicher Kunst, die aus dem Wasser des mit antiker Säulenkunst

As Malcolm de Chazal, famous Mauritian painter and poet, once so aptly remarked, "Mauritius looks as if it has been sculpted and painted by a giant". The island which belongs to the Mascarenes and is similar in area to Munich, is a fascinating place owing to the diversity of its scenery above and below water. The imposing mountain formations, bizarre plateaus and broad plains of seemingly unending fields of sugar cane across 730 square miles, extend into the warmest ocean in the world as a heavenly underwater garden. Its hardly surprising then that Mauritius has developed into one of the most popular holiday destinations for travellers from all over the world, not least because of its temperate climate all the year round. Depending on the season the average temperature is between 18 and 30 °C. Only 20 minutes away from the busy capital of Port Louis (in the evening you can see a myriad lights flickering on the horizon), the new Oberoi nestles beside a sensitively designed and beautifully landscaped coastal strip of the

geschmückten Hauptpools herausschauen, im subtropischen Park Spalier stehen oder in den privaten Villengärten für Aufmerksamkeit sorgen. Das Oberoi, Mauritius spricht die emotionalen Wünsche einer internationalen Gästeklientel an, die nach exklusiver Privatsphäre, friedvoller Ruhe und der Möglichkeit zur regenerierenden Entspannung sucht. Genuss und Erholung bestimmen den Tagesablauf, je nach Lust und Laune angeregt vom sportlich-aktiven Wassersportangebot.

Insgesamt 76 luxuriöse Garten-Villen, mit und ohne Pool, sowie als Reihenhäuschen angelegte Terrassen-Pavillons verteilen sich locker über den bezaubernden Tropenpark. Jedem Hobbygärtner geht das Herz auf beim Anblick der grandios gestalteten Pflanzungen, die in verschwenderischer Farbenpracht einen Querschnitt über die exotische Flora geben: rote und gelbe Krotons, Buntnesseln, dunkelrotes Indianergras, Geranien, Wandelröschen, Canna, Hibiskus, Bleiwurz sowie zahlreiche andere Blühsträucher und Stauden bilden einen blühenden Teppich zwischen verschlungenen Wegen, Villen und Rasenflächen.

Interieur sowie komplettes Innendesign der luxuriösen Logis stammen vom berühmten Singapurer Innenarchitekten H. L. Lim, der schon mehrere andere Oberoi-Hotels gefühlvoll und von der Natur inspiriert in Szene gesetzt hat. Muster, Strukturen und Farben der Einrichtung orientieren sich am multikulturellen Gesellschaftsbild der Insel. Deshalb entsprechen die Möbel auch keinem bestimmten Stil. Sie sind hell, rustikal und zeitgemäß. Besonders originell präsentieren sich die aus Zuckerrohrwedeln geflochtenen Betthäupter in sämtlichen Zimmern. Nur eine Glaswand trennt die vollendeten Luxusbäder mit der im Boden eingelassenen

Baie aux Tortues. Most of the stones excavated during construction have been re-used in the natural stone walls and partitions, including in the prominent 130 ft. high aqueduct which guards the entrance to the resort like a silent witness. It is the way Lek Bunnag, the hotel's renowned Thai architect responsible for this remarkable hotel project, has chosen to pay tribute to Mauritian culture. Ever since colonial times these aqueducts have been utilized to irrigate the sugar plantations. In the Oberoi the aqueduct feeds an idyllic pool in which masses of brilliant koi are darting about, and where in the evenings one can listen to an amusing concert of frogs croaking. Arranged in a semi-circle to the right of this central point are the resort's communal buildings, the main restaurant, the bar, a tea pavilion, a shop, conference rooms and the reception. Architecturally, it is African elements which dominate

Wie man sich bettet, so schläft man: nämlich exzellent unter dem Spitzdach.
Your sleep is as good as the bed you sleep in, in other words remarkably well beneath the pointed roof.

Badeträume werden wahr!
Dreams of luxury bathing come true.

in the shape of the open design and the high, pointed roofs thatched with sugar cane reed. Otherwise everything else the guest encounters within the 20-acre site clearly indicates the Oberoi's Asian roots. Some of the more conspicuous features are the Far Eastern stone sculptures which look out from the water of the main pool which has ancient pillars. They stand guard in the sub-tropical park and attract attention in the private villas. The Oberoi Mauritius meets the emotional desires of a cosmopolitan clientèle looking for exclusive privacy, peace and quiet, and the opportunity to recharge their batteries. The day revolves around enjoyment and relaxation whatever mood one is in, and might include trying the energetic water sports on offer. Altogether there are 76 luxurious Garden Villas, with and without pools, as well as rows of small Terrace Pavilions scattered informally across an enchanting tropical park. Every gardener is delighted at the sight of the lavish planting of flowers and shrubs creating a riot of colour. There is a cross-section of exotic flora – canna, coloured nettles, geraniums, climbing roses, hibiscus, and any number of herbs and herbaceous plants and shrubs which form a flowery carpet between the winding paths, the lawns and the villas. Responsible for the décor and the interior design is the famous Singapore architect H. L. Lim who, inspired by the natural surroundings, has designed several other Oberoi hotels with great sensitivity. The patterns, structures and colours of the furnishings reflect the island's multicultural society, the reason why the rustic yet contemporary furniture is of no particular style and held in light colours. The wicker bedheads in all the rooms woven from sugar cane reed are a notable example. Only a glass partition separates the living space from an atrium with tropical plants. The wonderful private

*Verwöhnprogramm von Kopf bis Fuß:
Im Oberoi Spa geht die Seele fliegen.*
**A pamper programme to cosset you from head
to foot. At the Oberoi your spirit takes flight.**

Marmorwanne von einem tropisch bepflanzten Atrium. Auch im Wohnraum holen großzügige Fensterfronten die herrliche Natur optisch ins Haus – den wundervollen privaten Blumengarten, umfriedet von einer sehenswerten Mauer aus Lavagestein, den erhöht angelegten Dinner-Pavillon über dem eigenen Pool oder die lustigen, zutraulichen Singvögel, die sich als Zaungäste ebenso wohl fühlen wie die Urlauber, die hier wohnen.

Zu den Highlights des Luxusdomizils gehört zweifellos der Spa, ein Himmel auf Erden, ein Ort, wo Körper, Geist und Seele auf angenehmste Art loslassen und neue Kräfte

sammeln können. Denn man ist, wie schon in den Villen, umgeben von absoluter Privatsphäre und sanfter Stille. Zu jedem Behandlungsraum gehört, das ist im Oberoi Konzept, natürlich ein (nicht einsehbarer) Garten. Paare relaxen gemeinsam während Simultanmassagen oder Körperbehandlungen in den exklusiven Behandlungssuiten mit Kalt- und Dampfdusche sowie Jacuzzi. Die Philosophie des Oberoi Spa basiert auf einer puren, natürlichen und ganzheitlichen Sichtweise. Das gilt auch für die verwendeten Produkte. Viele sind naturbelassen, hergestellt aus heimischen mauritianischen Früchten und Gemüse wie Kokosnuss und Papaya. Eines solcher Highlights ist die „Kokosnussschalen-Behandlung". In erster Linie umfasst das Spa-Angebot ayurvedische und mauritianische Therapien, basierend auf traditionellen Bräuchen und Heilmethoden. Zum Topangebot an Massagen, Körper- und Beautyanwendungen kommen noch Sauna, Dampfbad, Fitnesscenter und zwei

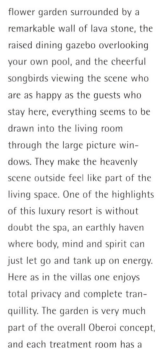

flower garden surrounded by a remarkable wall of lava stone, the raised dining gazebo overlooking your own pool, and the cheerful songbirds viewing the scene who are as happy as the guests who stay here, everything seems to be drawn into the living room through the large picture windows. They make the heavenly scene outside feel like part of the living space. One of the highlights of this luxury resort is without doubt the spa, an earthly haven where body, mind and spirit can just let go and tank up on energy. Here as in the villas one enjoys total privacy and complete tranquillity. The garden is very much part of the overall Oberoi concept, and each treatment room has a

Zu den Highlights der Körperbehandlungen gehört die „Kokosnussschalen-Behandlung" mit frischen Kokosraspeln und Kokosöl.
One of the highlights of the beauty treatment on offer is the coconut shell treatment using fresh desiccated coconut and coconut oil.

Dessertgenuss ohnegleichen: Orangen-Kürbis-Crème brûlée mit Schokoladenpudding "Mouilleaux" und Aniseiscreme.
Dessert beyond parallel: Orange-pumpkin crème brûlée with a mouilleaux chocolate blancmange and aniseed crème.

"The Restaurant" serviert eine exzellente Gourmetküche bestehend aus den Stilrichtungen international, orientalisch sowie kreolisch.
"The Restaurant" serves an excellent cuisine featuring international dishes and oriental and Creole cooking.

Andrew Skinners Cuisine ist phantastisch. Zur Freude der Gäste wechselt seine Karte täglich.
Andrew Skinner's cuisine is fantastic. Guests are delighted that his menu changes daily.

private one hidden from view. Couples relax together while being massaged. They can also receive treatment simultaneously in the exclusive treatment suites, enjoying cold and steam showers, or a jacuzzi. Oberoi has adopted a pure, natural and holistic philosophy, an approach also applied to the products being used. Many are natural substances produced from local Mauritian fruit and vegetables, such as coconut and papaya. One of the highlights is the coconut-shell treatment. However, the main focus of the spa is on ayurvedic and Mauritian therapies which are based on traditional practice and methods of healing. The superb range on offer includes massage, beauty treatment and body treatment, as well as a sauna, steam bath, gym and two floodlit tennis courts. Bordering the grounds is a 710-yard stretch of white sandy beach which marks the boundary of the resort beside the shimmering turquoise waters

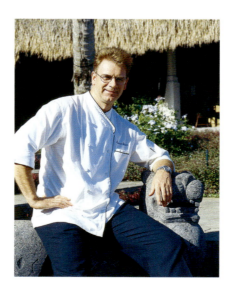

Flutlicht-Tenniscourts. Verschwenderisch trennt ein 650 Meter langer Strandabschnitt mit feinem weißen Sand das zauberhafte Domizil von den türkis schimmernden Fluten des Indischen Ozeans. Ob Sonnenbaden, Schwimmen im Meer, Tretboot fahren, Schnorcheln, Surfen oder Tauchen – im Oberoi, Mauritius ist man darauf eingestellt. Hinzu kommt eine geradezu mystische Poolanlage gleich parallel zum Strand. Drei Säulen mit Widderköpfen, an denen das Wasser ins Becken rinnt, bilden den einladenden Blickfang für dieses phantasievolle Konstrukt. Ein riesiges Fischmaul spuckt sprudelnd Wasser aus, an Längs- und Stirnseite erhellen lodernde Fackeln die Nacht. Exquisit wie das übrige Ambiente zeigt sich auch die Gastronomie. Im stilvollen Open-Air-Restaurant diniert man eine vorzügliche Fusion-Cuisine, bestehend aus kreolischen, indischen, orientalischen wie europäischen Komponenten. Der britische Küchenchef Andrew Skinner wechselt täglich (!) die Karte, das ist einzigartig für eine Hotelküche auf der Insel. Bestens umsorgt vom äußerst zuvorkommenden Service diniert man bei Kerzenschein Vorzügliches wie "Tandoori Jhinga", in Chili marinierte Hummerkrabben mit Yoghurt, Tasmanisches Lachsfilet aus der Cajun-Küche

auf Mais, Koreander und Okra Salsa mit Harissa-Dressing oder Australische Lammschulter mit Zwiebeln und roten Kashmir-Chilis, serviert mit hausgemachten Pickles. Passende Begleitung finden diese superben Spezialitäten in einer ausgezeichneten internationalen Weinauswahl. Für den Tagesappetit ist die schöne legere Pool Bar zuständig. Unter breiten Sonnenschirmen am Wasser sitzend, lässt man sich leichte Snacks, knackige Salate, Pasta und Pizza schmecken. Das Oberoi, Mauritius, Mitglied bei The Leading Small Hotels of the World, gehört ohne Zweifel zu den ertsen Adressen der Insel und ist rund ums Jahr eine Reise wert.

of the Indian Ocean. Whether you want to sunbathe, swim in the sea or go in a pedalo, snorkelling or surfing, the Oberoi is equipped with everything you need. In addition it has a mystical-looking pool area parallel the sea. Three pillars adorned with rams' heads from which water streams into basins, draw attention to this imaginative construction. A giant fish's mouth gushes water and to the side and beneath blazing torches illuminate the night. The gastronomy is as exquisite as the rest of the ambience. In the stylish open-air restaurant one dines on an excellent fusion cuisine created

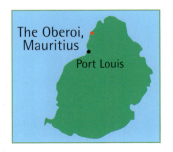

from Creole, Indian, Oriental and European components. Andrew Skinner, the British chef, changes the menu on a daily basis, quite unique for a hotel kitchen on the island. Pampered by outstanding service, guests dine by candlelight on "Tandoori Jhinga" – prawns marinated in chili and yoghurt; Cajun-blackened Tasmanian salmon filet on sweet corn, coriander and okra salsa with a harissa dressing, or on Australian lamb shoulder cooked with onions and Kashmiri red chillies served with home-made pickles. A fitting wine to accompany the meal can be selected from the excellent international wine list. During the day light snacks, crisp salads, pasta and pizza are available from the informal Pool Bar. The Oberoi, Mauritius, a member of The Leading Small Hotels of the World, belongs without doubt to the top addresses of this island, and is well worth visiting at any time of the year.

General Manager Wilhelm Luxem.

Südafrikanisches Bilderbuch
A South African picture book

KURLAND

COUNTRY HOTEL

Text: Jürgen Gutowski · Fotos: Martina Gutowski

Im Stil kapholländischer Bauernhäuser empfängt das Kurland Country Hotel seine Gäste an der idyllischen südafrikanischen Garden Route.
Built in the style of a Cape Dutch cottage, the Kurland Country Hotel welcomes its guests to the idyllic South African Garden Route.

The pastures stretch from the mountains down to the sea. Horses which even in winter look as if they have been painted on to this lovely landscape, graze the brilliant green expanse. Wooden paddocks painted white as snow are dotted about the landscape and high above eagles are quietly circling, concentrating on the land below. The towering oaks on the gentle hills resemble the trees in the German countryside, but the odd palm tree and the slightly curved gables of the Cape Dutch farmhouses signal that this landscape is at the southerly end of South Africa. This Mediterranean end is everything other than grey

Die Wiesen reichen von den Bergen bis zur Küste. Pferde grasen in der leuchtend grünen Weite, die selbst im Winter wie hineingemalt erscheint in diese Landschaft ganz aus Lieblichkeit. Koppeln aus Holz und weiß wie Schnee rastern die Natur, und über allem kreisen Adler, ruhig und konzentriert wie das Land, auf das sie schauen. Eichen auf den sanften Hügeln ragen auf wie in deutschen Landen, aber verstreute Palmen und die geschwungenen Giebel der kapholländischen Bauernhäuser stellen klar: Diese Landschaft finde ich in Südafrika, an seinem südlichen Ende, doch dieses mediterrane Ende ist alles andere als grau und trostlos, nicht umsonst trägt es den blumigen Kosenamen „Garden Route". Wie der Fingerabdruck eines erlauchten, naturgewaltigen Gärtners, wie ein Gemälde inmitten des Bildes, liegt seit

Jahrhunderten ein Grundstück von sechshundert Hektar Größe an dieser Route zwischen Indischem Ozean und Outeniqua Mountains, und sein lautmalerischer Name spricht für sich, ist sein Programm: „Kurland".

Schmiedeeiserne Tore öffnen sich unweit der Landstraße, die mich binnen zwei Stunden von Port Elizabeth hierher geführt hat, und schnurgerade liegt nun die kieselsteinige Allee dieses Kurlandes vor mir. Ich parke den Wagen auf dem beschaulichen Hof, wo ein friedlich dösender Haushund mich mit sanftem Augenaufschlag begrüßt und sich dann wieder seinen Tagträumen widmet. Im Rosengarten beschneidet der Gärtner den Stock, er winkt mir so freundlich zu, als würden wir uns lange kennen. Die zweiteilige Eingangstür des weißen Bauernhauses öffnet sich erst oben und dann unten, ein weiteres herzliches Willkommen, und nach dem Händeschütteln bin ich im Handumdrehen meine Koffer los. Ich stehe erst seit Sekunden im Flur des Anwesens, nie war ich vorher hier, und doch ist das Gefühl des Heimkommens so intensiv, wie ich es in einem Hotel nur selten erlebt habe. Nein, ein Hotel ist dies eigentlich nicht, denn statt an der Rezeption finde ich mich im Wohnzimmer wieder, statt hektischer Betriebsamkeit umfasst mich ruhige Beschaulichkeit. Im Kamin prasselt ein wärmendes Feuer, gelbes Licht aus Kristallleuchtern und Stehlampen fällt auf die warmen Terrakottafliesen zu meinen Füßen, auf die stuckschmucken Weinlaubmotive an den Wänden, auf die prachtvollen Blumensträuße auf den handgeschnitzten Tischen. Wohin ich auch blicke, in diesem Wohnhaus sammelt

Liebevoll arrangierte Details, warme Terrakottafliesen und gemütliche Sitzmöbel im original britischen Country style prägen die Interieurs.

Lovingly arranged details, warm terracotta tiles and cosy armchairs in original English Country house style, are a main feature of the interiors.

and boring. Not for nothing is it called by its flowery nickname, the "Garden Route". Like the fingerprint of an illustrious gardener, a 1,482-acre stretch of this Route between the Indian Ocean and the Outeniqua Mountains is called "Kurland", a name which speaks for itself. After a two-hour drive from Port Elizabeth, I arrive at the wrought iron gates just off a country road beyond which is a straight gravel path leading into Kurland. I park the car in the courtyard where a dog dozes peacefully. After acknowledging me with a tame upward glance it falls back sleep. A gardener is pruning the roses and give me a

In den zwölf Paddock-Suiten genießt man die Atmosphäre eines „home far away from home".
The twelve Paddock Suites have a sophisticated "home far away from home" feel.

friendly wave as if we have long known one another. The double-door main entrance of the white farmhouse opens first at the top then at the bottom and I receive another warm welcome. After handshakes I am relieved of my case in the twinkling of an eye. I have only been standing in the hall for a few seconds, I've never been here before yet have never had such an intense feeling of having come home as I have in this hotel. Well, actually it's not an hotel, because instead of a reception area I find myself in the living room where I am surround not by a hectic activity but by peace and tran-quillity. A warm fire crackles in the grate, and a yellowish light from the chandeliers and standard lamps falls on

Die im Kolonialstil eingerichteten Suiten lassen auch für weit gereiste Gäste keine Wünsche an Luxus und Komfort offen.
The colonial-style suites leave nothing to be desired in the way of luxury and the latest amenities, even for the widely travelled guest.

jemand Schönes und Wertvolles: Gemälde und Zeichnungen, Radierungen und Portraits, Menschen und Landschaften in goldenen oder hölzernen Rahmen. In einem Wandschrank sind nahezu alle Strohhüte der Welt versammelt, auf dem Ecktisch blühen Orchideen und Rosen, in silbernen Schalen knospen weiße Tulpen dem Frühling entgegen, wuchtige Sessel und schwere Sofas mit farbenprächtigen Kissen laden vor reich gefüllten Bücherregalen und mit Bildbänden beladenen Schreibtischen zum Ruhen und Relaxen ein. Der Gesang von Andrea Bocelli hängt leise in der kamingeschwängerten Luft, ich summe sein *Canto della terra,* das Lied dieses (Kur)Landes, leise mit. Durch ein weiteres Kaminzimmer mit raumhoch aufgestapeltem Feuerholz führt mich mein Weg weiter durchs herrschaftliche Bauernhaus. Nur am prall mit Spirituosen gefüllten Silbertablett erkenne ich, dass ich mich im nächsten Salon in der Bar des

Hauses befinde. Nebenan im Restaurant auf festlich eingekleideten und gedeckten Tischen reflektiert das Licht schlanker Kerzen in goldenen Wandspiegeln und silbernen Gefäßen. Hier wird morgens ein kräftiges Farmfrühstück serviert, mittags und abends hat man die Wahl unter zwei rustikalen Menüs. Fast überflüssig darauf hinzuweisen, dass der Kamin in diesem Refektorium fast so groß ist wie die begehbaren Kleiderschränke in den Gästezimmern. Zur anderen Seite der Bar öffnet sich eine Veranda, wie man sie aus kolonialen Kinofilmen kennt: Riesig, fletzig, plüschig und dabei kein bisschen vom Winde verweht, da überdacht und seitlich abgeschirmt. Auf den niedrigen Rattantischen lagern afrikanische Schnitzereien, Pflanzenbestimmungsbücher, bemalte Straußeneier, Windlichter, dazu ein Fernrohr, durch das ich die Pferde auf den nahen Wiesen beobachte. Polospieler in blauem Dress und gepunkteten

the warm terracotta floor tiles and the pretty vine leaf motif on the walls, illuminating the gorgeous flower arrangements on the hand-carved tables. Wherever I look I can see that someone in this house collects beautiful and precious things. There are paintings and drawings, engravings and portraits, figures and land-scapes in gold or wood frames.
In a wall cupboard nearly all the straw hats of the world are on display, and on a corner table orchids, roses in silver bowls and white tulip buds herald the Spring. Massive armchairs and solid sofas with bright cushions appear to be inviting you to relax in front of the bookcases and the writing desks piled with coffee table books. A song of Andrea Bocelli hangs in the air, and I start quietly humming his "Canto della terra", the song of this country. As I saunter through this splendid farmhouse, I pass through yet another room with a fireplace which has firewood stacked to the ceiling. In the next room it is only when I see a silver tray crammed with spirits that I realize I've reached the hotel bar. Adjoining it is the restaurant where the light of

Die Bibliothek lädt mit prasselndem Kaminfeuer zum Verweilen ein.
Browsing in front of a crackling fire in the library is an attractive prospect.

Im Obergeschoss der Paddocks befindet sich ein separates Kinderzimmer.
On the upper floor of the Paddocks is a children's room.

Wem der eigene Plunge-Pool zu klein ist, der zieht seine Bahnen im Schwimmbad.

If your private plunge pool is too small you can always try the swimming pool.

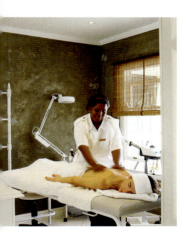

Im kleinen Spa des Landhauses können sich die Gäste nach allen Regeln der Massagekunst verwöhnen lassen.

Guests can indulge in all manner of massage in the country house's little spa.

slim candles on the beautifully laid tables is reflected in the gold frames of the wall mirrors and the silver. A substantial farm breakfast is served here in the morning. At midday and in the evening the guest has a choice of two menus of country food. It's hardly worth mentioning that the fireplace in this refectory is nearly as large as the walk-in wardrobes in the guest rooms!

On one side of the bar is a verandah just like the ones featured in films about colonial times. Spacious and plush, it is sheltered from the elements because it is covered and protected from one side. On the low rattan tables are African carvings, plant observer handbooks, decorated ostrich eggs, lanterns and even a telescope which I train on the horses in the nearby fields. Polo players clad in blue and wearing helmets are sweeping their mallets at ground level of the four private fenced in polo greens of the hotel's own polo club. Fans of the very British sport find an exemplary infrastructure at Kurland, including a 50 x 100

Schutzhelmen fegen dort drüben mit gesenkten Schlägern über die vier eingezäunten Greens des hauseigenen Poloclubs. Die Anhänger dieses eher britisch anmutenden Sportes finden im Kurland eine beispielhafte Infrastruktur, darunter eine 50 x 100 Meter große Poloarena, einen Übungssandplatz von einem Kilometer Länge und Ställe für bis zu 300 Pferde bzw. Ponys.

Unter Palmen wandere ich über den gepflegten Rasen, ich passiere den kleinen Spa des Landhauses, dann den Pool, umstanden von kissenweichen Sonnenliegen und naturfar-

above a separate children's room. The pampered traveller would find as little fault with all this as with the very well stocked minibar – the contents of which are free – or the Internet terminal over in the house. I am standing at the window of my paddock, my own little white Cape Dutch cottage looking out beyond the rose terrace to the fields and paths of Kurland. For a lingering moment I become part of this painting in the middle of a South African picture book, part of the work of that illustrious gardener.

Im Restaurant wird morgens ein kräftiges Farmfrühstück serviert, mittags und abends hat man die Wahl unter zwei rustikalen Menüs.
The restaurant serves a substantial farmhouse breakfast in the morning, and in the evening guests can choose between two country food menus.

benen Schirmen, und erreiche nach einer Minute meinen „Paddock", eines von insgesamt nur zwölf Gästezimmern des Kurland-Anwesens. Ganz klar, das fulminante Ambiente des kolonialen Manor-Hauses setzt sich in diesen individuell völlig unterschiedlich gestalteten Suiten fort. Eine edle Stimmung aus Samt und Seide, angereichert mit Ölbildern und echten Antiquitäten, umfängt mich in meiner geräumigen Suite. Schwere gewirkte Bettwäsche, Vorhänge und Teppiche, bemaltes Porzellan und frische Rosen, vielflammige Kronleuchter und die obligatorischen „Fire Places" erzeugen eine Atmosphäre ultimativer Behaglichkeit. Dass dazu auch technische Raffinessen wie Air-Conditioning, Fußbodenheizung und satellitengestützte Unterhaltungselektronik ursächlich beitragen, dass nebenan ein privater Plunge-Pool zum Bade lädt, dass sich im Obergeschoss ein separates Kinderzimmer befindet – dagegen hat der verwöhnte Reisende genauso wenig einzuwenden wie gegen die bestens sortierte Minibar, deren Inhalt dem Gast genauso kostenlos zur Verfügung steht wie die Nutzung des Internet-Terminals drüben im Haupthaus.

Ich stehe am Fenster meines Paddocks in meinem weißen kapholländischen Häuschen, mein Blick schweift über die Rosenterrasse hinüber zu den Wiesen und Feldwegen des Kurlandes. Und bin einen Augenblick lang Teil eines Gemäldes mitten im südafrikanischen Bilderbuch des eingangs schon erwähnten erlauchten Gärtners.

metre polo area, a practice field a kilometre long, and stabling for up to 300 horses or ponies. I walk across the well-tended lawn beneath the palms and pass by the little spa of this country house and the pool which is surrounded by soft upholstered sunbeds and sunshades in natural colours. A minute later I reach my own "paddock", one of the 12 guest rooms of this Kurland property. It was to be expected. The brilliant ambience of this colonial manor house is carried over into these suites, all of them with a different dècor. My suite has a refined atmosphere. Velvet and silk, oil paintings and genuine antiques are all around me in my spacious suite. Quality heavy-duty bed linen, curtains and carpets, painted porcelain and fresh roses, an opulent chandelier and the obligatory fireplace, create an atmosphere of ultimate luxury. A further factor enhancing the atmosphere are the technically sophisticated amenities such as air-conditioning, underfloor heating and entertainment thanks to satellite communication. What is more, next door is a plunge pool and on the floor

THE COLLECTION
BY LIZ MCGRATH

The Plettenberg
Plettenberg Bay

The Marine
Hermanus

The Cellars-Hohenort
Cape Town

Liz McGrath, die Grande Dame der südafrikanischen Top-Hotellerie, ist die einzige Frau auf der Welt, der drei Relais-&-Châteaux-Hotels gehören. Die stilvolle und kultivierte Lady verfügt nicht nur über außergewöhnlichen Geschmack und ein Händchen dafür, aus Hotels wahre *homes far from home* zu machen, sie ist auch eine sehr mutige Frau, die wenige Tage vor dem Ende der Apartheid statt wie viele andere aus dem Land zu fliehen ein Weingut kaufte und in ihre Hotels investierte. Ihre drei Juwelen „The Plettenberg" in Plettenberg Bay, „The Marine" in Hermanus und „The Cellars-Hohenort" bei Kapstadt gehören zu den absolut besten Hotels, die Südafrika zu bieten hat.

Liz McGrath, the grande dame at the pinnacle of the South African hotel business, is the only woman in the world with three Relais & Châteaux hotels. Not only has this stylish and cultured lady extraordinary good taste and the knack of making her hotels feel like homes far from home, she also has great courage. Only a few days before the end of apartheid, instead of fleeing the land like many others she purchased a vineyard and invested in her hotels. Her three gems, The Plettenberg in Plettenberg Bay, The Marine in Hermanus and The Cellars-Hohenort near Cape Town are three of the finest hotels that South Africa has to offer.

Text: Jürgen Gutowski
Fotos: Jürgen & Martina Gutowski

There are many ways of getting to Cape Town. I've lost count of the number of times I've been here, once on a train across the desert, another time by air and yet another by ship. All my journeys led to Cape Town, the magnetic city which draws me to it like no other in the world. This town with a lightness of being despite its contrasts is the metropolis of the Rainbow Nation, and the centre of a broad landscape, even now in the gentle South African winter. An indescribable steel blue sky is

Viele Wege führen nach Kapstadt. Wie viele Male bin ich hier angekommen, mal mit dem Zug quer durch die Wüste, mal mit dem Flugzeug, mal mit dem Schiff. Alle meine Wege führen jedenfalls nach Cape Town, in die magnetische Stadt, die mich anzieht wie keine andere auf der Welt. Stadt der Leichtigkeit des Seins trotz aller Gegensätze, Metropole der Regenbogennation, Zentrum einer gigantischen Landschaft. Auch jetzt im sanften südafrikanischen Winter, der mit dieser unbeschreiblichen stählernen Himmelsbläue über den weiten Dünen des Bloubergstrands ruht.

Vom Aschenputtel zum Königskind: Liz McGrath hat aus der ehemaligen Jugendherberge ein Refugium mit Stil gemacht.
From Cinderella to Princess: Liz McGrath has converted an old youth hostel into a stylish residence.

Hervorragende Weine vom eigenen Gut lagern im Keller des Plettenberg, der auch schon mal für ein Candle-Light-Dinner herhält.
Superb wines from the private estate are stored in the Plettenberg's cellar which is sometimes used for candlelight dinners.

Diesmal kam ich mit dem Auto in meine zweite Heimat, machte den Weg von Ost nach West auf einer der spektakulärsten Routen, die die Welt zu bieten hat, benannt nach ihren Farben und Pflanzen und Hainen – die südafrikanische Garden Route. Ich hatte den Mietwagen in Port Elizabeth übernommen und folgte der N2 westwärts, vorbei am Wild Flower Reserve und dem berühmten Tsitsikama National Park. Gut zu wissen: Drei Stationen der Gastlichkeit lagen auf meinem Weg nach Kapstadt, die drei kleinen Juwele aus der Kollektion von Liz McGrath, der Grande Dame und gleichzeitig Jeanne d'Arc der südafrikanischen Top-Hotellerie, die „The Plettenberg" im gleichnamigen Ort, „The Marine" in Hermanus und „The Cellars-Hohenort" bei Kapstadt zur Weltklasse führte. Eine mutige Frau, die wenige Tage vor dem Ende der Apartheid statt aus dem Land zu fliehen ein Weingut kaufte und in ihre Hotels investierte. Geadelt durch die Mitgliedschaft im Club der Besten von Relais & Châteaux sind die drei Perlen dieser Kollektion nun die erste Empfehlung für einen Besuch der *southernmost coast of Africa*.

The Plettenberg

Westerngleich empfängt mich das Küstenstädtchen Plettenberg Bay, kalifornisch muten die niedrigen Häuser mit ihren Holzbalkonen, Boutiquen, Grünanlagen und Healthfood-Läden an. Eine weite geschwungene Bucht öffnet sich direkt unter dem Hotel, Strandewigkeiten so weit das Auge reicht auf mehr als zehn Kilometer. Ich stehe barfuß auf dem beheizten Fußboden meiner Suite, eine helle, ganz in Pastelltönen gehaltene Kemenate, und kann es kaum glauben, dass dieses gediegene Haus oberhalb der fernen Dünen des Blouberg-Strandes liegt.

above the distant dunes of the Blouberg beach.
This time I arrived at my second home by car driving from east to west along one of the most spectacular routes the world has to offer, named after its colours, plants and groves – the South African Garden Route. I rented a car in Port Elizabeth and followed the N2 westwards, driving past the Wild Flower Reserve and the famous Tsitsikama National Park. Good to know there are three small hotels on my way to Cape Town, jewels of Liz McGrath's Collection, the grand dame of the South African hotel business. The three hotels, "The Plettenberg" in the place of the same name, "The Marine" in Hermanus, and "The Cellars-Hohenort" near Cape Town, are world class establishments.
Liz McGrath has courage.
A few days before the end of apartheid, instead of fleeing the country she bought a vineyard and invested in her hotels. Granted membership of the eminent Relais & Châteaux, the three gems of this collection now head the list of recommended hotels for a visit to the southernmost coast of Africa.

Unangefochtene Nummer eins der Garden Route: The Marine, Fünf-Sterne-Herberge mit Charakter.

The Marine is a hotel with character and is undisputed as the foremost five-star hotel on the Garden Route.

Das geschichtsträchtige Hotel präsentiert sich als Hort der Ruhe und Beschaulichkeit.

A hotel steeped in history, a place of great beauty and peace.

The Plettenberg

The coastal town of Plettenberg Bay resembles one in a Western. The low houses with their wooden balconies, the boutiques, the lawns and the health food shops remind one of California. The wide curving bay in front of the hotel has a beach over six miles long which stretches as far as the eye can see. I am standing barefoot on the heated floor of my suite, a light room in pastel colours, hardly able to believe that years ago this elegant house used to be a youth hostel. "The Lookout", as it was then called, was also a steak house. Steaks are still served today and "The Lookout" is as spectacular as it used to be, except that in the hands of Liz McGrath Cinderella has been transformed into a royal princess. The Plettenberg only has 37 rooms in its two houses on the cliff, but they are equipped with every luxury and electronic gadget expected by the discriminating traveller: air-conditioning, minibar, underfloor heating, electronic safe, phone and TV. The last never gets switched on because the view over the terrace and the pool which merges

gene Haus vor Jahren als Jugendherberge diente. „The Lookout" hieß es damals und beherbergte ein Steakhouse. Steaks gibt's auch heute noch und auch der *look out* ist so spektakulär wie damals, aber unter den Händen von Liz McGrath wandelte sich das Aschenputtel zum Königskind. Gerade mal 37 Zimmer bietet „The Plettenberg" in den beiden Gebäuden auf der Klippe, ausgestattet sind sie mit allem Komfort und Elektronik, die der High-End-Traveler erwartet: Air-Conditioning, Minibar, Fußbodenheizung, elektronische Safes, Phone & TV. Letzteres bleibt ausgeschaltet, denn der Blick über die Terrasse und den Pool, der mit der Bläue des Meeres zu verschmelzen scheint, ist Panoramafernsehen, wie es kein elektronisches Programm auch nur ansatzweise auszustrahlen vermag. Vom Zimmer, von den Terrassen, vom Restaurant – überall öffnet sich diese Weite, begleitet mich auf allen Wegen auf dieser hohen Klippe über dem Meer. In der Ferne springen Delphine im Abendlicht, perfekt synchronchoreographiert von Mutter Natur, während ich auf der Terrasse des neu renovierten Restaurants frischen Fisch und kühlen Chardonnay aus dem hoteleigenen Weinkeller genieße.

The Marine

Ein Monument über der Bucht von Hermanus. Weiß und lang gestreckt wie die stolzen Dampfer der historischen Union- und Castle-Lines ruht

das Hotel über der walfischreichsten Bay Südafrikas. Vor 100 Jahren schon das erste Haus am Platze, doch erst 98 Jahre später unter den kreativen Händen von Liz McGrath und ihrem Team begnadeter Designer zum unangefochtenen Fünf-Sterne-Haus der Garden Route avanciert, bietet es in 45 Räumen Platz zum Leben sowie überwältigende Ausblicke in die Walker Bay. Einige Suiten sind behindertengerecht, alle, selbst die vier Einzelzimmer, sind individuell möbliert in frischem viktorianischen Charme. Doch die acht Premier-Suiten, manche auf zwei Etagen, sind die Prunkstücke des Hotels Marine. Sie sind kolossale Beispiele historischer, englisch-afrikanischer Lebensart: Echte Kamine mit fulminanten Ausmaßen erwärmen die Erker und Räume, Kristallüster bescheinen die schweren Sessel und Sofas, riesige Sprossenfenster, die an die Kommandobrücke eines Ozean-

riesen erinnern, geben den Blick frei in mehrere Himmelsrichtungen. Natürlich sind auch Air-Conditioning, High Tech usw. überall vorhanden, doch steht man lieber auf dem großen Balkon in der Sonne, in der berühmten „Champagnerluft von Hermanus", um den Walfamilien bei der Buchtinspektion zuzuschauen, statt der Deutschen Welle oder CNN. Im Erdgeschoss, wo heute die Orangerie zu einem Glas Champagner einlädt, tanzte schon in den zwanziger Jahren Prinzessin Alice zu den Klängen der Bigbands vom Cape. Doch heute ist das geschichtsträchtige Hotel ein Hort der Ruhe und Beschaulichkeit, der Reading Room etwa besticht eher durch behagliche Kontemplation denn durch quirliges Businessgehabe. Auf dem Klippenweg durchstreift man den „Fynbos", die artenreichste Vegetation der Welt. Und steht dann doch immer wieder auf dem Balkon in seinem *room with a view!*

The Cellars-Hohenort

Zeit zu leben und zu schauen auf der gut einstündigen Autofahrt von Hermanus nach Cape Town. „Overberg", so heißt diese Region, und so fahre ich über den Berg, nur um *den* Berg Südafrikas zu erblicken, Table Mountain in ganzer 1000-Meter-Pracht, diesmal ein wenig Schnee als weiße Tischdecke oben drauf. Davor der schier unendliche Bloubergstrand und die ewig heranrauschenden Wellen in Sechser- oder Achterkolonnen. Vorbei an den *wine lands* und Golfplätzen von Constantia, ich passiere den Botanischen Garten von Kirstenbosch, rolle durch Wälder und über Serpentinen, und ich befinde mich schließlich an „hohem Orte" – The Cellars-Hohenort macht seinem erhöhten Namen alle Ehre. Die weiße Fassade des kapholländischen Weinguts gleißt in der tief stehenden Nachmittagssonne, der Gärtner schneidet Rosen, die hier nach dem legendären Capetonian Dr. Christiaan Barnard benannt sind, und ich parke meinen Wagen auf knirschendem Kies. Vorbei am Brunnen vor dem Tore und erntereifen Orangenbäumen, und ich

with the blue of the ocean, is a wide-screen TV in itself, unmatched by any electronic device. This vast panorama is spread out beyond the windows, the terrace and the restaurant, and is wherever I look on this high cliff above the sea. In the evening light, Dolphins are jumping in unison in the distance, perfectly choreographed by Mother Nature, while I sit on the terrace of the recently renovated restaurant enjoying fresh fish and a cool Chardonnay from the hotel's own wine cellar.

Prunkstück: Eine der acht Premier-Suiten des Marine Hotels mit raumhohen Sprossenfenstern und grandiosem Blick auf die Walker Bay.
Showpiece: one of the eight Premier Suites of the Marine Hotel. Its ceiling-high lattice windows afford fantastic views across Walker Bay.

The Marine

A monument above the bay at Hermanus. The hotel is a long, white building standing like a proud liner of the historic Union and Castle Line overlooking the bay with the most whales in South Africa. It was the first house to be built in this spot over a hundred years ago, and ninety-eight years later is has been elevated by Liz McGrath and her team of talented designers to the status of a five star hotel on the Garden Route. Its 45 rooms offer plenty of living space and overwhelming views of Walker Bay. Some of the suites have been adapted for the disabled, and the four single rooms are furnished in charming Victorian style with a personal note. However, it is the eight Premier Suites, some of which are on two floors, which are the showpieces of the hotel. They are superb examples of Anglo-African lifestyle. Grand fireplaces heat the oriels and rooms, crystal chandeliers cast their sparkling light on to the heavy armchairs and sofas, enormous lattice windows, reminiscent of the bridge of an ocean liner, look out in all directions. It goes without saying that they have air-conditioning, hi-tech etc. but you may to prefer to stand in the sun on the big balcony taking in the famous "champagne air of Hermanus" watching families of whales rather than watching CNN. On the ground floor in the Orangery where nowadays glasses of champagne are served, Princess Alice used to dance to the sound of the big bands of the Cape. Nowadays this historic hotel is a haven of peace and tranquillity. It is the contemplative atmosphere of the Reading Room which is its most distinctive feature, rather than the bustle of business. Walking along the cliff path one goes through fynbos, the most varied vegetation in the world, but then its back to the balcony of one's Room with a View.

The Cellars-Hohenwart

On the hour-long drive from Hermanus to Cape Town, one has time for simply looking and living. This region is called Overberg, so I drive over the mountain to be able to see *the* Mountain of South Africa, the 3,280 ft Table Mountain standing there in all its glory, covered on this occasion with a white tablecloth, a sprinkling of snow. At its foot is the endless Blouberg Beach, waves advancing in regular sixes and eights breaking on to the shore. Driving through wine country, I pass the golf courses of Constantia and the Botanical Garden of Kirstenbosch. I take winding roads through woods to arrive at last at the "high place" or Hohenort. The Cellars-Hohenort does its elevated name justice. The white façade of the Cape Dutch house of this wine-growing area gleams in the low afternoon sunlight, and a gardener is pruning roses which here have been named after legendary South African Dr. Christiaan Barnard. I park my car on the crunchy gravel, then walk past the fountain and orange trees laden with oranges in front of the door, and through into the hotel hall of this historic manor house. The hall which has a surrounding gallery beneath the ceiling, is an ensemble of wood, golden chandeliers

stehe in der Halle des historischen Manor Houses des Hotels, wo wie vor 300 Jahren der gigantische Kamin den Raum – ein Ensemble aus Holz und goldenen Lüstern und Ölgemälden und einer umlaufenden Galerie hoch oben unter der Decke – in eine Atmosphäre heimischer Behaglichkeit taucht. Die Zeit scheint stillzustehen, selbst die antike Standuhr verweigert sich der Zeitmessung. Auch die Räume, groß und hell und angereichert mit antikem Mobiliar, sind Reminiszenzen an eine *by-gone-era*, die allerdings in diesem Hotel eine Renaissance erfährt. Wohlbefinden für den Gast, das ist hier das Zauberwort, und diesem Zweck dient jeder Raum und jeder Mensch, der hier seine Aufgabe hat. Ich werde in mein Zimmer geführt, ein „Standardraum", wie ich erfahre, aber angesichts der Üppigkeit, der farblichen und räumlichen Grandeur, der verschwenderischen Architektur unterm Schrägdach oder im mö-

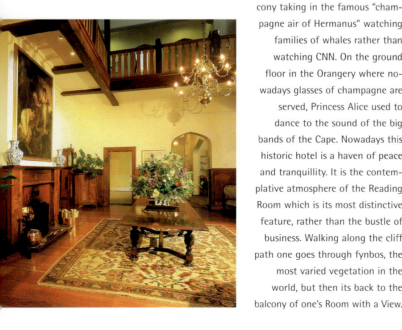

blierten Wintergarten kann ich nicht umhin, fortan nur von meiner „Suite" zu schwärmen. Und die echten Suiten mit ihren wuchtigen Himmelbetten, historischen Waschtischen, lodernden Kaminen und deckenhohen Panoramafenstern sind in der Tat eine Hommage an eine Jahrhunderte währende Ära des Geschmacks und der Gastfreundschaft. Der eilfüßige und perfekte 24-Stunden-Butler-Service, der legendäre Weinkeller des Hotels, der kleine von Gary Player entworfene Golfplatz, die beiden Gourmetrestaurants sowie der vielseitige und anerkannte „Carchele-Spa" unterstreichen die hohen Standards an diesem „Hohenort". Ob nun der Weg nach Kapstadt, Hermanus oder Plettenberg führt, es ist ein guter Weg zu den drei Perlen aus Liz McGraths Collection. Collection mit C – wie *Courtesy, Charm, Character, Cuisine* und *Calm* – der Stoff, aus dem Relais & Châteaux gemacht ist.

and oil paintings. It has a gigantic three hundred year-old fireplace which gives the room a really homely feeling. Time seems to stand still, even the antique grandfather clock refuses to measure the time. The rooms, large and light, are furnished with antiques and are reminiscent of a bygone era, albeit an age which in this hotel is experiencing a renaissance. The magic words here are "total wellbeing" for the guest. Every member of staff and every room are dedicated to this purpose. I am led into my room, one of the "Standard Rooms" which, I am told, are either beneath the sloping roof or in the furnished Wintergarten. Owing to its opulence and colour scheme, its space, grandeur, and lavish architecture, I come to regard it as my own "Suite", and I go into raptures about it. The real suites however have enormous four posters, antique washstands, blazing fires and ceiling-high picture windows, which are a tribute to a century of taste and hospitality. The fleet-footed, perfect butler-service, the hotel's legendary wine cellar, the little Putting Green designed by Gary Player, the two gourmet restaurants and the broad range of treatment on offer in the well-known "Carchele Spa", is further evidence of the high standards at Hohenort. Whether your journey takes you to Cape Town, Hermanus or Plettenberg, it is a good road that leads to the three gems of the Liz McGrath Collection. Their "five Cs", Courtesy, Charm, Character, Cuisine and Calm, the very stuff of which Relais & Châteaux is made.

Von der Sonne geküsst: eines der großzügigen „Standardzimmer" des Weingut-Hotels.
Sun-kissed: one of the spacious Standard Rooms in the vineyard hotel.

Very british: Süße Träume im Himmelbett sind hier Realität.
Very British: sweet dreams in a four-poster are reality here.

Verschwenderische Architektur unter dem Schrägdach und heimelige Behaglichkeit durch antikes Mobiliar machen jedes Logis des Cellars-Hohenort zu einem individuellen Zuhause auf Zeit.
The lavish architecture beneath the sloping roof and the homely comfort of the antique furniture make every room of the Cellars-Hohenort feel like temporary home from home.

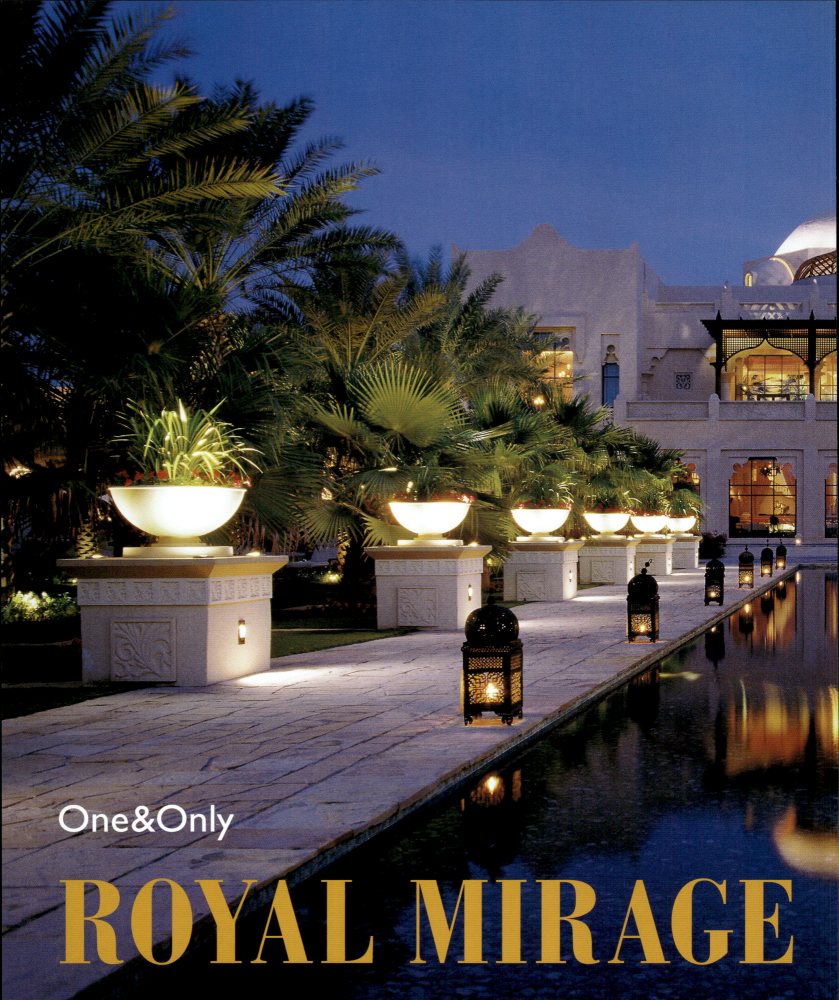

Verloren in einem Wüstensturm, so erzählt es die Legende, erscheint einem Beduinen eine majestätische Festung am Horizont. Wahrhaft königlich empfangen, prägen Pracht und Opulenz den Aufenthalt innerhalb der Mauern. Nachdem sich der Sturm gelegt hat, nimmt der Beduine wehmütig Abschied. Sein Blick geht ein letztes Mal zurück – die Festung ist wie vom Erdboden verschwunden. Inspiriert von dieser Legende verwöhnt das luxuriöse Fünf-Sterne-Hotel One&Only Royal Mirage seine Gäste mit prachtvoller Architektur und dem Zauber arabischer Gastlichkeit.

A legend tells of a Bedouin lost in a desert storm who sees a majestic fort on the horizon. He is received with all the splendour and hospitality accorded to royalty. After the storm has died down the Bedouin departs with a heavy heart. He takes a last look – the fort has vanished. Inspired by this legend, the luxurious five-star hotel One&Only Royal Mirage pampers its guests with magnificent architecture and the magic of the Arabian hospitality.

Text: Bernd Teichgräber · Fotos: Klaus Lorke

Erinnerungen an arabische Märchen und Sagen werden wach.
Stirring memories of Arabian stories and legends.

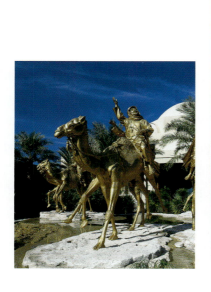

Pracht, Opulenz und Weite charakterisieren die Lobby.
Splendour, opulence and space define the lobby.

Approaching the hotel stirs memories of Arabian myths and legends. The navy blue BMW stretch limousine taking the guest to the entrance glides through a dream garden at night, past palms hung with hundreds of little lights. The walls, towers and turrets of the fort and a tremendous Moorish dome look like a film set for the Arabian Nights, and blazing torches illuminate a path over a bridge leading to the building. At this late hour the light is mysteriously reflected by giant bronze statues of Bedouins and their camels standing in front of the entrance to the palace. They seem to be part of an imaginary journey transporting the visitor to The Palace of the One&Only Royal Mirage into another time and place, and the feeling remains throughout one's stay. The feeling subsides as one goes into the imposing, echoing entrance hall. First sight of the vast space beyond leaves an overwhelming impression. Beneath a richly ornamented dome typical of the country, is a cathedral high hall with four tall palms. Quiet piano music from the lobby lounge accompanies the melody of the fountains which appear to be in every corner of the resort. The marble floors are a typical feature of this luxury hideaway, uniting splendour, opulence and elegance with traditional elements. Exceptional furniture and high quality fabrics and other materials are evidence of the great store put by quality, which displays the sumptuous nature of Arab lifestyle.

Bereits bei der Anfahrt zum The Palace of the One&Only Royal Mirage fühlt man sich an arabische Märchen und Sagen erinnert. Die dunkelblaue BMW-Stretch-Limousine, die den Gast ans Portal bringt, gleitet durch einen nächtlichen Traumgarten, vorbei an mit Hunderten von kleinen Lichtern geschmückten Palmen. Festungsmauern, Türme und Zinnen sowie eine stimmungsvoll beleuchtete maurische Kuppel präsentieren sich wie eine Filmkulisse aus 1001 Nacht, während lodernde Fackelfeuer den Weg über eine Brücke hinter die Gemäuer weisen. Geheimnisvoll spiegelt sich das Licht der späten Stunde in überlebensgroßen bronzenen Statuen vor dem Palasteingang wider, die Beduinen mit ihren Kamelen zeigen. Sie scheinen nur ein Teil einer Zeitreise zu sein, die den Besucher des The Palace of the One&Only Royal Mirage in eine

One's gaze is constantly being drawn to the graceful oriental arches and beautiful ornamentation. Every teacup, every chair leg, every mirror frame and every pillar is decorated. The guest is amazed to hear that every item of furniture has been handcrafted exclusively for the hotel, and every part of the décor and colour scheme has been carefully designed to integrate into this overall work of art. The wonderful view from lobby bar, the lounge and the sun terrace is over a rambling garden to the Arabian Gulf beyond. The ceremonial character of the entrance hall has a profound effect on the guest. You tend to stride rather than walk across the valuable Persian carpets which lead to the 173 Deluxe rooms, 53 Gold Club room, 18 suites and 2 Royal Suites, all of which have a balcony or terrace with sea views, air-conditioning, Sat TV, minibar, a walk-in wardrobe and a luxury bathrooms with a separate shower, toilet and bidet. From here one can observe the range and ever-changing colours of the sand, from the brilliant white sand on the beach to the light yellow of the dunes early in the day. Other rooms overlook a mélange of colour including the strong blue-greens of the sea. The Gold Club accommodation is really luxurious and provides an excep-

andere Zeit, in einen anderen Raum versetzt. Dieses Gefühl wird den Gast fortan nicht mehr verlassen. Nicht, wenn er die imposante Eingangshalle des Palace mit ihrer feierlich widerhallenden Weite betritt. Der erste Eindruck ist überwältigend, dem Auge erschließt sich die ganze Fülle des Raumes: Unter einer kunstvollen, mit landestypischer Ornamentik reich verzierten Kuppel erstreckt sich eine kathedralenhohe Halle mit vier emporstrebenden Palmen. Leise Pianoklänge aus der Lobby-Lounge untermalen die verträumte Melodie des Wasserspiels der Springbrunnen, wie man auch an fast jeder Stelle des Resorts die Geräusche von Wasser wahrnimmt. Auf dem glänzenden Marmor-Fußboden entfaltet sich der stilvolle Charakter dieses Luxus-Hideaways, das Pracht und Opulenz mit Eleganz und traditionellen Elementen vereint. Ausgesuchte Möbel, hochwertige Stoffe und Materialien verraten Qualitätsbewusstsein und zeigen den Reichtum arabischer Wohnkultur. Immer wieder zeichnet das Auge die anmutige Form orientalischer Bögen und Muster nach. Jede Teetasse, jedes Stuhlbein, jeder Spiegelrahmen und jede Säule trägt diesen Stempel. Der staunende Gast erfährt, dass sämtliche Einrichtungsgegenstände exklusiv für das Hotel von Hand gefertigt wurden und sich fein abgestimmt in Farbe und Anmutung in das Gesamtkunstwerk integrieren. Von der Lobby-Bar, der Lounge und der Sonnenterrasse geht der Blick herrlich über den weiträumigen Garten auf den Arabi-

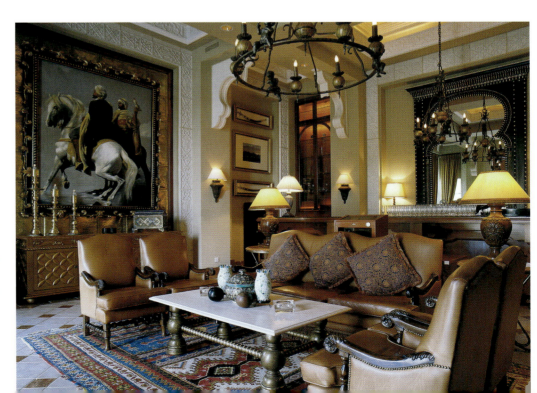

Jedes Zimmer zeigt Farbkombinationen, die harmonisch aufeinander abgestimmt sind.
Each room has a harmonious colour scheme.

Traumpool für wohlige Wasserwonnen.
Dream pool bliss.

tional level of personal care and attention. It has its own reception area, a separate lift and lounge, and round-the-clock valeting. When you go outside you notice how wide is the area covered by the resort. Around The Palace of the One&Only Royal Mirage are radiantly colourful flower borders, winding paths and lawns whose lush green could compete with any English lawn. One is constantly discovering something new and delighting in the picturesque pillared courtyards, the bright mosaics and the 1,300 palms which make The Palace of the One&Only Royal Mirage the green oasis that it is. A significant element of the courtyards is the light which is always creating new effects at different times of the

schen Golf. Der zeremonielle Charakter der Eingangshalle nimmt den Besucher so gefangen, dass man mehr schreitet als geht: über kostbare persische Teppiche zu den 173 Deluxe-Zimmern, 53 Gold-Club-Zimmern, 18 Suiten und zwei Royal-Suiten, die allesamt über Balkone oder Terrassen mit Meerblick, Klimaanlage, Sat-TV, Minibar, begehbare Kleiderschränke und luxuriöse Badezimmer mit separater Dusche, Toilette und Bidet verfügen. Die changierende Vielfalt der Farben des Sandes von strahlendem Weiß der Strände bis zum hellen Gelb der Dünen im Licht des heraufziehenden Tages kommt hier bestens zur Geltung, während andere Logis auf eine kräftig angemischte Farbpalette mit den lebhaften Blaugrüntönen des Meeres setzen. Luxus und eine ausgesucht persönliche Umsorgung bietet der Gold-Club-Bereich mit individuellem Empfang, separatem Fahrstuhl, Lounge und Butler-Service rund um die Uhr.

Tritt man vom Hotel ins Freie, bemerkt man sofort die Weiträumigkeit dieses feinen Resorts. The Palace of the One&Only Royal Mirage ist von leuchtenden Blumenrabatten, verschlungenen Wegen und Rasenflächen umgeben, die in ihrem satten Grün jedem englischen Park Konkurrenz machen könnten. Ständig entdeckt das Auge Neues, erfreut sich an malerischen Säulenhöfen, an bunten Mosaikfliesen und über 1300 Palmen, die The Palace of the One&Only Royal Mirage zu einer grünen Oase machen.

Wichtiger Hauptakteur in den Innenhöfen ist das Licht, das mit den wechselnden Tageszeiten immer neue überraschende Effekte schafft. Begleitend dazu bereichert die traditionelle orientalische Wasserkunst die moderne Garten-

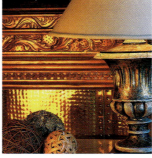

Träume aus 1001 Nacht werden wahr.
Dreams of Arabian Nights come true.

architektur. Kanäle, Rinnen und Springbrunnen untermalen den internationalen Stil. Ein wohltuend warmer Kontrast zu den grauen Tagen des europäischen Winters, zumal der mit 600 Quadratmetern größte Swimmingpool Dubais zu ausgiebigem Schwimmen lockt. Gerne verbringt man den Tag auf bequemen Sonnenliegen unter dem natürlichen Blätterdach des weiträumigen Palmengartens oder taucht in die Tiefen des Meeres ab. Wasserski, Windsurfen, Hochseefischen, Angeln, Tennis oder Volleyball sind nur ein Ausschnitt aus der Vielzahl der Sport- und Freizeitmöglichkeiten. Wohl mit Recht bezeichnet sich Dubai als *die* Golfmetropole der Region, denn keine andere Wüstenstadt der Welt hat fünf 18-Loch-Golfplätze zu bieten. Wer etwas für seine Schönheit und Gesundheit tun möchte, der ist im The Palace of the One&Only Royal Mirage Health & BeautyInstitut bestens aufgehoben.

Der vorbildlichen Gastlichkeit des Hauses entspricht die Gastronomie der Nobelherberge, denn lukullische Hochgenüsse gibt es reichlich am Arabischen Golf. Bereits zu Zeiten der Kalifen gehörten Kochkunst und Lebenskultur eng zusammen. Der Gast hat die kulinarische Freiheit zwischen dem hoch eleganten Gourmetrestaurant Celebrities und einer „Cuisine du soleil" in der heiteren und ungezwungenen Atmosphäre des „Olives". Im Stil eines nordafrikanischen Restaurants aufgemacht, verbreiten im Tagine marokkanische Zubereitungen von allerbestem Geschmack ihre Wohlgerüche. Aufmerksam wacht Executive Chef Paul Linz, der seine Kochkunst in namhaften Häusern rund um den Globus erlernte und verfeinerte, über die Qualität der Küchen. Was seine Küchenbrigade auf die Tische zaubert, darauf dürfen sich Feinschmecker freuen. Die Mezze im „Tagine" sind ein Erlebnis: ein Tisch, voll mit zahlreichen dekorativen Vorspeisen, köstlich gewürztes Gemüse wie Auberginenmus oder Kichererbsenpüree, Pilze, Oliven und viele Delikatessen mehr. Das zarte Lammfleisch mit Couscous und Gemüse setzt mit Recht auf den Gaumengenuss des erstklassigen Ausgangsproduktes. Ganz nah an Wind und Wellen sitzt der Gast im Strandhaus „The Beach". Während die Wogen des

day. Yet not only the light but traditional oriental water features are very much part of the modern garden design. The streams, channels and fountains are international in style. The place is a certainly a warm contrast to the grey European winter, especially since its pool covers an area of nearly 6,500 square feet, making it the largest swimming pool in Dubai. It's so simple to spend the day outside on a comfortable lounger in the shade of the palms in the large palm garden, or go skin diving in the sea.

Water skiing, wind surfing, deep sea fishing, angling, tennis and volleyball are only a few of the many activities and leisure time pursuits available. Dubai can justly claim to be the golf metropolis of the whole region, because no other desert city anywhere else in the world has five 18-hole golf courses. Visitors who are more interested in health and beauty are superbly catered for by The Palace of the One&Only Royal Mirage

Romantische Stätte der Gastlichkeit: das Strandrestaurant „The Beach".
"The Beach" restaurant – hospitality and romance rolled into one.

Marokkanische Ambiance für eine ebensolche Küche.
A Moroccan ambience for Moroccan cuisine.

Mediterrane Piazza-Atmosphäre im Restaurant „Olives".
The „Olives" restaurant has a Mediterranean piazza atmosphere.

Health & Beauty Institute. The exemplary hospitality of this smart hotel is well up to the standard of its gastronomy. The Gulf abounds in culinary delights. At the time of the caliphs, cuisine and a highly cultivated lifestyle went together. The guest can choose between the very elegant Celebrities restaurant and the cuisine du soleil served in the lively, informal Olives restaurant. The Tagine Restaurant has north African décor and serves very tasty, wonderfully aromatic Moroccan dishes. Executive chef Paul Linz, who learnt and refined his cooking skills in the finest hotels around the world, carefully monitors the quality of the cuisine. The dishes produced by his staff are sheer pleasure for any gourmand. The mezze in Tagine are an absolute must. Spread out on a table are numerous attractive starters including delicious spicy vegetables such as aubergines with chickpea puree, mushrooms, olives, and many other delicacies. The tender lamb with couscous and vegetables is definitely one of the most delicious dishes. You can be very close to wind and the waters of the Gulf at the Beach house.

Golfs sanft an den feinsandigen Strand rollen, genießt man auf rustikalen Holzplanken frische Grill- und Meeresspezialitäten. Dann wird es auch langsam Zeit, sich auf einen begeisternden kulinarischen Abend vorzubereiten – Romantik pur im Kerzenschein.

Nur wenige Schritte vom The Palace of the One&Only Royal Mirage entführen seit Dezember 2002 zwei weitere spektakuläre Luxus-Hideaways ihre anspruchsvolle Klientel in Oasen der Glückseligkeit. Die Hotels Arabian Court und Residence & Spa of the One&Only Royal Mirage sind ein Tribut an arabische Architektur und Gastlichkeit, wobei jedes Domizil über eine eigene Hotelzufahrt, Pool, Gartenanlage, Restaurants und privaten Strand verfügt.

Die stil- und prachtvollen Interieurs des Arabian Court sind beeindruckende Inszenierungen und thematisieren orientalisches Leben, Erleben und Fühlen, ohne ihren internationalen Touch zu verleugnen. Optisches Highlight ist die atemberaubende Grand Gallery: Sieben imposante Kuppeln symbolisieren die Anzahl der Vereinigten Arabischen Emirate. Hier wie in den Restaurants und 172 Zimmern und Suiten taucht man in eine Aura gehobener Wohnkultur.

Weltgewandter Gastgeber im The Palace of the One&Only Royal Mirage: Olivier Louis.
Olivier Louis, sophisticated host of The Palace of the One&Only Royal Mirage.

Als intime Luxus-Oase der Ruhe mit drei Garten-Villen mit privatem Pool, 18 Suiten und 32 Deluxe-Zimmern zeigt sich das Residence & Spa of the One&Only Royal Mirage. Das Hamam & Spa lässt die Schönheits- und Badekultur des Orients wieder auferstehen und verwöhnt mit vielfältigen kosmetischen und therapeutischen Behandlungsmethoden. Exklusiv für den Mittleren Osten bietet die französische Nobelmarke Givenchy ein umfangreiches Programm für gutes Aussehen und sich Wohlfühlen an, so dass in der entspannenden Atmosphäre dieses Kleinods der Alltag in weite Ferne rückt.

While waves are breaking on the shore, guests can sit on simple wooden benches enjoying freshly grill specialities and seafood, then get ready for a fantastic evening meal by candle-light – pure romance. Just a few yards from The Palace of the One&Only Royal Mirage, two new spectacular luxury hideaways are enticing their sophisticated clientele into oases of sheer bliss. The Arabian Court and Residence & Spa of the One&Only Royal Mirage are a tribute to Arabian architecture and hospitality. Each of the hotels has its own entrance drive, pool, garden, restaurant and private beach. The style and the opulent interiors of the Arabian Court resemble grand stage sets, but their central themes around oriental life and experience are not compromised by their international touch. The focal point must surely be the breathtaking Grand Gallery which has seven imposing domes symbolizing the number of Emirates which form the United Arab Emirates. As in the restaurants and the 172 rooms and suites, one is enveloped by an aura of exclusive living. The Residence & Spa hotel which has three Garden Villas with private pools, 18 suites and 32 Deluxe rooms, is an intimate and peaceful oasis. The Hamam & Spa has revived oriental traditions of beauty and bathing, and pampers guests with a wide variety of cosmetic treatment and therapies. The exclusive French Givenchy brand provides a wide range of cosmetic and feel-good treatment so that the daily grind can be firmly put aside in therelaxing atmosphere of this beautiful place.

Jumeira Beach: feinsandiger Strand mit Palmen.
Jumeira Beach: powdery sand and palms.

The Royal Coco Palm

The Royal Coco Palm Resort & Spa an den Traumstränden der Andamanen-See im Süden Thailands macht seinem Namen alle Ehre. Hinter den blütenweißen Ufergestaden erstreckt sich der über 6,5 Hektar große Palmenhain, unter dessen sattgrünes Dach sich die luxuriösen Villen des Resorts ducken. Umgeben von Palmen und exotischen Gärten, zauberhaftem Ambiente und vorbildlichem Service garantiert das vor zwei Jahren eröffnete Luxus-Resort wahrlich königliche Urlaubserlebnisse.
Text: Sabine Herder | Fotos: Christian Prager

Im Land des Lächelns
Resort & Spa
In the Land of Smiles

The Royal Coco Palm Resort & Spa beside the fantastic shoreline of the Andaman Sea in South Thailand does its name justice. Stretching beyond the brilliant white beaches is a 16-acres palm grove beneath whose lush green fronds are the luxurious villas of the resort. Surrounded by an enchanting ambience of palms and exotic gardens, the resort which was only opened two years ago provides an exemplary service which ensures that you have a truly royal holiday.

Herzlich willkommen im Land des Lächelns!
Welcome to the land of smiles!

Rechts und links des Resorts erstrecken sich die kilometerlangen hellen Sandstrände der Andamanen-See.
To the right and left of the Resort are miles of fine, light-coloured sandy beaches of the Andaman Sea.

There's no doubt about it, the Thai people know how to smile. You notice it as soon as you arrive at Phuket Airport. The driver of the air-conditioned Mercedes-Benz limousine taking us to the Royal Coco Palm Resort welcomes us with a disarming smile which is really infectious. Automatically we respond with broad smiles and sense that our wanderlust is now open to all the beauty of Thailand. The journey into the land of the coconut palms takes us in a northerly direction from the Phuket peninsula. We pass traditional little Thai villages, which are hives of activity just before the sun goes down. Straw-hatted peasant women are carrying large baskets into the houses; graceful young women in Thai dress are decorating the miniature temples outside the front doors with fresh flowers; washing flutters in the wind and a host of laughing children wave at us. Every now and again between the settlements in the hinterland of the Andaman Sea, one catches sight of roaring

Wie ein typisches Thai-Dorf gruppieren sich einige der palmgedeckten Stelzenhäuser um die Poolanlagen und den einen kleinen natürlichen See.
Like a typical Thai village, the houses on stilts are grouped around the pool landscape and a small natural lake.

Keine Frage: In Thailand versteht man zu lächeln. Davon können wir uns gleich bei unserer Ankunft auf dem Flughafen von Phuket überzeugen. Der Fahrer der klimatisierten Mercedes-Benz-Limousine, der uns ins Royal Coco Palm Resort bringen soll, empfängt uns mit einem entwaffnenden Lächeln, das wirklich ansteckend ist. Ganz automatisch setzen wir unser schönstes Sonntagslächeln auf und spüren, dass unserem Fernweh nun die Träume Thailands offen stehen. Die Fahrt ins kokosnussgelobte Land führt uns von der Halbinsel Phuket

Richtung Norden. Vorbei an kleinen traditionellen Thai-Dörfern, wo so kurz vor Sonnenuntergang rege Betriebsamkeit herrscht. Strohbehütete Bäuerinnen tragen große Körbe in die Häuser; anmutige junge Frauen in thailändischer Tracht schmücken die kleinen Haustempel vor der Tür mit frischen Blumen; Wäschestücke flattern im Wind und jede Menge fröhlich lachende Kinder winken uns zu. Zwischen den Siedlungen im Hinterland der Andamanen-See immer wieder Ausblicke auf rauschende Wasserfälle und die exotische Vegetation des tropischen Regenwaldes. Je weiter wir nach Norden kommen, umso ursprünglicher zeigt sich der immergrüne Monsunwald. Wir passieren den Kao Sok National Park, dem sich das Khlong Saeng Wildlife Sanctuary anschließt. Dort kann man laut unserem freundlich lächelnden Fahrer frei lebende Elefanten, Tiger, Leoparden, asiatische Schwarzbären, Gibbons, Warane, Wildschweine und unzählige exotische Vogelarten beobachten. Aber auch Kanufahrten, River-Rafting- oder Wandertouren finden in dem Nationalpark ihr spektakuläres Umfeld.

Nach einer Stunde Fahrt über eine sehr gut ausgebaute Straße erreichen wir kurz nach Sonnenuntergang das Royal Coco Palm Resort & Spa. Mit unzähligen Lichtern effekt-

waterfalls and the exotic vegetation of the tropical rain forest. The farther north we go, the more unspoilt the ever-green monsoon forest scene. As we pass the Kao Sok National Park which is joined to the Khlong Saeng Wildlife Sanctuary, our smiling driver tells us it is a place where you can observe animals in the wild, elephant, tiger, leopard, Asian black bear, gibbon, boar, and many exotic birds. This is a truly spectacular location for canoeing, river rafting and walking. After a good half hour's drive through the jungle we arrive at the Royal Coco Palm Resort & Spa. The numerous lights set the scene. The Resort sheltered by the long fronds of mighty palm trees, appears to have quite a mystical, romantic air about it. The illuminated silhouettes of the palm-thatched buildings scattered across the whole of the grounds, are reflected in the gigantic pool area which stretches

Vom Restaurant und der Bar „The Mariner" zeigt sich die Andamanen-See von ihrer schönsten Seite.

The Andaman Sea looks best from "The Mariner" Restaurant and Bar.

Das Royal Coco Palm Resort bietet jedem Gast die Möglichkeit, die Vielschichtigkeit der thailändischen Kultur zu erleben.

The Royal Coco Palm Resort provides every guest with the possibility of experiencing the many aspects of Thai culture.

Natürliche Materialien und viel Platz prägen die Wohlfühlatmosphäre der 150 qm großen Pool Villen.

Natural materials and lots of space create an atmosphere of total wellbeing in the Pool Villas (1.614 sq. ft.).

Absolute Privatsphäre garantieren die luxuriösen Pool Villen mit eigenem Garten und Privatpool.

The luxury Pool Villas which have their own gardens and private pools guarantee absolute privacy.

from the sea through the heart of the Resort and beyond, ultimately to flow into a small natural lake. To the left and to the right of the winding path to our villa there is a whistling and a chirping, and the air is heavily scented. Bathed in a warm light, our villa brings a spontaneous smile to our lips, a smile of rapture which remains fixed for the whole duration of our stay, and which always elicits warm smiles in response from the 80-strong staff. This evening it is Somchai who explains the technical equipment in our luxurious Pool Villa with the patience of a saint. Adjustable air-

voll in Szene gesetzt, präsentiert sich das Resort mit einer fast mystischen Romantik, über die die mächtigen Palmen schützend ihre „langen Finger" halten. Die illuminierten Silhouetten der palmstrohgedeckten Gebäude, die sich über das weitläufige Gelände verstreuen, spiegeln sich in der gigantischen Poolanlage, die sich vom Meer bis in das Herz des Resorts erstreckt und landeinwärts in einen kleinen, natürlichen See übergeht. Links und rechts des sanft geschwungenen Weges, auf dem wir unsere Villa erreichen, zirpt, pfeift und duftet es mächtig. In warmes Licht getaucht, zaubert unser Zuhause auf Zeit ein ganz spontanes Lächeln auf unsere Lippen. Ein fast entrücktes Lächeln, das unser Gesicht während unseres gesamten Aufenthaltes zieren sollte und das von den über 80 Mitarbeitern stets herzlich erwidert wurde. Heute Abend ist es Somchai, der uns mit einer Engelsgeduld in die technischen Finessen unserer überaus luxuriösen Pool Villa einführt. Individuell regelbare Klimaanlage, Minibar, Sat-TV, Safe, HiFi-Anlage und der eigene Wasserkocher für eine Tasse Tee oder Kaffee sind in den sieben Pool Villen und den 44 Deluxe Bungalows genauso selbstverständlich wie eigene Terrassen und wunderschöne Badezimmer. Mit zwei Waschbecken, Badewanne, separater Dusche, WC und Bidet und einer Open-Air-Dusche zeigt sich Badezimmerluxus von seiner exklusivsten Seite. Noch ganz vertieft in die Betrachtung der überaus

Die 44 Deluxe-Villen überzeugen durch ihre geschmackvolle Symbiose aus thailändischer Eleganz und westlichem Komfort.
The luxury Pool Villas which have their own gardens and private pools guarantee absolute privacy.

großzügigen Räumlichkeiten, die mit einer atmosphärischen Symbiose aus thailändischer Eleganz und westlichem Komfort glänzen, reißt uns der Blick auf die Uhr aus unserer Gedankenwelt. Obwohl das riesige Kingsize-Himmelbett süße Träume verspricht, ist der Ruf des Magens unüberhörbar. Bei der Aufzählung der Möglichkeiten für ein stimmungsvolles Dinner stellt uns Somchai vor eine wirklich schwere Entscheidung, denn das Royal Coco Palm Resort & Spa sorgt sich gleich mit drei Restaurants um das kulinarische Wohl seiner Gäste. Das „Palm Grove Restaurant" lockt morgens und mittags mit üppig bestückten Buffets und am Abend mit phantasievollen Spezialitäten aus der regionalen und internationalen Küche. Authentisch thailändisch und das auf höchstem Niveau geht es im „Ruam Jai Thai Restaurant" zu. Wogegen im „The Mariner Bar & Grill" direkt am Strand tagsüber leckere Snacks und Erfrischungen serviert werden:

Aber auch am Abend kann man die besondere Strandatmosphäre beim Barbecue oder einem legeren Dinner for two genießen. Glücklich können sich besonders die Gäste schätzen, die das „Dine-Around-Package" gleich mitgebucht haben. Denn die Location können sie für ihre Hauptmahlzeiten frei wählen. Noch etwas müde von der Anreise und ganz gefangen von der besonderen Atmosphäre unserer Pool Villa entsagen wir den Versuchungen der drei Restaurants und entscheiden uns für die romantischste Variante der Nahrungsaufnahme: ein Dinner am Privatpool im eigenen exotischen Garten, über den alle Pool Villen verfügen.

Und erst am nächsten Morgen machen wir uns auf, das Resort in all seinen Facetten zu erkunden. Wie es sich für einen Nordeuropäer gehört, führt uns der Weg zuerst an den Strand. Beim Anblick des in allen Blautönen schimmernden Meeres und der blütenweißen Küstenlinie lernt auch unser Herz zu lächeln. Erschien uns gestern die Erkundung der unberührten Dschungelwelt noch als das optimale Highlight für den ersten Urlaubstag, hält uns beim Anblick der blau-türkis schimmernden Fluten nichts mehr an Land. Bewaffnet mit Flossen und Schnorchel tauchen wir in die prachtvolle Unterwasserwelt der Andamanen-See ein, die ohne Frage zu den Highlights des luxuriösen Resorts zählt. Schon ganz in der Nähe begeistert die reizvolle, tropische Unterwasserfauna. Erfahrene Tau-

conditioning, minibar, Sat TV, safe, hifi equipment and one's own tea/coffee-making facilities are as self-evident in the Pool Villas as having one's own terrace and the wonderful bathroom. This really is a most luxurious place. It has two washbasins, a bath, separate shower, WC, bidet and an open air shower. Still reflecting on the extremely spacious rooms, which brilliantly manage to combine Thai elegance and western comfort, suddenly I awake from my reverie and look at my watch. Although the huge king-size bed holds out the promise of sweet dreams, one does need to eat. Reciting the choices we have of where to spend a romantic evening, Somchai faces us with a really difficult decision, because the Royal Palm Resort & Spa has three restaurants catering for the culinary needs of its guests. The "Palm Grove Restaurant" serves lavish buffets in the morning and at lunchtime, and in the evening regional and international food. Top quality authentic Thai food is available at the "Ruam Jai Thai Restaurant", and during the day the "Mariner Bar & Grill" serves delicious snacks and light

HIDEAWAYS 111

Kulinarisch glänzt das Resort mit phantasievoll dargebotenen internationalen und orientalischen Zubereitungen auf höchstem Niveau.
The Resort's cuisine is excellent. International and Oriental dishes of the highest quality are served.

Im Palm-Groove-Restaurant schlägt das kulinarische Herz des Resorts.
The Palm Grove Restaurant is the culinary heart of the Resort.

refreshments. In the evening one can enjoy the special atmosphere of a beach barbecue or an informal dinner for two. Guests who have booked the "Dine-around Package" are particularly lucky, because every evening they can choose a different venue for their three-course meal. Still somewhat weary from the journey and totally entranced by the special atmosphere of our Pool Villa, we decide against having dinner at the restaurant and opt for a romantic variation – dinner beside our private pool in our own exotic garden.

Next morning we set out to discover everything there is to know about the Resort. As is only right and proper for visitors from northern Europe, we first make our way to the beach. When we get there, we're simply stunned and delighted by the brilliant white coastline and the sea shimmering in every shade of blue. Even if our jungle excursion yesterday seemed to us to be the unbeatable highlight on the first day of our holiday, once we catch sight of the turquoise waters, there is nothing on land to hold us. Equipped with flippers and snorkel, we go snorkelling in the scintillating underwater world of the Andaman Sea, definitely one of the highlights of our stay at this luxurious resort. Only a few yards from the beach, there is a fantastic underwater world with lovely marine plant life. Experienced divers go the Similian Islands Marine National Park. These incredibly beautiful islands feature on the marine diving map amongst the

cher zieht es in den Similian Islands Marine National Park. Eine Bootsstunde vom Resort entfernt gehören diese traumhaften Eilande, umgeben von türkisfarbenem Wasser und feinstem weißen Korallensand mit den riesigen Granitblöcken zu einem der wohl etabliertesten Höhepunkte auf der Weltkarte der Tauchgründe. Die paradiesische Meereswelt mit einem extremen Reichtum an bunt schillernden tropischen Fischen lässt das Herz eines jeden Tauchfans höher schlagen.

Wieder an Land, bleibt noch genügend Zeit, um vor dem Sundowner im „The Mariner" – jeden Abend ein absolutes *must* – den Damen im Royal Coco Palm Spa, der ein breit gefächertes Spektrum natürlicher Treatments für Body und Soul bietet, einen Besuch abzustatten. Unter den kundigen Händen der erfahrenen Therapeutinnen meißelt sich das entrückende Lächeln fest ins Gesicht und wie auf Wolke sieben schwebe ich dem spektakulären Sonnenuntergang entgegen. Um die

most established diving grounds in the world. Surrounded by turquoise water and the very finest of white coral sand, they are also known for their enormous blocks of granite. This heavenly underwater world with its wealth of shimmering multi-coloured tropical fish sets the heart rate of every diver racing. On land once more there is still enough time before a sun downer at the "The Mariner" – an absolute must every evening – for the ladies to pay a visit to the Royal Coco Palm Spa which offers a wide range of treatment for body and soul. In the knowing hands of the professional therapists, my smile becomes fixed as I am swept up into seventh heaven as the sun sets in spectacular fashion. A small circle of holidaymakers has already gathered around the tables of "The Mariner".

They chat about what they have done during the day, and each of them is convinced of having had the ultimate holiday experience: golfers who have found their El Dorado at the nearby Blue Canyon Country Golf Club, ranked No. 14 by the Golf World Cup; amateur biologists who have seen tigers living in the wild at the Klongh Saeng Wildlife Sanctuary; divers and snorkellers, but also inquisitive globetrotters who have gone off on their own to discover nearby villages. The lower the sun sinks, the more dramatic the sky becomes and the quieter it gets. In the end even the hardest-baked realist falls silent in awe. Only the blissful smiles remain.

Ein Elefantenritt durch die grüne Welt des Dschungels ist nur eines der zahlreichen Highlights, die die Umgebung zu bieten hat.
An elephant ride through the world of thick jungle is just one of the experiences on offer at this location.

Urlaub für den Körper und die Seele: die traditionellen Techniken der Thai- und Ayurveda-Massage stellen das innere Gleichgewicht wieder her.
Vacation for body and mind: traditional Thai techniques and Ayurveda massage restore one's equilibrium.

Tische im „The Mariner" hat sich bereits ein kleiner Kreis Urlauber versammelt. Munter plaudert man über die Unternehmungen des Tages und jeder ist der festen Überzeugung, das ultimative Urlaubs-Event erlebt zu haben. Golfer, die auf dem nahe gelegenen Blue Canyon Country Golf Club, die Nummer 14 beim Golf World Cup, ihr Eldorado gefunden haben; Hobby-Biologen, die im Klongh Saeng Wildlife Sanctuary wild lebende Tiger beobachtet haben; Taucher und Schnorchler, aber auch neugierige Weltenbummler, die auf eigene Faust die umliegenden Dörfer erkundet haben. Je tiefer die untergehende Sonne sinkt und je dramatischer sich der Himmel färbt, umso stiller wird es. Schließlich verstummt selbst der hartgesottenste Realist ergriffen. Was bleibt, ist das selige Lächeln auf den Gesichtern.

Der Royal Coco Palm Spa verwöhnt mit einer großen Bandbreite natürlicher Treatments.
The Royal Coco Palm Spa pampers its visitor with a wide range of natural treatments.

Der Garten Eden auf Kreta

ELOUNDA MARE HOTEL

Garden of Eden on Crete

Text: Jürgen Gutowski · Fotos: Jürgen & Martina Gutowski

"To God a thousand years are as one day". I am reading the inscription above the ancient door of an equally old chapel up here in the bare mountains of Sitia. Time has stood still on the island of the Gods at this most southerly edge of the European continent within sight of Asia - through binoculars. Peasants still shake the best olives in the world from the 14 million silvery-leafed olive trees, just as they did a thousand years ago when Zeus, Father of the gods seduced "Europa" to Crete - giving the continent its name. Millions of sheep and goats lazily graze karstic plateaus as they did in ancient times, and the priest, attired as of old in ornate clerical dress, cycles as he always did through the tulip and orchid gardens to one of the 3,000 churches built in the Byzantine era. Down below on the dark blue waters of the Æean, the sun and the clouds still create the eternal, celestial play of light and shade. Who but Homer, ancient poet of poets, could have described the largest Greek island with more fitting words than, "land in the middle of a dark, heaving sea, lovely and fertile, bathed in waves". Beyond the mysterious caves and Grand Canyon-like ravines I catch sight of white monasteries close to white villages of white houses with blue windows, and in front of them are women clad in black and dozing dogs blinking in the

Vor Gott sind tausend Jahre wie ein Tag und ein Tag wie tausend Jahre, so lese ich auf der uralten Türinschrift der nicht minder betagten Kapelle hier oben in den kargen Bergen von Sitia. Die Zeit ist stehen geblieben an diesem südlichsten Rand des europäischen Kontinents, auf der Insel der Götter, nur einen Fernglasblick entfernt vom asiatischen Teil der Welt. Wie vor Jahrtausenden, als Göttervater Zeus die phönizische Königstochter „Europa" nach Kreta entführte, was zur Namensgebung des Erdteils führte, schütteln auch heute noch die Bauern die besten Oliven der Welt von den vierzehn Millionen silbrigblättrigen Ölbäumen. Millionen Schafe und Ziegen zuckeln grasend und Käse und Wolle spendend über die karstigen Hochebenen wie zu antiken Zeiten, der Pope radelt nach wie vor in vollem Ornat durch Tulpen- und Orchideengärten zu einer der dreitausend

Valery Giscard d'Estaing über Elounda Mare: „Ein Paradies!"

Valery Giscard d'Estaing on Elounda Mare: "It's paradise!"

Kirchen oder Kapellen aus der byzantinischen Epoche, und dort unten auf den dunkelblauen Wassern der Ägäis bringen Sonne und Wolken das ewige sphärische Schauspiel von Licht und Schatten zur Aufführung. Alter Homer, Dichter aller Dichter, wer könnte die größte griechische Insel treffender auf den Punkt bringen als du: „Land inmitten des dunkel wogenden Meeres, schön und fruchtbar und wellendurchflutet."

Vorbei an geheimnisvollen Höhlen und Grand-Canyon-gleichen Schluchten, erblicke ich weiße Klöster in der Nähe weißer Dörfer. Darin wiederum weiße Häuser mit blauen Fenstern, davor alte schwarzgekleidete Frauen und dösend blinzelnde Hunde im Schutze schattiger Johannisbrotbäume. Ich fahre nach Elounda, das Dorf im Norden Kretas ist mein Ziel für ein paar Tage. Zwei Kilometer außerhalb des Fischerdörfchens parke ich den Wagen im Schatten von Olivenbäumen und passiere das Tor einer massiven Natursteinmauer, auf der in unspektakulären Buchstaben „Elounda Mare" zu lesen ist. Daneben, etwas größer, das weltberühmte Logo von Relais & Châteaux – klar, dass man hier mit Recht stolz darauf ist, als einziges Hotel Griechenlands Mitglied dieser renommierten Hotelfamilie zu sein. Es ist nicht leicht, Aufnahme in diese Riege erlesener Domizile zu finden, Elounda Mare hat es geschafft. Über einen kleinen, mit Kopfstein gepflasterten Patio erreiche ich das niedrige weiße Haupthaus, das sich beim Eintreten zu einem großen am Hang gelegenen Herrenhaus entfaltet. Die kolossale Halle verdient diese Bezeichnung, beim Zeus! Links die Bar, in der Mitte Sofas und Sitzgruppen, rechts die Treppenaufgänge zu den Zimmern, hinter mir die kleine Rezeption mit dem Willkommens-Cocktail und nach vorne bis zum Horizont Weite, Bläue und Meer. Einkehr mit Aussicht für mich als Neuling, Rückkehr aus Einsicht für mehr als ein Drittel der Besucher, denn was sich gleich vorne hinter den riesigen gläsernen Schiebetüren eröffnet, ist Grund genug, der Hang-Herberge auf der Stelle zu verfallen. Ein Hotel im landläufigen Sinne entdecke ich nirgends beim Spaziergang durch die Gässchen dieses griechischen Dörfleins, dafür die landestypischen weißen Häuschen, vor deren Mauern Bananen gedeihen, über deren ummauerte Balkone vielfarbige Bougainvillea klettert, an deren blauen Pools weiße Sonnenschirme leuchten. Darüber hier und da gemauerte Kamine, die aber nur im Frühling und Spätherbst, die schlimmstenfalls mit gnädigen 14 Grad daherkommen, angezündet werden. Außer dem Zirpen der Zikaden höre ich nur die Wellen des Mittelmeers ans nahe Gestade

shade of carob trees. I am on my way to Elounda, a village in the north of Crete where I am to stay for a few days. I park the car about 1 1/4 miles from this fishing village in the shade of olive trees, and pass through the door set in a massive stone wall upon which is inscribed in simple letters "Elounda Mare", and beside it in somewhat larger letters is the world-famous logo of Relais & Châteaux. Obviously, the fact that this is the only hotel in the whole of Greece which is a member of this renowned hotel association is a source of great pride. It isn't easy to gain admission to its ranks to join the other member hotels, but Elounda Mare managed to do so.

Bungalow Suite: Kein Komfort fehlt, sogar offene Kamine sind vorhanden.
Bungalow Suite with every conceivable comfort, even an open fire place.

Für ganz private Badefreuden: Bungalow Suite mit eigenem Pool.
Bungalow Suite with its own pool for very private amusement.

Die Krone unter der 5 zeigt es an: Elounda Mare gehört zur vornehmen Hotelvereinigung Relais & Châteaux, wohlgemerkt: als einziges Hotel in Griechenland.
The crown beneath the "5" says it all. Elounda Mare is the only hotel in Greece to belong to the elite Relais & Châteaux.

I walk across a small cobblestone patio to the low, white main building which opens up into a large mansion built on the slope of a hill. The colossal hall certainly deserves this description, by Jupiter! To the left is the bar, in the centre are sofas and groups of armchairs, to the right are flights of stairs to the rooms, behind me is the little reception area with welcome drinks, and before me a vista of blue, the ocean stretching as far as the horizon. This is indeed a place for me, a newcomer, to tarry a while, but for more than a third of its guests it is a place to which they return, because what lies beyond the sliding glass doors is reason enough to become instantaneously addicted to this hillside hideaway. As I walk through the alleyways of this Greek village, I find no hotel in the ordinary sense of

fluten und von Zeit zu Zeit das Läuten einer einzelnen Glocke. Tatsächlich, als ich den schattigen „Dorfplatz" erreiche, rechts ein Kunstlädchen, daneben eine Galerie, erblicke ich die hoteleigene griechisch-orthodoxe Kapelle „Santa Marina". Seinen Namen hat das kleine weiße Kirchlein mit seinem wertvollen Ikonen-Interieur von der einzigen Tochter der Familie Kokotos, den Creatoren und Besitzern des Elounda Mare. Als der kretanische Student der Architektur Spyros Kokotos vor 30 Jahren hier in der Bucht von Mirabello zum Angeln rausfuhr, hatte er wie so viele Künstler in ägäischen Breiten eine kreative Vision: Ein Refugium absoluter

Unten: Die Interieurs zeigen Eleganz und feine Behaglichkeit, im Haupthaus ...
The interiors of the main house ...

... wie in den Bungalow Suiten.
... and the bungalows have elegance and distinction.

Privatheit in Verbindung mit First-Class-Unterkünften in unmittelbarer Nähe zum Meer zu schaffen, das den hohen Bedürfnissen jener gerecht würde, die 350 Tage hart arbeiten und in den verbleibenden wenigen Tagen des Jahres nichts sehnlicher wünschen als totale Entspannung, ein ultimatives Ambiente und genussvolles Einfach-so-Sein auf höchstem Niveau. Kein Zweifel, die Vision von Architekt Kokotos wurde Wirklichkeit und das Gelingen seines Konzeptes wird im Gästebuch des Hotels eindrucksvoll bescheinigt von denen, die hier zu Gast waren und es wissen müssen: Himmelstürmer John Glenn und die Eurythmics gehören zu den Wiederkehrern, Expräsident Valery Giscard d'Estaing beschreibt das Hotel als „Paradies", und US-Botschafter Nicholas Burns nebst Gattin vermerken „We've had a wonderful time!" Legion sind der Einträge, doch das führt hier zu weit.

Die Ursachen für derlei Begeisterung sind mir ja angesichts dieses kleinen griechischen Gartens Eden schon erklärlich, aber es finden sich noch weitere Anlässe zur Wiederkehr: Hinter efeubewachsenen Nischen und über hölzernen Treppen öffnen sich die Haustüren zu insgesamt nur 79 Wohneinheiten. Etwa die Hälfte der Zimmer und Suiten befindet sich im Haupthaus, die anderen in den Bungalows, die sich auf dem 30 000 Quadratmeter sanft abfallenden Gelände bis hinunter zum 300 Meter langen Küstenstreifen verteilen. Egal ob Suite oder Superior-Zimmer: Ausnahmslos alle haben den gigantischen azurblauen Meeresblick, alle verfügen über großzügige Veranden oder Balkone, alle haben jene Bäder und Fußböden, die man ohne Übertreibung als „Orgie in Marmor" bezeichnen kann. Ich frage mich, wie viele Schiffscontainer oder wie viel Flugzeugladeraum wohl benötigt wurden, um die Tausende riesiger Quader des edlen, polierten Gesteins aus dem fernen Kanada hierher nach Kreta zu schaffen.

Wem der öffentliche heizbare Meerwasserpool, der kleine geschwungene Sandstrand des Hotels oder die Leiterzugänge zum Meer nicht genügen, der sollte sich für einen

the word, but rather the typical little white houses where bananas thrive beside walls, colourful bougainvillaea climbs over walled balconies, and where white sun-shades are radiant beside blue pools. Here and there are walled fireplaces where fires are only lit in early spring when mercifully temperatures never drop below a mere 14 °C. Apart from chirruping cicadas I can only hear the Mediterranean surf breaking on the nearby seashore, and from time to time the tolling of a solitary bell. As I reach the shady village square which has a little art shop on the right and a gallery on the left, I catch sight of the hotel's own Greek Orthodox chapel of "Santa Marina". The little white church with its valuable icons inside is named after the single daughter of the Kokotos Family, the creators and owners of the Elounda Mare.

Thirty years ago, when Spyros Kokotos a Cretan architecture student came to the bay of Mirabello to go angling, like so many artists in the Ægean world he had a creative vision. He imagined a totally secluded hideaway close to the sea which would provide first class accommodation and meet the sophisticated needs of all those who have to work very hard 350 days of the year, and who just long to let go and relax completely during the year's few remaining days, surrounded by the ultimate ambience. Without a shadow of doubt the architectural vision of Kokotos has been realized, and the success of his idea has been impressively logged in the hotel's guest book by visitors who ought to know: Astronaut John Glenn and the Eurythmics are among the guests who have returned. Ex French President Valery Giscard d'Estaing describes the hotel as "Paradise", and US Ambassador Nicholas Burns remarks, "we've had a wonderful time". The entries are legion, too many for

Tafelfreuden mit paradiesischem Blick: Restaurant Yacht Club.
Gourmets enjoy divine views – the Yacht Club Restaurant.

Es wird exquisit gekocht, von den Garnelen mit Safranreis bis zum erfrischenden Dessert.
The dishes are exquisite, whether the prawns served with saffron rice or the refreshing dessert.

Highlight im Yacht Club, immer wieder freitags: das Seafood-Buffet.
Highlight in the Yacht Club – the Friday seafood buffet.

Treue Begleiter, wohin man spaziert: vielfarbig blühende Bougainvilleen.
Multicoloured bougainvillaea flowers wherever you walk.

now. The reasons for this level of enthusiasm are easy to understand in view of this little Greek Garden of Eden, but there are many other reasons to come back here. Behind ivy-clad niches and above wooden steps, front doors open into only 79 units. About half the rooms and suites are in the main building, the other in the bungalows scattered across the sloping 7 $^1/_2$ acre estate which descends to a 328 yard long stretch of coast. Whether suite or Superior Room, all of them have a stupendous view of an azure sea, all have large verandahs or balconies, and all have bathrooms and floors which can be described without exaggeration as veritable "orgies in marble". I ask myself how many ships' containers or aeroplane holds were needed to bring to Crete the thousands of giant slabs of finest, polished marble from far-off Canada. Guest who wish more than a public heated seawater pool, a small curved sand beach that belongs to the hotel or the a ladders down to the sea, should opt for one of the 42 bungalows which have private seawater pools, and are heated in springtime and autumn. Depending on category, some of

der 42 Bungalows entscheiden, die ausgestattet sind mit privaten Meerwasserpools und im Frühjahr und Spätherbst beheizt werden. Je nach Kategorie teilen sich einige Bungalows einen gemeinsamen Pool, andere verfügen über ihr eigenes Schwimmbecken nebst privatem Garten und uneinsehbarer Sonnenterrasse. Die Shooting Stars unter den Kemenaten jedoch sind die vier Präsidenten Suiten, benannt nach legendären Herrschergestalten wie König Minos und Prinzessin Ariadne; diese Domizile liegen in unmittelbarer Nähe des Meeres, man hat die Wahl zwischen einem oder zwei Schlafzimmern, die eigenen Pools sind noch größer als die der restlichen Bungalows, und „King Minos" offeriert sogar einen privaten Fitnessbereich mit entsprechenden Geräten, eigener Sauna und Dampfbad. Bleibt noch zu erwähnen, dass alle Unterkünfte im Haupthaus und die meisten Bungalows außerdem über Jacuzzi-Badewannen, teilweise separate Duschen, regelbare Air-Conditioning, Telefon plus PC-Connection, Satelliten-TV mit Musikkanal, Minibar, Safe und Fön, Bademäntel, Hausschuhe und Waage verfügen. Es gibt genügend Sonnenschirme, Liegen und Badetücher, kurzum: alles drin, alles dran! Und wenn mal etwas fehlt, sorgt der 24-Stunden-Room-Service binnen Minuten für Ausgleich. Es soll, so erfahre ich von einer Dame des Hauses, eine nicht unerhebliche Zahl von Gästen geben, die man angesichts der oben beschriebenen privaten Grundstücksverhältnisse so gut wie nie zu Gesicht bekommt. Doch auch

für die gibt es drei Lockmittel, derer man sich kaum entziehen kann, und die heißen „Yacht Club", „Old Mill" und „Deck Restaurant". Während es sich bei Letzterem um die gelungene Kombination von Observations-Deck und Frühstücksraum handelt, gelten die Alte Mühle und der Yacht Club als zwei der anerkannt besten Restaurants von Kreta. Im Yacht Club wird Internationales sowie Griechisches à la carte und mit frischer Leichtigkeit serviert, und immer freitags wacht der Geist Poseidons über dem berühmten mediterranen Fischbuffet. Und im „Old Mill", wo tags-

über im Schatten der mächtigen Johannesbrotbäume Snacks und Kleinigkeiten erhältlich sind, endet der Tag im Elounda Mare bei leiser Klaviermusik als elegantes Fine Dining Experience mit erlesenen internationalen Köstlichkeiten, die, flankiert von vornehmen griechischen Weinen und französischem Champagner, auch flambiert gereicht werden. So ist es heute, und so war es schon vor 20 Jahren. Und der tiefste Grund dafür, dass so viele Gäste immer wiederkehren, besteht in der Erkenntnis, als sei seit dem letzten Besuch kein einziger Tag vergangen.

the bungalows share a pool, while others have their own, as well as a private garden and a secluded sun terrace. The shooting stars amongst the apartments are however the Presidential Suites named after the legendary King Minos and Princess Ariadne. They are situated very close to the sea and have one or two bedrooms. The pools however are larger than those of the other bungalows, and the "King Minos" even has its own fitness zone equipped with the necessary apparatus, and its own sauna and steambath. What is more, all the accommodation in main building and in most of the bungalows have jacuzzi baths, partly separate showers, adjustable airconditioning, telephone plus PC connection, satellite TV with music channel, minibar, safe and a hairdryer as well as bath robes, slippers and balances. There are plenty of sunshades, loungers and bathtowels. However there is all what you need and its all inclusive. A lady in the house tells me that owing to the privacy prevailing on the estate, a not inconsiderable number of the guests never even show their faces. Yet, even for them there are three attractions which are nigh on irresistible - the Yacht Club, the Old Mill and the Deck Restaurant which is a combination of observation deck and breakfast room. The Old Mill and the Yacht Club are two of the best known restaurants in Crete. The Yacht Club serves an international cuisine and a Greek à la carte menu of light, fresh food. On Fridays the ghost of Poseidon watches over the famous fish buffet. All day long, snacks and light dishes are available at the Old Mill in the shade of the mighty carob trees. However the day ends at the Elounda Mare to the strains of quiet piano music where you can have the fine dining experience whilst being served exquisite international culinary delicacies which, accompanied by select Greek wines and French champagne, can also be flambé.
So it is today and so it was 20 years ago. The real reason why so many guests return is that when they do, it seems not a day has gone by since their last visit.

Die Kapelle Santa Marina. Der griechische Architekt Spyros Kokotos erfand Elounda Mare vor 30 Jahren. Die Kapelle ist nach seiner Tochter benannt.
The Chapel of Santa Marina. The Greek architect, Spyros Kokotos, founded Elounda Mare over 30 years ago. The Chapel is named after his daughter.

Meerblick von einem der größten privaten Pools.
Sea view from one of the largest private pools.

HIDEAWAYS 121

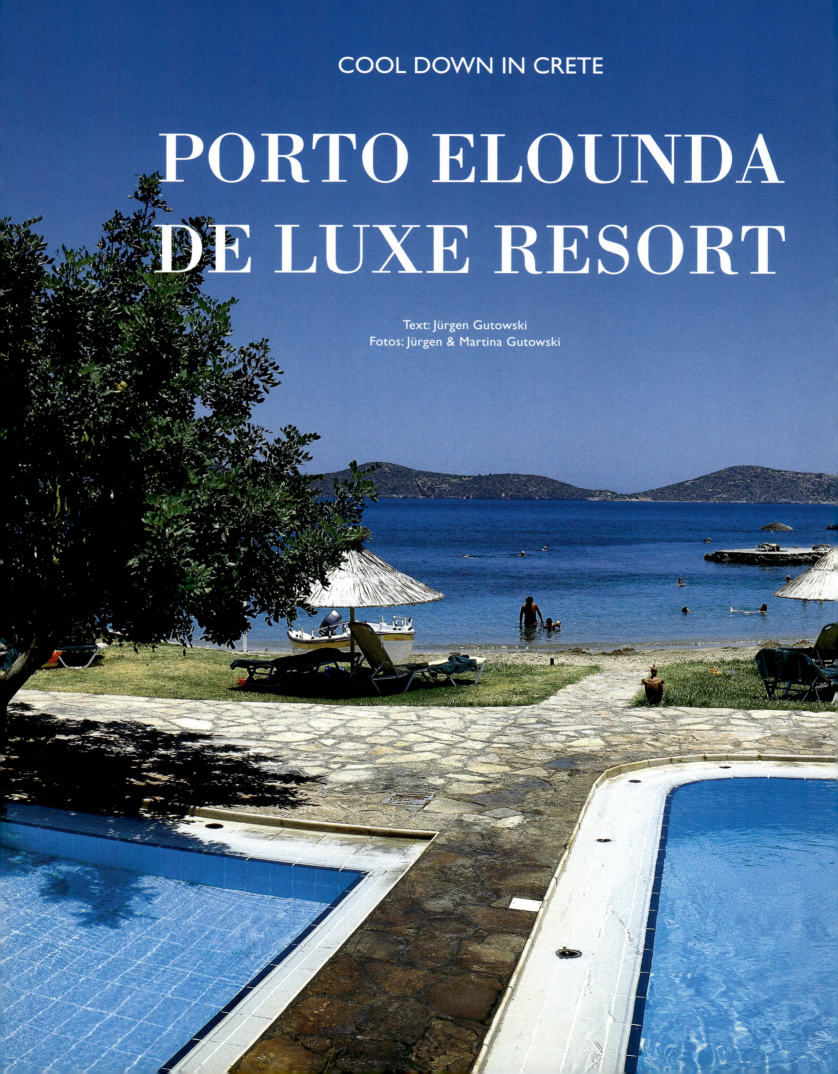

COOL DOWN IN CRETE

PORTO ELOUNDA DE LUXE RESORT

Text: Jürgen Gutowski
Fotos: Jürgen & Martina Gutowski

shower and a jacuzzi. Spaciousness is the trump card of Kokotos the architect, something which is true of the whole peninsula. The home cinema – I have never experienced anything like it in an hotel – is a real picture palace like the cosy ones of the 1970s. The Calypso Restaurant seems to merge with the ocean because of its panoramic window and the adjoining water garden outside. Next to the wine cellar with the best Greek and international wines, the indoor swimming pool in the hotel's relaxation zone deserves its description because you can really swim in it instead of having to turn after a few strokes. I take a stroll through the garden where hibiscus and bougainvillaea are coming into flower. The garden is on a gentle incline down to the water's edge where the Presidential Suites are located. Here, the rooms in the seven waterside Presidential Suites are even more lavishly appointed, and have floors of Greek marble and teak. The garden has a

Schlafgemach einer Superior Suite. Jede Suite hat mindestens 100 Quadratmeter Raum.

Bedroom in a Superior Suite. Every suite has an area of at least 1,076 sq. feet.

HIDEAWAYS 127

private pool, and the living area (1,614 feet) inside has state of the art hi-fi and video equipment, and a writing corner with PC link. Grandeur unmatched anywhere else in the Aegean is to be found in the Grande Suite, which stands in over an acre of its own grounds. Inside it has nearly 2,700 feet of living space on three floors, conveying a palatial feel to the place. This becomes even more evident if one considers the features of this mega-suite: there are two bedrooms, a marble bathroom with a jacuzzi, shower, and a balconies, one on the ground floor and one on the third floor. Between the ground and the upper floors is a dining area with fine porcelain and fresh flowers. One can go down a flight of stairs or take the lift to the ground floor where there is a huge living area with panoramic views of the Aegean. Opposite is the private indoor pool surrounded by flowers, and adjoining this are the gym, the sauna and a Turkish Bath. Anyone not satisfied with the number of baths has the option of the heated and illuminated outdoor pool in the garden or private access to the sea. Right at the end of the peninsula beside the private landing stage, one can observe the sunset from a private bar hidden in a rock grotto right beside the sea.

det sich ein privater Pool, im 150-Quadratmeter-Innenraum stehen *state of the art* Hi-Fi und Video sowie eine Schreibecke mit PC-Anschluss zur Verfügung. Die Grandeur, unangefochten auf den Inseln der Ägäis, finde ich zu guter Letzt in der Grande Suite auf ihrem 1000-

Die „Admiral's Bar" eröffnet einen Rundumblick auf das Blau der Agäis.
"The Admiral's Bar" opens a panoramic view to the blue colour of the Aegean.

Fine Dining am Abend: das Restaurant Calypso.
Fine dining in the evening: the Restaurant Calypso.

Quadratmeter-Grundstück. Mehr als 250 Quadratmeter Raum auf drei Ebenen sorgen hier für ein mediterranes Palastgefühl, das noch verstärkt wird, betrachtet man die inneren Werte dieser Mega-Suite: Zwei Schlafzimmer mit Marmorbad, Jacuzzi, Dusche und Balkon gibt es, eines im Erdgeschoss, das andere auf der dritten Ebene. Eine Essecke befindet sich auf der mittleren Ebene, bereichert durch edles Porzellan und frische Blumen. Wahlweise über die Freitreppe oder mit dem Aufzug gelangt man ins Erdgeschoss, wo sich ein riesiger Wohnbereich mit Panoramaausblick auf die Ägäis öffnet. Gegenüber betritt man das private, von Pflanzen umgebene Hallenbad. Nebenan finden sich auch der Gymnastikbereich, die Sauna und das Türkische Bad. Und wem so viele Bäder noch immer nicht genügen, der hat im Garten die Wahl zwischen einem beheizten und beleuchtbaren Meerwasser-Außenpool und dem privaten Zugang zum Meer. Und ganz am Ende dieser Peninsula, neben dem privaten Bootsanleger, genießt man den Sonnenuntergang in der eigenen Bar, versteckt in den Felsgrotten direkt am Meer.

Im Weinkeller lagern beste griechische und internationale Tropfen.
In the wine cellar store just the best greece and international capital wines.

GRECOTEL MYKONOS BLU

Blue and white symphony in the Ægean

Text: Jürgen Gutowski · Fotos: Jürgen Gutowski / Grecotel Mykonos Blu

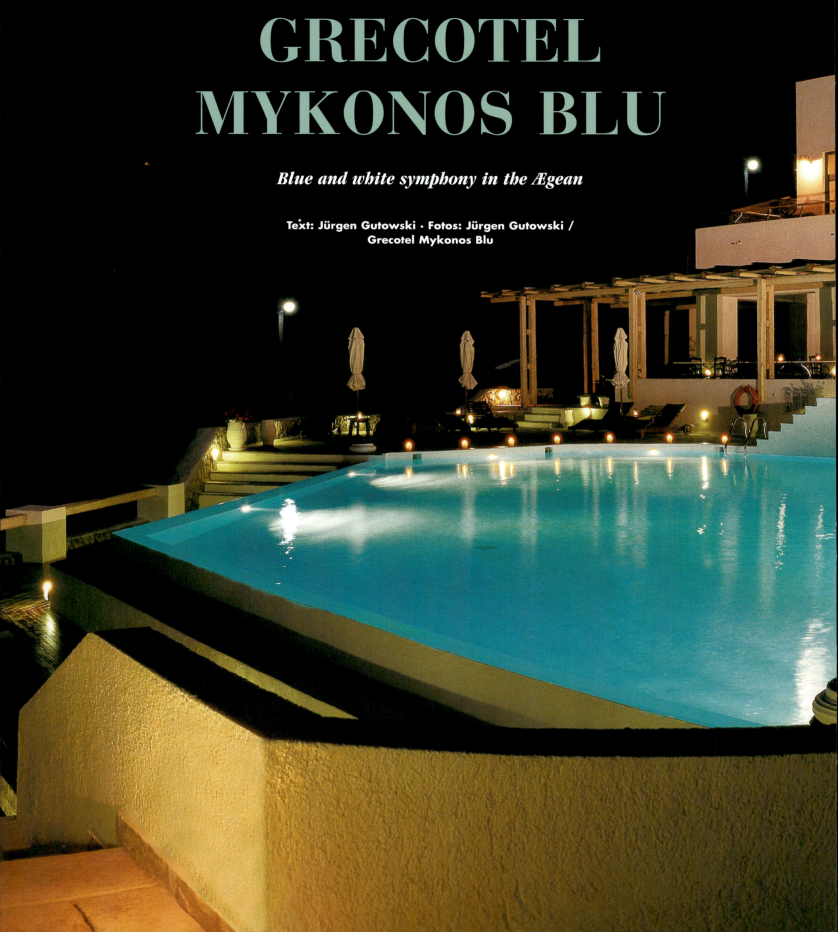

Past the bus station I go and the tavern where taxi drivers wait for custom, then into the labyrinth that is "Chora", the capital of the small towns and the centre of Mykonos, a melting pot for jet setters and backpackers alike. The narrow alleys bustle with life, gesticulating blustering men, and on the pavements women with eyes modestly cast down yet confident enough. Another ace is slapped down on the table at the kafenion, a Greek-style café-bar. I can feel the cobblestones pressing through my leather soles as I dodge an oncoming roaring moped with sidecar in which a cobbler is transporting a sewing machine. The little white houses are tightly packed side by side as if to provide one another with shade in this sunny land, and steps of wood or stone lead up to their flat roofs where washing is fluttering in the salty breeze. Church bells toll the hours but orthodox or not, here time doesn't really matter.

Everything is swish and spotless just like Rodeo Drive or the Kö, yet its all in miniature, fitting perfectly into the Greek island architecture - boutiques, perfumeries, golden gates into sophisticated galleries, typical Green taverns and beside it caviar in tins. You can get a genuine Rolex for 8,000

Am Busbahnhof vorbei, an der Taverne, vor der die Taxifahrer auf Kundschaft warten, hinein ins Labyrinth von „Chora", Hauptstadt der Kleinstädte, Zentrum von Mykonos, Schmelztiegel von Jetset und Rucksacktourismus. In den engen Gassen wirbelt das Leben, man gestikuliert und schwadroniert, frau flaniert gesenkten Blicks doch selbstbewusst auf dem Bürgersteig, man trinkt und spielt – und noch ein Ass knallt auf den Tisch des Kafenions! Das Kopfsteinpflaster drückt durch die Sohlen meiner Schuhe, ich weiche einem röhrenden Dreiradmoped samt Anhänger aus, auf dem der Schuster eine Nähmaschine transportiert. Weiße Häuschen dicht an dicht, als würden sie sich gegenseitig Schatten spenden in diesem Sonnenland, hölzerne oder steinerne Außentreppen führen auf ihre flachen Dächer, dort weht die Wäsche in der salzigen Luft. Kirchenglocken läuten die Zeitansage herüber, so genau nehmen sie's nicht dabei, orthodox hin oder her. Pieksauber und piekfein wie am Rodeo Drive oder auf der Kö, doch eingepasst in die Winzigkeit der griechischen Inselarchitektur: Boutiquen und Parfümerien, goldene Portale vor mondänen Galerien, daneben typisch grie-

chische Tavernen, wieder daneben Kaviar in Dosen. Rolex echt für 8000 Bucks, keine 100 Meter weiter die Kopien für „'nen Heiermann". Weiter geht's das abschüssige Kurvensträßchen runter zum Hafen, vorbei an träge rotierenden Windmühlen, und dort liegt die offene Bucht, unwillkürlich breite ich die Arme aus. Die Luft riecht nach Fisch, der hier so frisch wie nirgends in den Einkaufstaschen der griechischen Hausfrauen verschwindet. Im schattigen Eingang des Hafenkirchleins schmusen Jugendliche, die es kaum interessiert, dass da draußen im Hafen die teuersten Yachten der Welt und Kreuzfahrtschiffe aus aller Herren Länder anlanden. Mykonos. Früher warst du mal das Aschenputtel der Kykladen, als karg und unfruchtbar verschrien. Doch jetzt bist du auferstanden von den Totgesagten. Deine Farben, das Blau und das Weiß haben uns überzeugt. Deine edlen Galerien, deine rot gedeckten Kirchen ebenfalls, und auch ein Hotel.

Grecotel Mykonos Blu – ganz klar, einen anderen Namen kann dieses Hotel nicht tragen angesichts des Farbspiels zu seinen Füßen. Blau und Türkis, eingerahmt von einer hellen geschwungenen Bucht, leuchtet die Ägäis herauf zu dem weißen Haus hoch oben über dem

bucks and just a hundred yards farther on a fake for peanuts. Down the steep winding road I go to the harbour, past slowly turning windmills to the open bay, and involuntarily I spread out my arms.

The air smells of fish which disappears in a trice into the shopping bags of Greek housewives.

Canoodling in the shady entrance to the church are youngsters who aren't the slightest bit interested in the cruise ships and the luxurious yachts from every major country in the world anchored in the bay. Mykonos, once the Cinderella of the Cyclades and written off as bare and barren, is now risen from the dead. Its colours, the blue and the white, have won us over, as indeed have the superb

In der Bucht leuchtet das Türkis der Ägäis in den schillerndsten Farben.
The turquoise water of the Ægean shimmers in the bay.

galleries, the red-topped churches and now the hotel. Grecotel Mykonos Blu. Clearly this hotel could have no other name owing to the colours at its feet, blue and turquoise. Set beside a gently curving bay, the white house high above Psarou Beach reflects the light of the Ægean, a peaceful idyll yet only a five-minute drive away from the pulsating city centre. Even the designer reception area is a symphony in blue. The massive counter like the ones in dispensing chemists has 50 glass drawers through which sun rays stream in fifty shades of blue. Every room key is kept in its own metal drawer on the back wall, and below the ceiling 12 giant preserving jars reflect the blue tones of the Ægean sea. Mykonos Blu indeed! In stark contrast however, but only to be seen in the evening together with the colours at sundown, are the two giant red neon hearts between the windows opposite. A couple of paces further on I find myself in the spacious and lavishly furnished lounge of the hotel which has seating virtually hidden away in the corners. The colour scheme is warm and there is a wooden floor. Between the pillars are "Sesoules", sofas suspended to the ceiling

Psarou-Strand, in ruhige Idylle getaucht und doch nur fünf Autominuten entfernt von der pulsierenden Innenstadt. Eine Sinfonie in Blau allein schon die Designer-Rezeption. Sie besteht aus einem wuchtigen Apothekentresen mit 50 gläsernen Schubladen, aus denen fünfzigmal verschieden blaues Licht strömt. Jeder Zimmerschlüssel „wohnt" in seiner eigenen Metallschütte an der Rückwand, und unter der Decke spiegeln 12 riesige Einweckgläser die Blautöne des Ägäischen Meeres. In kräftigem Kontrast, jedoch erst abends zu bewundern und in Harmonie mit den Farben des Sonnenuntergangs, erstrahlen zwischen den gegenüberliegenden Fenstern zwei überdimensionale rote Neonherzen. Ein paar Schritte weiter, und ich stehe in der weitläufigen Lounge des Hotels mit üppigen Wohnmöbeln und beinahe verborgenen Sitzgruppen in den Ecken. Hier dominieren warme Farben und ein hölzerner Fußboden, zwischen den Säulen schweben *Sesoules*, durch Seile an der Decke befestigte Sofas, drum herum eine verschwenderische Vielzahl leuchtender Kerzen. Zwei Stufen hinauf, am Ende des Saals, erhebt sich in Form einer Walflosse die Bar, ganz aus Chrom und Holz.

with ropes, and all around a myriad candles flicker. Up two steps at the end of the room is a bar of chrome and wood designed like a whale's fin.

I go down the stairs to the floor below, and notice a many branched, fairy-tale chandelier of the finest glass as I cross the lobby to go into the restaurant, or is it a library? Between speckled beige-coloured pillars are hundreds of books, folios and manuscripts on the poets of the Ægean after which the restaurant has been called. The "Poets of Ægean" ranks as one of the best restaurants in Greece, a meeting place not only for hotel guests but also for gourmets from all over the world whose yachts lie at anchor down in the bay. Guests from other hotels hasten here too, to dine on the award-winning grilled seafood of the Ægean served with herbs, or on the popular "Sofrito" fillet of pork with garlic sauce. The menu is wide-ranging and includes international dishes beside local food, and the wine list too should satisfy the most discriminating of the wine-drinking cognoscenti.

But enough of that for now. What about the breakfast buffet, often a great disappointment for Germans in the hotels of southern

Ich wandere die Treppe hinab, ein Stockwerk tiefer erblicke ich einen märchenhaften Kronleuchter, vielarmig, aus feinstem Glas gesponnen. Ich gehe durch den Vorraum, den er schmückt, und stehe im Restaurant. Oder ist es eine Bibliothek? Zwischen beige gesprenkelten, mächtigen Säulen lagern Hunderte Bücher, Folianten, Manuskripte. Und von den bläulich gesprenkelten Wänden blicken ernst die Söhne Mykonos' von schwarz-weißen Fotografien. Es handelt sich dabei um die Poeten der Ägäis, nach denen das Restaurant benannt wurde: „Poets of Ægean" gilt als eines der besten Restaurants Griechenlands, hier treffen sich nicht nur die Hotelgäste, sondern auch die Gourmets aus aller Welt, deren Yachten unten im Hafen liegen oder die aus anderen Hotels herbeieilen, um die preisgekrönten gegrillten Meeresfrüchte vom Spieß mit Kräutern der Ägäis oder das beliebte *Sofrito,* Schweinefilet mit Knoblauchsauce, zu genießen. Die Karte ist enorm vielseitig, international und landestypisch zugleich, auch die Weinliste dürfte selbst ausgefallene Geschmäcker begeistern, aber das führte hier zu weit, und deshalb nur noch ein Wort zum Frühstücksangebot, denn dieses

Das Restaurant „Poets of Ægean" gehört zu den besten in Griechenland.
The "Poets of Ægean" is one of the best in Greece.

Europe? Grecotel Mykonos Blu is the exception to the rule. I'm willing to bet that in the not too distant future, a "Five Star Breakfast Award" will be created which the Grecotel Mykonos Blu resort will win. Of that I have no doubt whatsoever. Laid out are thirty different kinds of bread and bakery goods, cakes and biscuits, honey, smoked salmon, mackerel, trout, eggs cooked in every conceivable way, baked beans, platters of German sliced sausage, multicultural cheese boards with feta as well as central European cheese, dishes of vegetables including warm cauliflower and fried tomatoes, and more kinds of muesli than you have ever seen in your life. In addition there is ice-cold champagne and coffee which actually deserves its name. Breakfast at Grecotel Mykonos Blu is a stylish experience, like the whole of one's stay here. I meander across the grounds past the shimmering pool and down a few steps. Suddenly I catch sight of a few of the 100 bungalows, blue and white with flat roofs typical of the country, grouped in small clusters on the gently sloping sub-tropical garden where date palms, giant agaves and large cacti grow. Roses climb the natural stone walls, as if they straining upwards for a view from the ubiquitous blue balconies. A cool elegance prevails inside, a reminder

Der romantische Hafen von Mykonos.
The romantic harbour in Mykonos.

Thema ist in Südeuropa ja leider oftmals ein Trauerspiel, jedenfalls aus deutscher Sicht, und deshalb dieser kleine Exkurs über die Ausnahme, die die Regel bestätigt: Das Grecotel Mykonos Blu wird in naher Zukunft mit dem noch zu erfindenden „Five Star Breakfast Award" ausgezeichnet werden, daran gibt es für mich keinen Zweifel: dreißig verschiedene Brot- und Gebäcksorten, Kuchen, Plätzchen, dazu Honig, geräucherter Lachs, Makrele, Forelle, Eier in allen erdenklichen Darreichungsformen, britische *baked beans*, deutsche Aufschnittplatten und multikulturelle Käseplatten mit Feta sowie zentraleuropäischen Sorten, Gemüseplatten mit warmem Blumenkohl und geschmorten Tomaten, nebenan das volle Müsli-Arsenal und und und. Dazu eisgekühlter Sekt und ein Kaffee, der diese Bezeichnung verdient. Frühstück im Grecotel Mykonos Blu – ein Erlebnis mit Flair wie der ganze Aufenthalt. Doch genug gefrühstückt, jetzt wandere ich übers Gelände. Vorbei am

Überall kann man ursprüngliche Idylle entdecken.
Idyllic scenes are everywhere to be found.

blau schimmernden Pool, ein paar Treppen hinab, und ich erblicke einige der 100 Bungalows – in Weiß und Blau und mit den landestypischen Flachdächern versehen, sie verteilen sich in verwinkelten Gruppen im sanft zum Meer abfallenden, subtropischen Garten, in dem Dattelpalmen, riesige Agaven und Ohren-Kakteen sprießen. Rosen klettern an Natursteinmauern empor, als hätten sie dieselbe „Sehn-Sucht" nach der gewaltigen Aussicht von den allgegenwärtigen blauen hölzernen Balkonen. Im Innern dominiert kühle Eleganz als Reminiszenz an die Klarheit der Kykladeninseln. Vier unterschiedliche Raumkategorien gibt es, fast alle verfügen über Meerblick von der privaten Veranda, alle haben ein romantisches Himmelbett und eine Sitzgruppe in den typischen Farben Hell- und Dunkelblau. Technisches von der Air-Con über Sat-TV mit 30 Programmen, Safe und CD-Player bis hin zum automatischen Wake-up call – nichts fehlt, was man in einem Fünf-Sterne-Haus erwartet. Blumen, Pralinen und Tageszeitung kommen täglich neu, die Minibar ist reichlich bestückt, und im Kleiderschrank findet sich eine „Wunderkiste" aus Metall mit Rotwein, Einmalkamera, getrockneten Mangos, Nagellackentferner, Olivenöl, Bvlgari-Taschentüchern und Halstabletten und noch mehr. Die Raum-Highlights des Grecotels Mykonos Blu sind die Deluxe Junior Bungalow Suiten, deren große private Terrasse mit bambusgedecktem Halbdach und privatem Pool auch den weit gereisten Luxus-Traveler überzeugen. Im Innern ist alles größer, der Raum, der Fernseher, das Bad mit seinen Bvlgari-Accessoires.

Ich stehe auf der Terrasse, eingetaucht in die Farbe, die dem Grecotel Mykonos Blu den Namen gab: um mich herum blaue Balkone, vor mit die blaue Bucht, über mir der Azur – man muss gar kein Dichter sein, um dieses Licht zu genießen wie einen Rausch.

of the clear atmosphere of Cyclades islands. There are four categories of accommodation but all afford sea views from private verandahs, and all have a beautiful, romantic four-poster, and easy chairs upholstered in light and dark blue throughout. Also provided, every amenity and all the hi-tech one would expect in a five-star hotel, including air-conditioning, satellite TV with 30 programmes, safe, CD-player and automatic wake-up call, everything is there. Flowers, chocolates and a daily paper are supplied on a daily basis, and the minibar is well stocked. In the wardrobe there is a metal "treasure chest" containing red wine, a disposable camera, dried mangoes, nail varnish remover, olive oil, Bvlgari handkerchiefs and throat tablets and much else. The most outstanding Grecotel Mykonos Blu accommodation are the Deluxe Junior Bungalow Suites. Each has a large private terrace, a thatched roof and a private pool which could not fail to impress even the frequent globetrotter. Inside there everything is bigger, the space, the television and the bathroom with its Bvlgari toiletries.

I am standing on the terrace bathed in the colour which has given the hotel its name. All around me are blue balconies, ahead of me is the blue bay, and above me is an azure sky. You don't have to be a poet to be intoxicated with this light.

Im Zeichen des Rosmarins

HOTEL ROMAZZINO

Surrounded by rosemary

Ganz im Nordosten Sardiniens liegt die Region Gallura mit der legendären Costa Smeralda. Ein karger steiniger Landstrich, dessen wildromantisches Flair seit 40 Jahren Betuchte aus aller Welt anlockt. Wer keine eigene Villa besitzt, logiert in einem der Top-Hotels an den smaragdfarbenen Buchten des Tyrrhenischen Meeres. Das Hotel Romazzino zählt zu den Spitzenadressen.

In the north-east of Sardinia is the Gallura region and the legendary Costa Smeralda. A bare, stony landscape, its wild, romantic scenery has been attracting the well-to-do for over 40 years. Visitors who do not have their own villas stay at one of the best hotels along the emerald green coastline of the Tyrrhenian Sea, the Romazzino Hotel.

Text: Gundula Luig · Fotos: Klaus Lorke

Einladend: die gemütliche Veranda mit ihren Rundbögen.

The comfortable verandah and its arches is an inviting sight.

Chef-Concierge Roberto Marin am wunderschön gestalteten Empfang.

Chef-concierge Roberto Marin in the beautifully designed reception area.

Schöner wohnen: Die maurisch inspirierte Baukunst fügt sich harmonisch ins Terrain.

The Moorish-style architecture merges harmoniously into the terrain.

It's intriguing how the smell of a place can figure so prominently in the memory. Each time I think of Sardinia I can smell the aroma of wild rosemary and thyme, which is why I could hardly wait to return there, this time to the most romantic and best known coastal district on this Mediterranean island, the Costa Smeralda. The scenery is fantastic, bizarre rock formations, crystal clear unpolluted water, and sparse vegetation which is a beautiful feature of this landscape. Yet, the best part of all this is that even after forty years, tourism has left the area unchanged. It's a very long time since the jet setting Aga Khan, the Ismaili Prince Karim IV. and others like him dis-covered the ancient beauty of Sardinia. In search of a new, unspoilt place for the millionaires of this world, he stumbled on the wild Gallura coast, at the time the poorest part of the island. Today the very opposite is true. Nowadays, those who want to spend a holiday

E igenartig, wie sehr Düfte einen Ort und das eigene Empfinden prägen können. Jedes Mal, wenn ich an Sardinien denke, steigt mir der aromatische Duft von wildem Rosmarin und Thymian in die Nase. Und so konnte ich es kaum erwarten, wieder dort zu sein, diesmal an der romantischsten und wohl auch bekanntesten Küste der Mittelmeerinsel, der Costa Smeralda. Eine großartige Naturlandschaft mit bizarrem Fels, glasklarem, noch unverseuchtem Meerwasser und einer Vegetation, deren Kargheit die Schönheit dieser Region ausmacht. Und das Beste ist, auch nach 40 Jahren Tourismus hat sich daran nichts geändert. Denn so lange ist es her, dass der Ismailiten- und Jetsetprinz Karim Aga Khan IV. die archaische Schönheit Sardiniens für sich und seinesgleichen entdeckte. Auf der Suche nach einem neuen, unberührten Plätzchen für die Millionäre die-

Zurückhaltend und reduziert präsentieren sich Zimmer und Suiten im typisch sardischen Stil.
The Sardinian style rooms and suites are minimalist and understated.

Folkloristische Blumenmotive schmücken die Kissen der bequemen Fauteuilles.
The cushions on the comfy leather armchairs have ethnic flower designs.

ser Welt, stieß er auf die wilde Gallurakūste, zu diesem Zeitpunkt noch das Armenhaus der Insel. Heute hat sich das freilich ins Gegenteil gewandt. Wer an dem 55 Kilometer langen Küstenstreifen im Nordosten Sardiniens urlauben will, muss tief in die Tasche greifen. Als Gegenwert erwartet das internationale Gästeklientel eine natürlich und organisch gewachsene Ferienlandschaft mit kleinen exklusiven Hotelanlagen in einer sagenhaften Natur.

Dreißig Minuten dauert die Fahrt vom Costa-Smeralda-Airport in Olbia zu einem der etabliertesten und romantischsten Hotels an somewhere along the 35-mile coastline have to dig deep. The international clientele stay in exclusive hotels surrounded by fantastic scenery which are all part of the holiday area which has developed organically over the years to accommodate them. The drive from Costa Smeralda Airport in Olbia to the Hotel Romazzino the best known and most romantic hotel on the emerald coast, takes thirty minutes. The natural, unspoilt landscape slipping by is virtually virgin territory. Why isn't it like this in other holiday areas? The air-conditioned limousine turns suddenly into a driveway. Before us the brilliant white façade of a Moorish-style building stands in stark contrast to the deep blue of

Breakfast is ready!

Die traditionellen Muster inseltypischer Stickereien zieren Polster, Bilder und Draperie.
Traditional island embroidery can be found on the upholstery, in pictures and curtains.

Der betörende Duft des Rosmarins erfüllt die Luft in der Dämmerstunde.
A beguiling smell of rosemary fills the air at dusk.

Seafood vom Feinsten: Gebratene Hummerkrabben mit gegrilltem mediterranen Gemüse.
Finest seafood: fried king prawns with grilled Mediterranean vegetables.

Machen einen tollen Job: Köche und Kellner des Nobelhotels.
This chefs and waiters of this super hotel do a great job.

the sky above. Well, having left behind the daily grind, here I am surrounded by the pampered world of the Hotel Romazzino. The famous Italian architect, Michele Busiri Vici, designed this luxury hotel in 1965 as part of the development of the area for tourism by the Costa Smeralda consortium. Traditional building materials – stone, gravel, curved tiles, bricks and the wood of the indigenous juniper tree, lend the hotel its unique character. The garden too has been planted plants local to the area. Romazzino for instance (rosemary in the Gallurian dialect) is everywhere. Tall hedges of rosemary are in the beautifully laid-out garden, it is an ingredient of Sardinian cuisine and can be seen as a corporate motif throughout the hotel on tiles, hand towels, bedspreads and glasses.

der Smaragdküste, dem Hotel Romazzino. Die Landschaft zieht an meinen Augen vorbei, so unverbaut, so natürlich, geradezu jungfräulich. Könnte das nicht auch in anderen Urlaubsregionen so sein?! Die klimatisierte Limousine biegt plötzlich in eine Einfahrt ab.

Blendend weiß, im maurisch-mediterranen Stil konzipiert, zeichnen sich die Fassaden des verschachtelten Häuserensembles vom tiefen Blau des Himmels ab. Ich bin drin – in der den Alltag vergessen lassenden Verwöhnwelt des Hotels Romazzino! Michele Busiri Vici, der berühmte italienische Architekt, entwarf das Luxushotel 1965 im Zuge der touristischen Erschließung durch das Consorzium Costa Smeralda. Traditionelles Baumaterial – Steine, Kiesel, gebogene Fliesen, Ziegelsteine und Wacholderholz aus der Region – verleiht dem Hotel seinen einzigartigen Charakter. Auch bei der Bepflanzung des Gartens griff man auf heimische Pflanzen zurück. Romazzino zum Beispiel, im gallurischen Dialekt der Begriff für Rosmarin, ist allgegenwärtig. Als mannshohe Hecke (!) im zauberhaft angelegten Garten, in der Küche Sardiniens sowie im Corporate Design des Hotels auf Fliesen, Handtüchern oder Gläsern und als intensiver ätherischer Duft.

Von meinem Zimmer aus habe ich eine phantastische Aussicht auf das türkis schimmernde Meer, auf die zerklüftete Küste, weiße Strandabschnitte und die herrliche dunkle Macchia. Auch beim Interieur der 94 Zimmer und Suiten, die entweder Meer- oder Gartenblick bzw. beides haben, stand die sardische Kultur Pate. Polster und Fensterdekorationen schmücken sich mit den typischen, farbenfrohen Stickereien Sardiniens, die Möbel kommen aus kleinen Handwerksbetrieben der Bergdörfer, die pastellfarbenen Keramikfliesen für Bäder und Böden stammen von der Inselmanufaktur Cerasarda. Nichts wirkt überladen, die Ambiancen wirken allein durch gewollten Purismus und Authentizität. Selbstverständlich machen

Features wie individuell regelbare Air-Con, Minibar, Direktwahltelefon sowie internationales Sat-TV die Annehmlichkeiten erst komplett. Beim Rundgang durch das Hotel Romazzino fallen die geschwungenen Formen von Wänden, Fensternischen, Treppenstufen und Fluren sofort auf, rechte Winkel sind die Ausnahme. Lange bevor eine Thematik wie Feng Shui in Europa Beachtung fand, scheint diese asiatische Tradition hier unbewusst Anwendung gefunden zu haben. Man fühlt sich ganz einfach wohl und geborgen.

Wie ein Stern strecken sich die einzelnen Flügel des Urlaubsdomizils dem längsten privaten Hotelstrand der Küste entgegen. Wandelpfade führen durch den herrlich blühenden und vom Aroma zahlloser Kräuter- und Gewürzpflanzen erfüllten Garten bis zum großen Freeform-Pool mit zahlreichen bequemen Sonnenliegen. Auf dem Weg dorthin komme ich am Outdoor-Gym vorbei. Eine grandiose Idee. Fitness an frischer Luft mit persönlichem Trainer – da kann kein noch so schöner Spiegelkeller mithalten. Ein paar Treppenstufen vom Pool entfernt befindet sich die legere Tagesbar mit dem Barbecue-Restaurant. Durch ein Strohdach vor zuviel Sonne geschützt, genießt man dort seinen Latte Macchiato oder einen erfrischenden Drink, und zum Lunch erwartet einen eines der köstlichsten Antipasti-Buffets der Insel. Fangfrische Meeresfrüchte und knackiges Gemüse in allen Varianten. Ein Gedicht. Parallel dazu werden die Hauptgerichte – Pasta-, Fisch- und Fleischzubereitungen – in einer offenen Showküche zubereitet und anschließend vom äußerst freundlichen und zuvorkommenden Serviceteam am Tisch serviert. Während man in mediterranen Genusswelten schwelgt, wandert der Blick über den unmittelbar angrenzenden Strand hinaus aufs Meer. Am Horizont hebt sich der schroffe, fünf Kilometer lange Tavolara-Felsen beinahe senkrecht 565 Meter aus der See. Wer dieses Naturphänomen von seiner Strandliege aus erleben möchte, braucht auf einen aufmerksamen Hotelservice übrigens nicht zu verzichten. Drinks und Snacks werden auch dorthin gebracht. Zum kulinarischen Highlight am Abend treffen sich die Gäste im Restaurant Romazzino (dort nimmt man auch das beeindruckend reichhaltige Frühstück), das über der Lobby des Hauptgebäudes eingerichtet ist. Am beliebtesten sind die Plätze auf der zauberhaften Speiseterrasse mit ihren perfekt eingedeckten Tischen und der wundervollen Aussicht. Die Brigade unter Chef de Cuisine Giovanni Raccagni zieht alle Register der Kochkunst. Ob Sashimi-Salat mit Thunfisch und Schwertfisch, Parmesankörbchen, Sellerie, Birnen und Pecorino, ob

The air too is pungent with the aroma of rosemary. The view from my room is fantastic, shimmering turquoise sea, a jagged coastline, white beaches and the wonderfully dark macchia. Sardinian architecture has inspired the décor of the 94 rooms and suites which overlook either the sea or the garden. Curtains and upholstery are embroidered with typical brightly coloured Sardinian designs, and the furniture is produced by small furniture-makers in mountain villages. The pastel-coloured ceramic tiles in the bathroom and on the floor are manufactured on the island by Cerasarda. There's no clutter, the ambience is effective because of its clean lines and authenticity. It goes without saying though that such amenities as the adjustable air-conditioning, DDI telephone and international TV are present. Going round the Hotel Romazzino, one notices the curved design of the walls, window niches, flights of steps and the corridors. Right angles are the exception. Long before something like Feng Shui found recognition in Europe, the principle of it seems to have been unconsciously absorbed here. One has a strong sense of wellbeing and security. The separate wings of this holiday resort hotel extend towards the longest private hotel beach on the island. Paths lead through a flowering garden, its air heavy with the

Vor der intensiven Sonne geschützt, lunchen die Gäste im Barbecue-Restaurant direkt am Strand.
At the Barbecue Restaurant on the beach guests can lunch in the shade.

aromas of innumerable herbs and plants, towards an irregular-shaped pool surrounded by numerous sun loungers. On the way there I pass the outdoor gym - a great idea. There's nothing to touch exercising in the open air with one's personal trainer. However luxuriously equipped, no mirror-walled basement gym can compete. Just a few feet away from the pool is an informal day bar and BBQ restaurant. Beneath the straw-thatched roof

Fettuccine mit Entensauce, Seebarsch parfümiert mit Vernaccia oder Kalbsfilet in Trüffelsaucen mit mediterraner Caponàta – jeden Abend steht man vor dem gleichen Problem: man würde gern mehr von diesem superben Speisenreigen probieren, aber die Kapazität des menschlichen Magens ist nun einmal begrenzt. Schade!

Ein Abend im Romazzino ist jedoch erst perfekt, wenn man mindestens einen Drink in der originellen wie kultivierten Ginepro-Bar genommen hat. Man beachte den Fußboden der Bar. Er besteht aus verlegten Baumscheiben des Wacholders, der zahlreich auf der Insel wächst. Daher auch der Name Wacholder = Ginepro. Chef-Keeper Dino Scalmana zaubert nicht nur hervorragende Cocktails, sondern ist zudem ein interessanter Gesprächspartner. Sein gutes Deutsch hat er vor vielen Jahren im Hause Oetker gelernt – als privater Servicemitarbeiter.

Ich habe mich oft gefragt, warum das Hotel Romazzino so eine Anziehungskraft auf mich und offensichtlich die zahlreichen Stammgäste hat. Es muss der Duft des Rosmarins sein, der einen nicht mehr loslässt!

Beliebter Treff am Abend: die originelle Ginepro-Bar
Popular evening rendezvous – the Ginepro Bar.

Die Aussichts-Sonnenterrasse der Ginepro-Bar.
The viewing terrace of the Ginepro Bar.

Eine Superidee: Body & Soul tanken auf im Outdoor-Gym.

A super idea: an outdoor gym where body and soul can recharge their batteries.

shading you from too much sun you can enjoy a latte machiato or a refreshing drink, and for lunch you can indulge in one of the most delicious antipasti buffets on the island. It's sheer poetry, freshly-caught fish and a wide variety of crunchy vegetables. Nearby, main dishes such as pasta, fish and meat are prepared in an open show kitchen, and then served by the very friendly and obliging staff. Steeped in the delights of this pampered Mediterranean existence, your eyes wander involuntarily beyond the adjoining beach across the water to the horizon where the 3-mile long Tavorala Rock rises over 1,850 feet out of the sea. Incidentally, if you want to view this sight from your beach lounger, you don't have to go without the obliging hotel service. Drinks and snacks can also be brought over to you there too. In the evening guests gather for dinner in the Romazzino Restaurant above the lobby (where the impressive breakfast buffet is laid out in the morning). The most popular place to eat is the terrace where the perfectly laid tables afford wonderful views. The kitchen brigade under the direction of the chef Giovanni Raccagni, pulls out all the stops. Whether the sashimi salad with tuna fish or swordfish, the parmesan basket, celery, pears and pecorino, the fettuccine in a duck sauce, the vernaccia-scented sea bass or the fillet of veal in a truffles' sauce with Mediterranean caponata, every evening one is faced with the same problem, what to choose. One wants to sample more of this superb variety of dishes, but the capacity of the human stomach is limited. Such a shame! An evening at Romazzino can be perfect though, as long as one has at least one drink in the very original but sophisticated Ginepro Bar. Note the floor. It is created from inlaid horizontal sections of tree-trunk of the juniper tree which grows all over the island. Hence the name, the Ginepro (juniper) Bar. Dino Scalmana, Chief barman, not only conjures up excellent cocktails, he is a most interesting conversationalist. He learnt his good German during his time at the Oetker company, when he was a member of the Service team.
I have often asked myself why the Hotel Romazzino exerts such magnetic attraction on his numerous regulars. It must be the aroma of rosemary, it never lets you go.

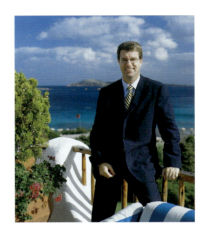

Souveräner Gastgeber: General Manager Milton Sgarbi.

The consummate host – General Manager Milton Sgarbi.

Alternativ zum Meer: Gern relaxen Gäste am großen Meerwasserpool.

A change from the sea – it's nice to relax by the large seawater pool.

Das Hotel Romazzino verfügt über den längsten Privatstrand der Costa Smeralda.

The Hotel Romazzino has the longest private beach on the Costa Smeralda.

Sonnenuntergang am Galatzo

SON NET

Sunset at Galatzo

Mallorca ist voller Schönheiten. Eine von ihnen war vorzeiten eines der vornehmsten Landgüter der Insel. Heute erlebt Son Net eine elegante Renaissance.

Majorca is an island set with gems. One of them, Son Net, once ranked alongside the grandest estates on the island. Today Son Net is experiencing an elegant renaissance.

Text: Günter Ned · Fotos: Ulrich Helweg

Son Net hat seine eigene Magie. Jeder wird sie auf seine Weise beschreiben. Wir fanden sie im geglückten Einklang zwischen Vergangenheit und Gegenwart. Der kalifornische Eigentümer David Stein und sein mallorquinischer Architekt Antonio Obrador haben nicht nur alles freigelegt und mit Liebe zum kleinsten Detail restauriert, was an Son Net historische Substanz ist (Herrenhaus und Landgut stammen so, wie sie erhalten geblieben sind, aus dem Jahr 1672; die Wurzeln der Finca, einer der nobelsten Mallorcas, gehen bis hinter die Maurenzeit zurück). Die Erfinder des Luxushotels Son Net haben viel mehr geschafft. Sie haben den Charme und die Schönheit vergangener Jahrhunderte aufgefangen und neu zum Blühen gebracht in einer Wohn- und Erlebnislandschaft, die edelsten zeitgenössischen Stil zeigt.

Was ist zu erleben auf Son Net? Die Gran Suite Maria de Napoles zum Beispiel. Sie ist eigentlich die Nummer 21. Aber alle Wohneinheiten: zwei Gran Suiten, eine Suite mit eigenem Swimmingpool, vier Royal Suiten – sie bieten mit 130 bis 150 Qualität das größte Logis – und die fünfundzwanzig Zimmer und Suiten sind nach Königen, Königinnen und Menschen benannt, die für Mallorca wichtig waren. In der Suite Maria de Napoles geht der Blick vom Bett, der erstklassigen Reproduktion eines mallorquinischen Himmelbetts aus dem 18. Jahrhundert, zum Fenster durch original erhaltene, sorgsam restaurierte Sandsteinbögen. Die blau-weißen Fresken im Salon, oben an den über vier Meter hohen Wänden, wurden erst während der Restaurierungsarbeiten freigelegt. Sie stammen ebenfalls aus dem 18. Jahrhundert, nicht anders der goldgerahmte französische Spiegel über dem Marmorkamin. Doch bei aller Nostalgie erfüllt der Wohnkomfort verwöhnteste Ansprüchen von heute. Herrlich bequem zum Beispiel die weiß-orange-gestreiften Sofas, Fauteuils und Ohrensessel. Sie sind natürlich neu von exzellenten Mallorquiner Handwerkern maßgefertigt. Aber auch hier ist elegant der Faden der Tradition aufgenommen. Die Stoffe zum Beispiel stammen von Bujosa aus Santa Maria. Sie entstanden nach alten mallorquinischen Mustern auf hundert Jahre alten englischen Webstühlen. Vater und Sohn Bujosa verwenden nur feinste Materialien, Leinen, Baumwolle, italienische Seide. Ihre Webkunst ist im ganzen Haus zu sehen, in der Bar zum Beispiel auch. Dort zeigen die Sessel unter dem jahrhunderte-

Son Net liegt malerisch eingebettet ins Tramuntanagebirge.
Son Net nestles in a picturesque spot in the Tramuntana Mountains.

Son Net has a magic all of its own which everyone describes in a different way. We experienced it as a happy harmony of past and present. Its Californian proprietor, David Stein, and his Majorcan architect Antonio Obrador not only stripped everything down and restored every detail with loving care and attention, but achieved much more than that. The historical origins of the mansion and the estate go back to 1672, but the very beginnings of the finca, one of the finest in Majorca, can be traced right back to Moorish times. The founders of the Son Net luxury hotel have managed to capture the charm and beauty of past centuries and the place is now flourishing anew, providing stylish living in the finest contemporary surroundings. What does Son Net have to offer? Well, the Gran Suite Maria de Napoles, for example. It is actually No. 21, but all the accommodation – two Gran Suites, one suite with

alten, sonnig getönten steinernen Kreuzgewölbe eines der ältesten Webmuster, die sich auf der Insel gehalten haben, die zungenförmigen „Lenguas mallorquinas".

Auf Schritt und Tritt präsentiert Son Net diese Symbiose von Ursprünglichkeit und raffiniertem modernen Interior Design. Wichtig dabei: das Spiel der Farben. Immer wieder ergibt es harmonische Übergänge zwischen den Zeiten, unter anderem zwischen kostbaren Antiquitäten und nicht weniger wertvoller moderner Kunst. Auf dem Flur im ersten Stock bleibt man unwillkürlich vor einem alten Mahagoni-Sekretär stehen. Hinreißend die figurenreich geschnitzten Elfenbeinintarsien. Gleich daneben sieht man 130 Jahre alte weißblaue Fliesen (auch sie kamen während der Restaurierung zum Vorschein). Der Clou kommt eine Ecke weiter: Über einer blauen Sitzgruppe hängt – weiß-braun auf blauem Grund – Andy Wahrhols Porträt-Lithographie von Jane Fonda. Ähnlich feinfühlig sind Bilder von Christo (sein verpackter Pont Neuf), Chagall, Frank Stella, David Hockney und Roberto Longo ins Interieur der Bar eingestreut.

Und wo findet sich dieses zeitnah gefasste Musterbild mallorquinischer Architektur? An einem der schönsten Flecken der Insel, mitten im Tramuntanagebirge (dabei nur zwölf Autominuten von der Hauptstadt Palma entfernt). Wir haben uns den Blick vom gegenüberliegenden Höhenzug gegönnt. Im Tal liegt weiß und noch ganz unberührt und unverfälscht vom Tourismus das Dorf Puigpunyent, überragt wie es sich gehört von seiner Kirche, und hoch darüber und über den typischen, einst von den Mauren terrassierten Olivenhainen schmiegt sich an einen Vorhügel am

a swimming pool, four Royal Suites which are the largest (floor space 1,400 to 1,615 square feet) and the twenty-five rooms and suites – is named after kings, queens and others who were important figures in Majorca. The Maria de Napoles Suite affords a view from the bed – a superb reproduction of an 18th century Majorcan four-poster – through the original, carefully restored sandstone arches to the window. In the salon there are blue and white frescoes on the 13ft-high walls which were first exposed during the restoration work. They too are 18th century, as indeed is the gilt-framed French looking-glass above the marble fireplace. Even with all this nostalgia, the luxurious furnishings and fittings meet the most demanding requirements of today's clientele. The orange and white striped sofas for example, and the armchairs and the wing chairs. They are new of course, made to measure by skilled Majorcan craftsmen. But even here, the thread of tradition is followed through. The Bujosa fabrics from Santa Maria have an old Majorcan pattern which has been woven on hundred-year-old English looms. Mr Bujosa and his son only use the finest materials, linen, cotton and Italian silk. Their skill as weavers is on display throughout the whole house,

Edelste mallorquinische Handarbeit: die Stoffe, in der Bar (oben mit Kamin und Bild von Christo darüber) wie in den Suiten (links unten die Suite Maria de Napoles mit Fresko aus dem 18. Jhdt. über der Tür).

Finest handmade Majorcan fabrics – in the Bar (above: over the fireplace a painting by Christo), and in the suites (below left: the Maria de Napoles Suite with 18th century fresco above the door).

Herrschaftliche Finca-Interieurs: Man schläft in typisch mallorquinischen Himmelbetten.
Magnificent finca interiors: you sleep in a typical Majorcan four-poster.

Die Bäder der Suiten sind Salons für sich.
The bathrooms in the suites are virtual salons.

Unten: Zimmerflucht einer Royal Suite.
Below: wing in one of the Gran Suites.

including the bar. The chairs beneath the centuries-old, sun-coloured stone cross vaulting are covered with one of the oldest woven designs still to be seen on the island, the tongue-shaped "Lenguas mallorquinas". Wherever you go you find this symbiosis of the natural and the latest style and sophistication in interior design. A significant aspect is the play of colour. Throughout the house an harmonious transition between periods has been achieved, for instance priceless antiques stand beside no less valuable modern art. In the hall on the first floor, one stops automatically in front of an old mahogany desk inlaid with charming ivory marquetry figures. Right next to it are 130-year old blue and white tiles which were also discovered during the restoration work, but the best is still to come just around the corner. Hanging above a blue suite of chairs is Andy Warhol's lithographic print of Jane Fonda. Pictures by Christo (the artist who packages monuments), Chagall, Frank Stella, David Hockney and Roberto Longo are sensitively hung around the bar area. Where can one find this exemplary model of contemporary Majorcan architecture? At one of the most beautiful spots on the island, in the middle of the Tramuntana mountains yet only a 12-minute drive away from Palma, the capital. Down in the valley is the white village of Puigpunyent, still untouched therefore unspoilt by tourism, and towering over it, as is only right, is the village church. Higher up still, even higher than the typical walled terraces of olive groves, standing on a foothill of the Galatzo mountain (3,400 ft) is the imposing, pastel red house. If you drive on for a few miles in the direction of Andtratx to the village of Galilea, there is a fantastic view of the sea beyond the mountains. Everything Majorca has to offer is no more than 30 minutes away, beautiful beaches, golf courses, the urban sophistication of Palma de Mallorca and many other sights worth seeing. One of the things you notice as a guest is that one never really

Fuß des 1035 Meter hohen Galatzo das imposante, in rotem Pastell gehaltene Herrenhaus.

Fährt man einige Kilometer weiter Richtung Andtratx zum Bergdorf Galilea, hat man übers Gebirge hinweg einen atemberaubenden Blick bis zum Meer. Innerhalb von dreißig Autominuten erreicht man alles, was Mallorca zu bieten hat, malerische Badestrände, Golfplätze, die urbane Schönheit von Palma de Mallorca und viele andere Sehenswürdigkeiten.

Auffallend nur – die Gäste beobachten es an sich selbst und aneinander –, dass sich Ausflugsstimmung auf Son Net gar nicht so richtig herstellen will. Die Magie des Ortes hat uns längst eingefangen. Man wird ruhig hier oben, umgeben von diesem feinen Stil und von dieser faszinierenden Berglandschaft. Das Panorama hat man überall, auf den Zimmern, in den Restaurants, auf den Terrassen und in den Gärten, und vor allem von einem wahren Schmuckstück im Ambiente, dem dreißig Meter langen Pool. Er ist umsäumt von luftig gestellten Liegen und zehn grünen Cabañas, schattigen Salonzelten. Buchsbaumhecken schützen das Fürsichsein bis zur privaten Treppe in den Pool.

Was soll einen hier wegziehen. Erfrischungen kommen von der Poolbar unter der 500 Jahre alten Zypresse. Wer Appetit auf Lunch bekommt, nimmt gleich nebenan im „Gazebo" Platz, einem Grill-Restaurant unter freiem Himmel, und lässt sich tagesfrischen Fisch,

Stilechte Ambiance: das Gourmetrestaurant L'Orangerie in der ehemaligen Olivenpresse.
Authentic ambience: the L'Orangerie gourmet restaurant in the old olive press.

Highlights für Feinschmecker: gebratene Foie gras (o.), Salat Caprese mit Langostinos (u.).
Highlights for gourmets – (above) fried foie gras, (below) Caprese Salad with crayfish.

Fleisch, Salat und Gemüse schmecken. Viele, die Son Net schon kennen, kommen auch am Abend zum Pool. Sie lieben diesen Tagesausklang: Treiben im Wasser, während vor ihren Augen die Sonne hinter dem Galatzo versinkt.

Ein Genuss dann die Suite, das Zimmer, die traumhaft schönen Bäder. Später ein Aperitif in der Bar, im Sommer draußen auf der Terrasse über den Rosenbögen, und schließlich das Diner im Gourmetrestaurant L'Orangerie. Bleibt man drinnen, hat man das Flair der Tafona, der alten Olivenpresse, um sich. Lässt man sich auf der Terrasse nieder, genießt man das Tal und die Berge von Puigpunyent im letzten Abendlicht.

wants to leave Son Net, for an excursion or anything else. The magic of the place is enthralling from the start. The visitor is able to unwind up on the hill surrounded by such exquisite style and the fascinating mountain scenery. The panorama is ever present, in the rooms and the restaurant, on the terraces, and in the gardens, but above all from a sparkling spot within this ambience, the 30-metre swimming pool. Around it are loungers with plenty of room between them, and ten green cabañas – shady marquees.

Lende und Koteletts vom mallorquinischen Lamm.
Majorcan loin of lamb and lamb chops.

Chefcuisinier Francisco Martorell aus Sóller.
Chef de cuisine, Francisco Martorell from Sóller.

HIDEAWAYS 153

Rechts: Gazebo, das Grill-Restaurant unter freiem Himmel. Unten: Der alte Mahlstein im L'Orangerie.
Right: Gazebo, the open-air grill restaurant.
Below: the old millstone in L'Orangerie.

Box hedges along the path to the pool protect your privacy up to your private steps into the pool. Why should one want to go anywhere else? Refreshments are availableat the Pool Bar beneath the 500 year-old cypresses. If you feel like lunch, you go next door and take a seat at he Gazebo, an outdoor grill restaurant where you can enjoy fish fresgly caught daily, meat, salad and vegetables. Many who already know Son Net go to the pool in the evening where they love to see out the day in the water as the sun sets behind the Gazebo. The suite, the room and the beautiful bathrooms are then pure delight. Later on you can have an aperitif at the bar which in summer can be taken out on the terrace above the rose bowers, then proceed to dinner at the L'Orangerie gourmet restaurant. If you choose to stay inside, you're surrounded by the flair of the tafona, the old olive press. On the terrace however, you have the valley and mountains of Puigpunyent in the fading evening light.

The chef, Francisco Martorell, comes from Sóller. His cuisine is just right for the whole atmosphere of Son Net, an imaginative, creative, beautifully prepared Mediterranean cuisine. Francisco

Küchenchef Francisco Martorell kommt aus Sóller. Seine Küche passt zur Stimmung von Son Net, stilvolle, anregend kreative, perfekt zubereitete Mittelmeer-Cuisine. Francisco bringt viel von der Insel auf die Tafel, das wunderbare Gemüse, Lamm, Spanferkel, den frischen Fang der Fischer aus Port de Sóller. Ein Genuss für Feinschmecker, wenn er Lammlende und -koteletts in Thymian brät, köstlich seine Foie gras, ein Gedicht so eine Schöpfung wie das Garnelen-, Gemüse- und Algengratin mit Seeigelsauce. Man trinkt beste spanische und mallorquinische Weine, hat eine schöne Nacht im Himmelbett, und irgendwann, wenn die Sonne längst wieder den Galatzo bescheint, beginnt ein neuer Tag auf Mallorca.

Vielleicht mit der Trauung in der hauseigenen Kapelle? Oder mit ein paar Stunden im

Die historische Architektur wurde brillant restauriert.
The historic architecture has been brilliantly restored.

Aussicht vom Balkon einer Suite in die Tramuntanaberge.
View of the Tramuntana Mountains from the balcony of a Suite.

Beauty Center? Oder kann uns Direktor Carlos Batista vielleicht doch zu einer kleinen Ortsveränderung animieren? Man braucht dabei die Atmosphäre von Son Net gar nicht so richtig zu verlassen. Längst sind uns die kulinarisch inspirierten Skulpturen aufgefallen. Im L'Orangerie etwa die Paravents aus sich drehenden, mannshohen Messern und Gabeln oder draußen vorm alten Haustor der Brunnen aus riesigen, oben umgebogenen Löffeln. Die Künstler, Ben Jakober und seine Frau Yannick, arbeiten auf der Insel, drüben in der Bucht von Alcudia. Sie zeigen gerne ihre Sammlung von Kinderporträts aus dem 16. bis 19. Jahrhundert. Unter Umständen lassen sie sich auch bei der Arbeit über die Schulter blicken.

Um sie zu besuchen, fährt man quer übers ganze Eiland, und wer das mit offenen Augen und Sinnen tut, der spürt, dass ihn Schönheiten wie die, von denen er aufgebrochen ist, auch unterwegs berühren. Sie ist überall zu spüren, die Magie von Son Net, die Magie von Mallorca.

integrates much from the island into his dishes: the wonderful vegetables, lamb, sucking pig and freshly caught fish from Port de Sóller. Bon vivants delight in his loin of lamb and chops roast with thyme, and his foie gras is simply delicious. His prawns and vegetables with a seaweed gratin and sea urchin sauce is out of this world. To accompany the food you have the best Spanish and Majorcan wines, then its off for a wonderful night's sleep in your four-poster. When the sun's rays are shining on the Galatzo once again another day begins in Majorca, maybe with wedding in the hotel's own chapel, or a couple of hours at the beauty centre. Perhaps Carlos Batista, the hotel's General Manager, will be able to persuade you to go somewhere else for a change of scenery but there's no real need to leave the atmosphere of Son Net. We have already noticed the inspired "culinary sculptures". In L'Orangerie for instance, there are mansize knives and forks turning slowly, and outside the old front door is a fountain of giant, bent spoons. The artists, Ben Jakober and his wife Yannick,

work on the island over in the Bay of Alcudia. They like to show their collection of portraits of children of the 16th to 19th centuries. Under certain circumstances you can watch them working. To visit them you have to cross the whole island, and those with eyes to see and the sensitivity to feel note that the beauty they leave behind can be found on this journey too. The magic of Son Net and of Majorca is everywhere.

Sinnvolles Requisit für Blicke ins Land: das Fernrohr im Salon.
Telescope in the lounge – useful for surveying the landscape.

Iris Hülle leitet das Beauty Center von Son Net. Sie pflegt mit Produkten von Maria Galland.
Iris Hülle manages the Son Net Beauty Centre. She uses Maria Galland beauty care products.

Relaxen in der Sauna, Wohltat im milden mallorquinischen Winter.
Relaxing in the sauna is wonderful in the mild Majorcan winters.

Idylle in der Mecklenburgischen Schweiz

SCHLOSSHOTEL BURG SCHLITZ

A Mecklenburg Idyll

In einer der landschaftlich reizvollsten Gegenden Mecklenburg-Vorpommerns findet sich eine der feinsten architektonischen Sehenswürdigkeiten, die das Land zu bieten hat, die Burg Schlitz. Seit 1999 empfängt der Herrensitz aus der Biedermeierzeit seine Gäste als zauberhaftes Schlosshotel.

Set in a scenically beautiful part of Mecklenburg-Vorpommern in Germany is one of the finest architectural sights in the region – Burg Schlitz. Now an enchanting hotel, this mansion built in the Biedermeier period has been welcoming guests since 1999.

Text: Günter Ned · Fotos: Klaus Lorke

Direktoren seit Januar 2002: Thomas und Maja Kilgore, ein Paar, das trotz seiner Jugend schon ein großes Renommee hat, wenn es darum geht, ein Hotel zum Blühen zu bringen (unter anderem als General Manager des Matahari Beach Resort auf Bali). Thomas Kilgore ist zugleich Chef der Gastronomie, ein Glücksfall für Feinschmecker.

General Managers since January 2002 – Thomas and Maja Kilgore, a couple who despite their youth already have a splendid reputation for bringing a hotel to life (General Managers of the Matahari Beach Resorts in Bali, among others). Thomas Kilgore is also the chef de cuisine, a stroke of luck for bon vivants.

The state of Mecklenburg-Vorpommern is over-endowed with scenic beauty. Its vast forests and fields, flowering meadows and endless shady avenues make Mecklenburg-Vorpommern a rural idyll par excellence. The Baltic in the north and Mecklenburg's lowlands scattered with lakes around the Müritz - the largest continental lake in north Germany - lend a maritime charm to the most thinly populated state in Germany. Another beautiful area known as "Mecklenburg's Switzerland", is a picturesque hilly landscape between Teterower, Kummerower and Lake Malchin. If you climb Röthelberg hill, the whole panorama lies at your feet. Not far from Hohen Demzin is Burg Schlitz, the most important classical mansion in Mecklenburg and a popular destination for excursions.

This grand residence has been an enchanting hotel since 1999. During the communist GDR period, the building was used as an old people's home among other things, but it has since undergone superb renovation made possible by an investment of 30 million Euro, and is now restored to its former glory. The Relais & Châteaux hotel has been the property of Matthias Stinnes and Elisabeth Schrader since the year 2000, and their hotel guests experience a brilliant blend of rural and architectural beauty at Burg Schlitz.

The mansion was built by Count Hans von Schlitz between 1806 and 1823. Born Hans von Labes, he was a diplomat by profession, a Second Secretary in the Prussian Diplomatic Service, and later on a gentleman farmer with estates in the immediate vicinity of the mansion built at a later date. He became a Count in a rather romantic way. Von Labes fell in love with Luise, the daughter of the Johann Eustrach von Schlitz-Görtz, a Count of the German Empire. To circumvent his daughter entering into an unsuitable marriage, the Count, now a potential father-in-law, adopted his daughter's intended which of course raised him to the ranks of the nobility.

Mecklenburg-Vorpommern ist überreich an landschaftlichen Idyllen: Weite Wälder und Felder, blühende Wiesen, endlose, schattige Alleen. Die Ostsee im Norden und die Mecklenburgische Seenplatte rund um die Müritz, den größten norddeutschen Binnensee, geben dem am dünnsten besiedelten deutschen Bundesland maritimen Charme. Schließlich das Herzstück, die Mecklenburgische Schweiz: eine malerische Hügelgegend, eingebettet ins Land zwischen dem Teterower, dem Kummerower und dem Malchiner See. Wer den Röthelberg besteigt, dem liegt das ganze Panorama zu Füßen. Ein traditionelles Ausflugsziel liegt ganz in der Nähe, etwas außerhalb von Hohen Demzin: Burg Schlitz, die bedeutendste klassizistische Schlossanlage Mecklenburgs.

Seit 1999 präsentiert sich die ehemals herrschaftliche Residenz als zauberhaftes Schlosshotel. Zu DDR-Zeiten unter anderem als Seniorenheim genutzt, blüht Burg Schlitz nach einer erstklassigen Restaurierung, möglich gemacht durch eine Investition von 30 Millionen Euro, in seiner ganzen Schönheit wieder auf. Seit dem Jahr 2000 ist das Relais-&-Châteaux-Haus im Besitz von Matthias Stinnes und Elisabeth Schrader. Wer auf Burg Schlitz logiert, erlebt eine geniale Verbindung von landschaftlicher und architektonischer Schönheit.

Erbaut wurde das Schloss in den Jahren 1806 bis 1823 vom Grafen Hans von Schlitz. Des Bauherrn ursprünglicher Name war Hans von Labes, von Beruf zunächst Legationsrat im preußischen diplomatischen Dienst, später Landwirt mit Ländereien in der unmittelbaren Nachbarschaft des späteren Schlosses. Zum Grafen wurde er durch eine romantische Geschichte. Herr von Labes verliebte sich in Luise, die Tochter des Reichsgrafen Johann

Eustrach von Schlitz-Görtz. Damit die Verbindung keine Mesalliance würde, adoptierte der Schwiegerpapa in spe den Auserwählten seiner Tochter und beförderte ihn damit zum Grafen. Graf von Schlitz machte sich einen Namen als liberaler Adeliger, der der Region erste Reformen brachte, als Freund der Künste und Künstler, als feinsinniger Gesellschafter, der auf dem Schloss Dichter wie Achim von Arnim und Johann Wolfgang von Goethe zu Gast hatte, und als passionierter Architektur-Fan. Er begnügte sich nicht damit, das Schloss und gleich daneben die Karolinen-Kapelle (benannt nach seiner einzigen Tochter) zu bauen. Er legte auch einen heute 130 Hektar großen, zauberhaften Park an – ein Werk, das nach seinem Tod von der Tochter und ihrem Gatten fortgeführt wurde und an die fünfzig Jahre in Anspruch nahm.

Wer sich hier in die Natur begibt, der geht nicht einfach spazieren, der lustwandelt. Ein Wäldchen mit jahrhundertealten Bäumen tut sich auf, es gibt kleine Seen, den Luisensee zum Beispiel, den Graf Schlitz seiner Frau widmete (in der Mitte gibt es die „Liebesinsel", man erreicht sie über eine Holzbrücke), und an den lauschigsten Plätzen hat der Schlossherr Denkmäler errichtet, 36 an der Zahl. Es sind Obelisken, Grotten, Säulen etc., sie sollen an Zeitgenossen erinnern, die der Graf liebte und verehrte. Am schönsten ist wohl der Nymphenbrunnen, 1905 von Walter Schott im Jugendstil geschaffen.

Des Grafen Liebe zur Skulptur und Architektur floriert natürlich nicht nur im Park, sondern auch im Schloss selbst. Das heutige Hotel integriert die historischen, glänzend restaurierten Kostbarkeiten geschickt in seine Ambiance, das Entree zum Beispiel mit seinen phantastisch bemalten, aufwändig restaurierten Tapeten und seinem sonnenförmig gelegten Parkettboden; den Schinkel-Saal, für die festliche Tafel ebenso geeignet wie für die Tagung, mit den beiden Kachelöfen, die nach

Graf von Schlitz made a name for himself as a liberal-minded aristocratic who introduced many reforms to the region. He became a patron of the arts and artists, hosting such poets such as Achim von Arnim and Johann Wolfgang von Goethe at the mansion. He was also passionately interested in architecture. Not only did he build the mansion and the adjacent chapel which he dedicated to his only daughter Caroline, but also created the enchanting 320-acre park which, after his death, his daughter and her husband continued to maintain right up to the 1950s.

Visitors to these parts don't just go walking, they stroll through the countryside for pleasure and amusement. Little woods with centuries-old trees come into view, and small lakes – Lake Luisensee for instance dedicated by Count Schlitz to his wife which has a "love island" in the middle of it connected by a wooden bridge. The Count placed

Oben: eines der stilvollen Doppelzimmer. Die Möbel wurden von den Deutschen Werkstätten Hellerau maßgefertigt.
Above: A stylish double room. The furniture was made to measure by the German Hellerau workshops.

Vielleicht das schönste Kunstwerk im 130 Hektar großen Schlosspark: der Nymphenbrunnen von Walter Schott. Unten links: die Holzbrücke zur Liebesinsel im Luisensee.
Possibly the most decorative feature in the 321 acre park is Walter Schott's Nymphs' Fountain. Below left: the wooden bridge to the island of love in the Luisensee lake.

Der prachtvoll restaurierte Schinkel-Saal. The superbly restored Schinkel Room.

Versierter Gastgeber im Restaurant: Maître d'hôtel und Sommelier Birger Kluth. Oben: die Salons fürs Private Dining. Rechts: der Samowar am Frühstücksbuffet.

The restaurant's experienced maître d'hôtel and sommelier Birger Kluth. Above: the rooms for private dining. Right: the samovar on the breakfast buffet.

Entwürfen des berühmten Baumeisters Karl Friedrich Schinkel angefertigt wurden, oder den Rittersaal, heute das Schlossrestaurant. Gäste dinieren unter einem neugotischen Gewölbe mit Spitzbögen aus Stuck, Tageslicht fällt durch Buntglasfenster aus dem Jahr 1820, die fein gedeckten Tische stehen auf Intarsienparkett.

Auch in den vierzehn Zimmern und sechs Suiten genießen Gäste immer wieder den Charme der Vergangenheit (wunderschön etwa die vergoldete Kassettendecke in der Grafen-Suite). Die Interieurs schmücken sich mit originalen Biedermeier-Antiquitäten, geschmackvoll angepasst dazu die maßgefertigten Möbel aus den Deutschen Werkstätten Hellerau, vom Biedermeier- wie vom Bauhausstil inspiriert. Elegante Wohnlichkeit bestimmt die Szene.

Das Schlosshotel Burg Schlitz wird von Thomas und Maja Kilgore geleitet, einem engagierten, liebenswerten Paar, das trotz seiner Jugend (30 und 31 Jahre) schon ein großes Renommee hat, wenn es darum geht, ein Hotel zum Blühen zu bringen (unter anderem als Direktoren des Matahari Beach Resorts auf Bali). Thomas Kilgore ist zugleich Chef der Gastronomie – ein Glücksfall für die Feinschmecker unter den Gästen. Tagsüber zeigt er sein geschliffenes Können im Schlosscafé mit leckerer Bistroküche (feine Salate, Entenstopfleberterrine auf Zwiebelkonfit, Mecklenburger Kalbstafelspitz). Fürs Diner im Schlossrestaurant entwickelt er mit einer gut ausgesuchten Crew (Souschef: Dirk Eichhoff, Restaurantleiter und Sommelier: Birger Kluth) eine Gourmetcuisine, die raffiniert drei Komponenten mischt: regionale Produkte (die Müritzer Fischer liefern ihren frischen Fang, der Spargel kommt von Hubertus Heinemann aus Redefin, das Holzofenbrot und die Marmeladen aus Jördenstorf, die Wildkräuter bringt Patissiére Sabine Marschner aus ihrem privaten Garten mit), dazu mediterrane Leichtigkeit (Olivenöl statt Butter) und dann der Clou: indonesische Gewürze und Garweisen. Thomas Kilgore hat die Zeit auf Bali selbstverständlich auch dazu genützt, sich in fernöstlicher Küchenkunst zu perfektionieren.

Aber die Kilgores machen nicht nur das Speisen zum Event, der ganze Aufenthalt auf Burg Schlitz wird mit ihnen zum Erlebnis. Was für ein perfektes Plätzchen, wenn es darum geht, einfach nur in stilvoller natur-

statues and memorials in leafy places, obelisks, grottoes and columns, thirty-six of them in all, intended to commemorate contemporaries whom Count loved and admired. The most beautiful has to be the Art Nouveau Nymph Fountain, designed in 1905 by Walter Schott. The Count's love of sculpture and architecture didn't only flourish in the park but also inside the mansion. Today's hotel integrates brilliantly restored, historic treasures within their own ambience. Take the entrance for instance which has

Das Schlossrestaurant im Rittersaal: neugotisches Gewölbe mit Spitzbögen aus Stuck, Buntglasfenster aus dem Jahr 1820, Intarsienparkett.
The Schloss Restaurant in the Knights' Chamber: neo-Gothic vaulted ceiling with pointed stucco arches, stained glass dating back to 1820 and parquet floor.

schöner Atmosphäre zu relaxen: bei einem Spaziergang (auf Wunsch mit fein gepacktem Picknick-Köfferchen), auf dem Goetheweg zum Beispiel, einem beschaulichen Rundpfad durch den Wald, oder auf dem Lustwandelweg. Er führt hinunter zur Burgruine aus dem fantastically painted, expensively renovated wallpaper, or the parquet floor which has been laid down in the shape of the sun.

Then there is the Schinkel Room which has two tiled stoves constructed to the design of the famous architect Karl Friedrich Schinkel. The Room is eminently suitable for celebration dinners as well as for conferences. The former Knights' Chamber is now the mansion restaurant. Guests dine at beautifully laid tables standing on an inlaid parquet floor beneath a neo-Gothic vaulted ceiling with pointed stucco arches. During the day the light shines through stained glass windows dating back to 1820. Guests are surrounded by the charm of the past in the rooms and suites too. Yet another wonderful feature is the coffered ceiling in the Graf Suites. Original Biedermeier antiques grace the interiors, and made-to-measure furniture in Biedermeier and Bauhaus styles from the Hellerau workshops discreetly complements the older pieces. The scene is that of a homely elegance.

The Schloss Hotel Burg Schlitz has been run by Thomas and Maja Kilgore, a charming and dedicated couple who despite their youth (30 and 31 years old) already have a splendid reputation in the business of bringing an hotel to life, having already managed the Matahari Beach Resort in Bali. Thomas Kilgore is also a chef de cuisine, a stroke of luck the bon vivants amongst the guests. During the day his expertise becomes evident in the mansion's Café which serves delicious salads, terrine of duck pâté with onion chutney, and Mecklenburg soured boiled rump of veal. For dinner in the mansion's Restaurant he has developed, together with his carefully selected staff (sous chef Dirk Eichhoff, and restaurant manager and sommelier, Birger Kluth), a gourmet cuisine which cleverly blends three components: regional products, Mediterranean lightness (olive oil instead of butter) and Indonesian spices and cooking techniques.

As to local products, the fish is freshly caught by Müritz fishermen, the asparagus comes from Hubertus Heinemann of Redefin, the bread baked in a wood-burning oven and the jam come from Jördenstorf, and

Thomas Kilgores rechte Hand in der Küche: Souschef Dirk Eichhoff. Links zwei Kreationen aus Kilgores gekonnter Gourmet-Cuisine: Presalée-Lamm mit zweierlei Bohnen und Rosmarin-Jus, Rhabarbermousse mit Erdbeersorbet.
Sous chef Dirk Eichhoff, Thomas Kilgore's right hand man in the kitchen. Left: two examples of Kilgore's skill – presalée lamb with two different kinds of beans in rosemary juice, and rhubarb mousse with strawberry sorbet.

Die restaurierten Schönheiten der Schlossarchitektur mischen sich stilvoll in die Hotel-Interieurs. Unten Mitte: das Entree mit Rezeption und strahlenförmig gelegtem Parkett. Unten rechts: die Grafensuite mit vergoldeter Kassettendecke.

The beautiful restored architectural features blend stylishly with the hotel décor. Below centre: entrance and reception area, and the rays of parquet floor. Below right: the Graf Suite and its gilded coffered ceiling.

the wild herbs are supplied by the pastry cook Sabine Marschner from her private garden. Clearly, Thomas Kilgore used his time well in Bali to perfect his Asian cooking skills. Yet, it is not only meals which the Kilgores make into an event. The whole stay at Burg Schlitz is an experience, a perfect place indeed to relax in stylish surroundings in the heart of beautiful countryside. For instance, you can go for a ramble along the Goetheweg, a lovely path through the woods, taking

9. Jahrhundert und an einem alten Ginkgobaum vorbei. Das hohe Gewächs mit den fächerförmigen Blättern – seine Art wird in Japan und China heilig gehalten – könnte eine schöne Anregung sein, sich einmal das Verwöhn- und Entspannungsprogramm des Ginkgo-Spas anzuschauen. Die exklusiv konzipierte Wellness-Oase des Schlosshotels pflegt und verschönt unter anderem mit klassisch europäischen wie fernöstlichen Massagen, mit Entspannungstechniken, einer vielfältigen Bade- und Saunalandschaft. Im Mittelpunkt stehen die renommierten Kosmetikprogramme von Kanebo.

Die Karolinen-Kapelle ist, zumal in der warmen Jahreszeit, als Hochzeitskirche sehr gefragt. Die Fußbodenheizung macht Trauungen aber auch im Winter komfortabel. Zur Feier lädt man in die eleganten Salons von Burg Schlitz oder, wenn es ein größeres Fest geben soll, in den Schinkel-Saal. Er ist auch Treffpunkt für erlesene kulturelle Highlights, die Konzertreihe der Festspiele Mecklenburg-Vorpommern zum Beispiel (von August bis Dezember, für Hausgäste reserviert die Direktion Karten der Kategorie I).

Die Traditionsverbundenheit des Hauses, die so harmonisch Hand in Hand mit seinem

zeitbetonten Luxus geht, hat Freunden der Reiterei ein ganz spezielles Highlight zu bieten: Schleppjagden durch den Schlosspark. Schon Graf Bassewitz, der Schwiegersohn des Grafen von Schlitz, hielt sich auf dem Schloss eine eigene Hirschmeute. Maja und Thomas Kilgore haben die traditionsreiche Jagddisziplin wiederbelebt, mit einer Strecke, die sich sehen lassen kann. Sie ist 30 Kilometer lang, mit 22 Sprüngen ausgelegt, und Tierschützer bleiben dabei völlig ruhig. Schleppjagden dürfen in Deutschland seit langem kein tierisches Opfer haben. Hundemeute und Reiter jagen hinter einer Schleppfährte her, die vom Menschen gelegt wird.

Man sieht, es gibt viele Möglichkeiten auf Burg Schlitz, die Sorgen des Alltags zu begraben und die schönen Seiten des Lebens zu genießen, ganz so wie es sich der Graf Schlitz von seinen Gästen erbat. Neben dem Einfahrtstor unterhalb des Schlosses ließ er einen Obelisken errichten. Sein Sockel trägt einen steinernen Kasten, die lateinische Inschrift hat eine Forderung an die Geladenen: „Gast, der Du hinaufsteigst, übergib dieser freundlichen Urne Deine Sorgen! Das wünscht Hans Graf Schlitz. 1816."

with you if you wish a delightfully packed little picnic box.
Alternatively, you could simply go for a short walk down to the ruins of a 9th century castle, passing a tall old ginkgo tree on the way whose fan-like leaves are venerated in China and Japan. It might prompt you to take a look at the pamper and relaxation programme of the Ginkgo Spa which provides a whole range of treatment, from European and Asian massage, relaxation techniques and a bathing and sauna area offering many possibilities. At the heart of it all is the renowned Kanebo cosmetics' programme. The Caroline Chapel is very popular for weddings, especially during the warmer months. However, the underfloor heating makes winter weddings possible also. Wedding receptions are held in one of the elegant function rooms at Burg Schlitz, though the Schinkel Room is used for larger weddings. It's also used as a venue for exclusive cultural events, for example the series of concerts held during the Mecklenburg-Vorpommern Festival which lasts from August to December. (The hotel management can book Category-I tickets for hotel guests.)

The hotel's close attachment to its tradition which goes so harmoniously hand in hand with the very latest in luxury, is exemplified by a special highlight it offers guests who ride i.e. drag hunting in the grounds of the mansion. Even Count Bassewitz, the son-in-law of Count von Schlitz kept a pack of hounds here. Maja and Thomas Kilgore have revived this country sport across a wonderful stretch of land 18 miles long with 22 jumps, and what is more animal conservationist are quite happy with it. Drag hunting animals to death has long been banned in Germany. It has no animal victims nowadays. The participants ride to hounds along a trail of scent laid by humans.

Burg Schlitz offers many opportunities to lay aside the stress of the daily round to enjoy the better things of life, exactly what Count Schlitz would have wanted for his guests. Beside the entrance which is at a lower level than the mansion, he erected an obelisk, and on its plinth is a stone container on which these words are inscribed into the stone: "Guest, before you go up, leave your cares behind in this friendly urn. This is the wish of Hans Count Schlitz. 1816".

Von oben: Barterrasse mit Parkblick, Hochzeitskapelle, idyllisches Plätzchen am See. Zum Picknick ist vorm Nymphenbrunnen gedeckt.
From above: Bar terrace with view of the park, wedding chapel, idyllic little spot beside the lake. Picnic laid in front of the Nymphs' fountain.

HOTEL FÄHR

Kultivierte Wohnoase am Wattenmeer

Lange vor der Eröffnung des legendären Hindenburgdamms am 1. Juni 1927 war der Fährhafen im idyllischen Munkmarsch Sylts Tor zur Welt und für Feriengäste und Insulaner erste Station auf der schönen Frieseninsel. Hier, direkt am Wattenmeer, spiegelt das traditionsreiche Fährhaus Munkmarsch ein wenig von dieser Vergangenheit wider – ein Stück vom alten Sylt, in das die Gegenwart behutsam eingezogen ist. Die stilvolle L'art de vivre-Gourmetresidenz zählt nicht nur zur exklusiven Vereinigung der „Small Luxury Hotels of the World", das Luxushotel vereint auch alle Annehmlichkeiten eines wahrlich luxuriösen Hideaways.

HAUS SYLT

Sophisticated oasis on the mud flats

Long before the opening of the legendary Hindenburg dam on the 1st June 1927, the ferry house on the Munkmarsch mud flats on Sylt a door to the world and the first stopping point for holiday visitors and the inhabitants of this beautiful Frisian island. Located right beside the mud flats, the Fährhaus Munkmarsch so very rich in tradition, reflects this past a little. It is a piece of Sylt in which the present has been cautiously integrated. Not only is this stylish l'art de vivre gourmet residence a member of the exclusive Small Luxury Hotels of the World organization, it unites under one roof all the amenities of a truly luxurious hideaway.

Text: Bernd Teichgräber · Fotos: Klaus Lorke

Kümmern sich rührend um ihre Gäste: Gerhard Pohl und Jasmina Klessa.

Gerhard Pohl and Jasmina Klessa lavish attention on their guests.

The interesting history of the Munkmarsch Ferry House began over 135 years ago when Thomas Selmer had a simple wooden house built beside Munkmarsch harbour which was intended as no more than a harbour guest house, plain and simple. Mussel fishermen felt completely at home in this idyllic place, and steamers and cargo ships laden with goods from East Frisia, England and Norway docked here. If and when holiday visitors reached this fishing harbour, they were simply transported by a horse-drawn carriage to the up-and-coming resort of Westerland. Even then the ferry house was a popular refuge for sea captains and fisherfolk, longshoremen and locals. It served as overnight lodgings and was a place to eat and to celebrate. Many a nautical yarn has been spun here in the cosy company of seafaring friends, but today the sophisticated Fährhaus Hotel Sylt has little in common with that rough Frisian charm of a bygone age.

The fresh breeze, the island atmosphere and a sparkling esprit makes the hotel an ideal place for gourmets, health and fitness disciples and nature-lovers. It provides everything you need to relax as well as the pleasure of enjoying superb hospitality in sophisticated, stylish surroundings. Guests are pampered in a cultivated environment where their needs are catered for with very personal care and attention. When asked about the more striking features of their hotel, Gerhard Pohl

Vor mehr als 135 Jahren begann die abwechslungsreiche Geschichte des Fährhauses Munkmarsch, als Thomas Selmer am Munkmarscher Hafen ein schlichtes Holzhaus errichten ließ, das wohl nicht mehr als eine einfache Hafengaststätte war. Muschelfischer waren an diesem idyllischen Ort zu Hause, Dampfschiffe und Frachtensegler, beladen mit Gütern und Waren aus Ostfriesland, England und Norwegen, kamen hier an. Erreichten Badegäste den Fischerhafen, wurden sie per Pferdekutsche kurzerhand ins aufstrebende Seebad Westerland kutschiert. Kapitänen und Fischern, Schauerleuten und Einheimischen diente das Fährhaus schon damals als beliebter Anlaufpunkt. Hier wurde übernachtet, gegessen, gefeiert und in feucht-fröhlicher Runde so manche Seemannsgeschichte zum Besten gegeben. Doch mit dem rauen friesischen Charme jener Zeit hat das noble Hotel Fährhaus Sylt heute weit

and Jasmina Klessa don't need long to reflect. "Its essentially southern elegance and airy lightness are the things which give the Fährhaus Munkmarsch Hotel its special character. There is nothing formal or artificial. The entire house has a bright and carefree atmosphere." Those who stay at the Fährhaus Hotel Sylt become aware of the beauty of the elements – the wind, the sun and the sea, its changing colours and its ebb and flow. Everything appears to contrast perfectly with the peaceful, stylish interior of the hotel, providing a kind of framework within which the guest can move during his stay.

The elegant design of the complex is a prime example of timeless hotel architecture on the island. The residence, which has sensational views of the marina and the mud flats, has 14 elegant rooms and six suites with modern décor. The four parts of the building which are linked by a glass construction, have different colours schemes. No room is the same. The Blue House has a nautical feel, and the rooms are named after ships which have anchored here. The décor and furnishings of the sand-coloured house have been lovingly assembled around a mud flats theme. The Green and Red Houses have grasses and birds as their theme. The ground floor of the hotel has light larch floors, hand-painted linen wall covering and wooden furniture varnished in the traditional way. The bathrooms are most attractive with their Harlinger tiles, antique marble and terracotta floors.

The modern feel of the light and airy hall extends to the first floor. Rare wood such as maple and

Zurückhaltende Materialien und Muster sind der Rahmen für das stilvolle Ambiente.
Muted colours and a tasteful décor provide a stylish ambience.

Zimmer mit Terrasse und Aussicht auf den Yachthafen.
Room with terrace and view of the marina.

HIDEAWAYS 169

Viel Licht und Atmosphäre hat das Gourmetrestaurant Fährhaus.

The Fährhaus gourmet restaurant is very light and has a tremendous atmosphere.

cherry dominate the style. In the bathrooms, basins made of cocciopesto, a handmade material from Italy, convey a southern flair. Lava stone washbasins have been specially produced for the Frisian part of the hotel; their colour matches the hand-painted tiles exactly. To ensure the guest wants for nothing, each room is equipped

weniger gemein. Angereichert mit einer frischen Brise Inselflair und stets taufrischem Esprit bietet es Gourmets, Wellnessfans und Naturliebhabern alles, was man sich heute an Erholung, feinen Genüssen, Gast- und Wohnkultur auf hohem Niveau wünscht.

Die kultivierte Wohnoase verwöhnt ihr Publikum mit ausgesucht persönlicher Umsorgung, besticht durch Individualität und exklusiven Anspruch. Gerhard Pohl und

Jasmina Klessa, befragt nach den Auffälligkeiten ihres Hauses, müssen nicht lange überlegen: „Es ist eine beinahe südliche Eleganz und helle Leichtigkeit, die das Fährhaus Munkmarsch auszeichnen. Nichts wirkt feierlich oder getragen, sämtliche Interieurs zeigen sich von beinahe unbeschwerter Heiterkeit." Wer im Hotel Fährhaus Sylt logiert, der bemerkt die ganze Schönheit der natürlichen Elemente: der Wind, die Sonne

Sternekoch Alexandro Pape leitet die Geschicke der hoch gelobten Fährhausküche.

Top chef Alexandro Pape is in charge of the highly praised Fährhaus kitchen.

Kross gebratener Loup de mer auf Radicchiorisotto mit gratinierter Ziegenkäsehaube und Noilly-Prat-Sauce.

Crisp fried Loup de mer served on a radicchio risotto au gratin and Noilly Prat gravy.

und das Meer mit seinem wechselnden Spiel von Ebbe und Flut scheinen perfekt mit dem friedlichen stilvollen Inneren des Hotels zu kontrastieren und sind jederzeit der einladende Rahmen, in dem sich der Gast während seines Aufenthaltes bewegt.

Mit dem eleganten Entwurf des Ensembles setzte der Betreiber ohne Zweifel einen Glanzpunkt für zeitlose Hotelarchitektur auf der Insel. Das Domizil mit sensationellem Blick auf Yachthafen und Wattenmeer beherbergt 14 elegante, modern gestylte Zimmer und sechs Suiten, die allesamt keine Wünsche offen lassen. Die vier Gebäudeteile, durch eine gläserne Konstruktion verbunden, wurden in unterschiedlichen Farben gestaltet. Kein Zimmer gleicht dem anderen. So neigt sich das Blaue Haus dem Meer zu und die Zimmer tragen Namen der Schiffe, die einst im Fährhafen ankerten. Das sandfarbene Haus ist mit Motiven des Wattenmeeres liebevoll ausgestattet und im Grünen und Roten Haus findet man Namen von Gräsern und Vögeln. Helle Lärchenböden kleiden die Logis im Untergeschoss, handgemalte Leinentapeten ebenso wie Holzmöbel mit traditioneller Strichlacktechnik oder Käseholz. Schmuck sehen die Bäder aus, mit ihren Harlinger-Kacheln, antikem Marmor oder Terracottaböden. Der moderne Eindruck der lichtdurchfluteten Halle setzt sich auch in der ersten Etage fort. Edles Holz wie Ahorn, Kirsche, Wenge oder Elsbeere prägen hier den Stil. Südländisches Flair vermitteln in den Bädern Waschtische aus Cocciopesto, einem handgefertigten Material aus Italien. Für den friesischen Teil des Hotels wurden eigens Lava-Waschtische gefertigt, deren Farbton exakt auf die handgemalten Fliesen abgestimmt ist.

Gemütlich mit ländlicher Eleganz: das Friesenzimmer.

The Frisian Room is cosy and has a country style elegance.

with television, video-recorder, stereo and a Bose sound system, room safe, minibar, kettle and two telephones, one of them cordless. The large pool area is an ideal place to relax and indulge in the health and beauty aspects of life. Adventure showers, whirlpool, steam bath, sauna and solarium aid the flight from the daily round. To meet the needs of physical fitness enthusiasts there is a gym with the very latest equipment including a cross trainer, climber, treadmill and power training apparatus.

Discriminating health and fitness disciples can experience the various beauty treatment packages, and

Ein wahrer Genuss: Törtchen von Flusskrebsen und Physaliskompott auf Rettichcarpaccio.

Sheer delight – crayfish tartlet and stewed Physalis on carpaccio of radish.

Exklusiv im Hotel Fährhaus: Produkte von Ligne St. Barth – eine der edelsten und begehrtesten Pflegeserien überhaupt.

Exclusive to the Fährhaus Hotel: Ligne St. Barth products are amongst the very finest and most sought-after cosmetics.

Ein Erlebnis: die wie Muscheln gestalteten Duschen aus Cocciopesto.

An experience: shell-shaped showers.

even have a Caribbean experience. The Beauty Farm – the only one on Sylt - uses the high quality products of Ligne St Barth, one of the finest and most sought-after lines in cosmetics. They are made exclusively from natural ingredients derived from Caribbean plants whose healing and care properties were known to generations of the Caribbean islands' native Arawak people, and which have been handed down to Ligne St Barth. A healthy swim in the sea taking in the salty air, or cycling can be beneficial in a quite a different way. Golf lovers too can experience yet another aspect of this beautiful place on one of the three golf courses.

Back at the hotel the first class cuisine and wines make dining a delight. While the guest admires the nostalgic, elegant Victorian style of the gourmet restaurant, the young chef, Alexandro Pape prepares samples of his culinary arts which have been awarded a Michelin star and 17 Gault Millau points. Guests enjoy a constantly changing menu depending on the season and the kitchen staff. Fish dishes of every kind are the chef's speciality. Whether barbel, lobster or loup de mer, the connoisseur experiences in the most wonderful way how the flavours of the oceans and the Mediterranean can be blended, seasoned and celebrated. Where else can you eat grilled turbot with

Um auf keinen Komfort verzichten zu müssen, findet der Gast selbstverständlich in jedem Zimmer Fernseher, Videorecorder, Stereoanlage mit Bose-Sound-System, Zimmersafe, Minibar, Wasserkocher und zwei Telefone – eins davon schnurlos.

Mit Wohltuendem für Körper und Seele ist die großzügige Badelandschaft ein Ort für entspannende Freuden rund um Schönheit und Gesundheit. Erlebnisduschen, Whirlpool, Dampfbad, Sauna und Solarium runden die „Flucht aus dem Alltag" ab. Für sportlich ambitionierte Gäste steht ein Fitnessraum mit modernsten Geräten wie Crosstrainer, Climber, Laufband und Krafttrainer zur Verfügung.

Anspruchsvolle Wellness-Liebhaber erleben mit individuellen Beauty-Arrangements gar karibische Träume, denn exklusiv auf Sylt bietet die Beauty-Farm hochwertige Produkte von Ligne St. Barth an, eine der edelsten und begehrtesten Pflegeserien überhaupt. Dabei kommen nur natürliche Wirkstoffe aus karibischen Pflanzen zum Einsatz, deren heilende und pflegende Eigenschaften schon vor Generationen von den indianischen Ureinwohnern der Insel, den Arawaks, an Ligne St. Barth überliefert wurden. Ganz andere Wohltaten lassen sich bei einem Bad im Meer, in der heilkräftigen Sylter Salzluft oder bei einer Radwanderung erleben. Auch Freunden des „grünen Sports" zeigt sich die Perle der Nordsee beim Spiel auf einem der drei Golfplätze von ihrer schönsten Seite.

Zurück im Hotel sind die erstklassigen Darbietungen aus Küche und Keller ein verlockender Anlass für unbeschwerte Tafelfreuden. Während der Gast noch den viktorianischen Stil des nostalgisch-eleganten Gourmetrestaurants bewundert, liefert der junge Cuisinier Alexandro Pape Kostproben seiner veritablen Kochkunst, die mit einem Michelin-Stern und 17 Gault-Millau-Punkten ihre entsprechende Würdigung findet.

In diesem Rahmen führt das ständig wechselnde Menü vor, was die Saison und die Küchencrew zu bieten haben. Vor allem Fischgerichte in allen Variationen sind die Spezialstrecke des Herdkünstlers. Ob Rotbarbe, Hummer oder Loup de mer – der Feinschmecker erlebt, auf welche wunderbare Weise Geschmack und Würze von Ozeanen und Mittelmeer zelebriert werden. Denn wo sonst werden bei gegrilltem Steinbutt mit

Die lichtdurchflutete Eingangshalle mit Fischaquarellen des Künstlers Tom Drake Bennet.
The light and airy entrance hall with water colours of fish by the artist Tom Drake Bennet.

karamellisierter Gänsestopfleber auf gefüllter Kartoffel-Mousseline mit Barolo-Schalotten oder Atlantik-Hummer in der Karkasse gebraten auf grüner Tomatenmarmelade und Tomatenbutter solch geschmackvolle kulinarische Meeresgeschichten erzählt. Nicht weniger gut das „Ende vom Ochsen" mit Laugenbrezeln gefüllt, Meerrettichmousse und Radicchiokompott. Dazu kredenzt Sommelière Birgitta Blaschko nach sachkundiger Beratung den passenden Tropfen aus der grandiosen Weinauswahl. Vinophile Liebhaber sollten nicht versäumen, der Vinothek in der ersten Etage einen Besuch abzustatten. Auf 70 Quadratmetern offeriert der begehbare Klimaschrank edle Rotweine und feinste Rauchwaren, die man in der stilvollen Raucherlounge genießen kann.

Vornehmlich regionale Gerichte offeriert die Küchenbrigade in der Käpt'n Selmer Stube, wobei das Friesenzimmer mit seinen originalen blauweißen Kacheln und antiken Sitzmöbeln durch landestypischen Charme besticht.

Bestens auf sein Tagwerk eingestimmt wird man bereits frühmorgens mit einem verführerischen Frühstücksbuffet, das von frischen Krabben über Eierspeisen bis zu leckeren Petitessen aus Italien, Frankreich, Skandinavien und Fernost alles bietet, was einen Start in den Tag noch schöner macht.

In der warmen Jahreszeit lockt die feudale Veranda mit Blick über den Yachthafen. Hier lässt sich besonders gut der Aperitif oder Digestif bei einem gemütlichen Plausch einnehmen. Und wer einmal am Nachmittag die köstliche Friesentorte aus der hauseigenen Patisserie genossen hat, mag zwar meinen, ein wenig beschwipst zu sein, hat dafür aber eine neue Sylter Leidenschaft entdeckt.

caramelised pâté de foie gras on stuffed potato mousseline with barolo shallots, or fried Atlantic lobster on a green tomato chutney served with tomato butter? Such tasty dishes tell their own tales of the sea. No less delicious is the rump of ox stuffed with pretzel sticks, a horseradish mousse and stewed radicchio. On consulting sommelière Birgitta Blaschko, a suitable wine from the hotel's vast selection can be served to accompany the food. Wine-lovers shouldn't forget to visit the vinoteque on the first floor. The air-conditioned walk-in repository (750 sq.ft.) stores top quality wines and the very best tobacco products. The Käpt'n Selmer Stube serves mainly regional dishes. The blue and white tiles and antique chairs lend the Frisian room typical local country charm.

Early in the morning guests can prepare themselves for the day's activities with breakfast from the tempting breakfast buffet. Laid out is a wide range of food, from fresh shrimps and egg dishes to delicious snacks from Italy, France, Scandinavia and the Far East. A wonderful start to the day. During the warm season the enormous verandha overlooking the marina is an ideal place for an aperitif or an afterdinner drink and a cosy chat. In the afternoon, anyone who samples the delectable Frisian cake from the hotel's own patisserie may feel a little tipsy, but will have discovered a new passion on Sylt.

Die atemberaubende Schönheit der Bergwelt, Schneesicherheit von Ende November bis Ende April, weite Hänge mit traumhaften Abfahrtmöglichkeiten und nicht zuletzt die exklusive Hotellerie und Gastronomie prägen die beschauliche Atmosphäre in Zürs am Arlberg. Mitten in diesem einzigartigen Winterparadies verwöhnen Elfi Thurnher und ihre Tochter Dr. Beatrice Zarges in ihrem bezaubernden Privathotel ihre anspruchsvollen Gäste.

Ein österreichisches Wintermärchen

An Austrian Winter-fairytale

Text: Sabine Herder • Fotos: Ulrich Helweg

Deep in the Austrian Alps you will find one of the most exclusive wintersport hotels. Thurnhers Alpenhof, a family-run establishment in the peaceful mountainious location of Zürs, is close to heavenly ski slopes where snow is guaranteed from the end of November to the end of April. Thurnhers Alpenhof pampers its guests with superb food, charming accommodation and outstanding service.

Much to the delight of Beatrice Zarges who manages the hotel with her mother, Elfi Thurnher, the American Academy of Hospitality awarded her its 5-star Diamond Award at the 2003 International Tourism Fair in Berlin already for the fifth time. She is the very first woman in Europe which has been honoured with the "Oscar" of the hotel branch, and Thurnhers Alpenhof is the only Austrian hotel ever

Das Lächeln zum Empfang kommt wirklich von Herzen.
The receptionist's smile is genuine.

Natürlich war die Freude groß, als Beatrice Zarges, die gemeinsam mit ihrer Mutter Elfi Thurnher den Alpenhof leitet, im Jahr 2003 auf der ITB in Berlin den „5-Star Diamond Award" der American Academy of Hospitality zum fünften Mal in Folge überreicht bekam. Nicht nur, dass sie als erste Frau in Europa mit dem „Oscar" der Hotelbranche ausgezeichnet wurde, nein, Thurnhers Alpenhof ist auch das einzige österreichische Hotel, das diese begehrte Trophäe sein Eigen nennen kann. Die fünf Ehrungen sind eigentlich nur die Bestätigung einer Philosophie, die schon seit fast vierzig Jahren den besonderen Charme von Thurnhers Alpenhof prägt. Eine Philosophie, in der der Begriff Service kein Relikt längst vergangener Jahrzehnte ist, sondern Tag für Tag von den bestens geschulten Mitarbeitern auf vorbildliche Art und Weise bis ins kleinste Detail mit Leben gefüllt wird – das fängt schon vor der Ankunft an und hört auch bei der Heimreise noch lange nicht auf. Auf 1720 Metern Höhe wird man von einer herrlichen Schneepracht, die von Ende November bis Ende April Skivergnügen pur verspricht, und von zuvorkommenden Mitarbeitern empfangen, deren Lächeln wirklich von Herzen kommt. Das Auto wird geparkt, die Koffer verschwinden fast unmerklich und die verbindliche Begrüßung vermittelt jedem das Gefühl, als Freund zu kommen. Die entwaffnende Freundlichkeit des Serviceteams, von denen viele schon seit Jahren in der Saison in Thurnhers Alpenhof arbeiten, wirkt nie aufgesetzt oder künstlich. Die große Kunst, schon vorab zu ahnen, was der Gast wünscht, und sich die individuellen Gewohnheiten, die akribisch in der Gästekartei gelistet werden, zu merken, dabei aber dezent im Hintergrund zu bleiben, prägt die gastliche Atmosphäre des familiengeführten Privathotels. Automatisierte Abläufe, einhergehend mit Personalabbau, heute leider auch in vielen Top-

Nach einem anstrengenden Skitag schmecken die hausgemachten Torten nochmal so gut. Daneben: An der bestens bestückten Bar klingt ein ereignisreicher Tag stimmungsvoll aus.
After a strenous day of skiing the homemade cakes are even more tastier. Beside: An eventful day draws to a close in the well-stocked bar where there is a tremendous atmosphere.

Hotels üblich, sind für Beatrice Zarges überhaupt kein Thema. Bei ihr steht immer der Mensch im Mittelpunkt – auf der Seite ihrer Gäste genauso wie bei ihren Mitarbeitern.

Ganz im Sinne dieser klassischen Servicephilosophie gilt das Luxusrefugium als eine der ersten Adressen im alpenländischen Raum, als Institution der Gastlichkeit für Gäste mit gehobenen Ansprüchen, die nicht auf den Komfort eines der „Leading Small Hotels of the World" verzichten möchten. Dies belegen nicht nur die fünf „5* Diamond Awards". Die große Zahl der Stammgäste, die immer wieder in „ihren" Alpenhof zurückkehren, ist eine Bestätigung dafür, dass die besondere Servicebereitschaft der Mitarbeiter und die persönliche Ansprache durch die Gastgeberfamilie besonders geschätzt werden. Dass unter den „Wiederholungstätern" viele Prominente sind, ist natürlich kein Zufall. Der beschauliche Ort, einer der schönsten und

to have received this distinction. All awards are clear evidence of the deep commitment of the hotel's owners and staff to service, a tradition which goes back 35 years. From the moment visitors arrive and until after they leave they are the focus of attention. They receive the warmest reception from a highly trained and most obliging staff who are alert to every request and every detail. Your car is parked for your, and you don't have to worry about your luggage because it's immediately taken off your hands. If you wish, it can be unpacked for you and crumpled clothing quickly ironed. The warmth of the welcome immediately makes you feel like a family friend. The kindness of the staff is genuine, in fact many have been doing seasonal work for years at Thurnhers Alpenhof. They are able to sense in advance the wishes of each guest and make notes, yet they remain discreetly in the background. The perfect alliance of warm hospitality and discretion is the most striking feature of this family hotel. Nowadays many hotels, even the best, have had to resort to automated procedures to make up

Im Winter sind die Suiten mit eigenem Kamin natürlich besonders begehrt.
In Winter the suites with the fireplace are the most sought after.

Individualität auch in den komfortablen Bädern.
Individual settings also in each comfortable bathroom.

for serious staff shortages. For Beatrice Zarges this is not an option because the needs of her guests remain paramount. This luxury hotel embodies the old understanding of service. As a top alpine hotel it attracts an elite, guests with sophisticated tastes who expect the comfort and luxury associated with a Leading Small Hotel of the World. Their total satisfaction is reflected in the five 5* Diamond Awards but also in the fact that they return year after year. The hotel's many regulars amongst whom are VIPs, appreciate

mondänsten Wintersportplätze der Welt, die erstklassigen Pisten, auf denen man von Ende November bis Ende April bis zur Hoteltür abschwingen kann, und nicht zuletzt der Charme des Fünf-Sterne-Domizils, in dem sich familiäre Tradition und internationales Flair harmonisch mit dem Komfort von heute und außergewöhnlichen Serviceleistungen verbinden, eröffnen nahezu grenzenlose Möglichkeiten. So auch bei den 40 komfortablen Zimmern und Suiten, die teilweise mit eigener Whirlpool-

wanne und offenem Kamin ausgestattet sind. Kein Raum gleicht dem anderen, nur den großzügigen Zuschnitt und die vielen liebenswerten Details haben sie alle gemeinsam. Dabei findet sich für jeden Geschmack genau das Richtige, mal mediterran inspiriert, mal zurückhaltend-elegant, mal romantisch-verspielt.

Die Winterurlauber, die noch bei Tageslicht die Höhe des Flexenpasses erreichen, sind wirklich zu beneiden, denn bei dem Anblick der glitzernden Schneemassen wird jedem Skifahrer warm ums Herz. Gut, dass der Skipass schon bereitliegt und die im Hotel eingelagerten Skier fit für die neue Saison sind. Selbst um das Gepäck braucht man sich keine Gedanken zu machen. Auf Wunsch werden die Koffer ausgepackt und wenn nötig verknitterte Hemden und Blusen schnell und unbürokratisch übergebügelt. Das nenne ich Urlaub von Anfang an! Sehr zur Freude passionierter Skifahrer liegt der Lift direkt vor der Haustür und „Schlangestehen" ist durch den konsequenten Ausbau der Liftanlagen am Arlberg ein unbekanntes Fremdwort. Ohne Zeitverlust gelangt man auf die weiten Hänge, um allein oder mit Roman, dem kundigen Freizeitbetreuer des Hauses, 260 Kilometer bestens präparierte Pisten, 180 Kilometer ungespurte Pulverschneeabfahrten oder den Snowboard-Fun-Park zu erkunden. Der Arlberg gilt mit seinen 88 Bahnen und Liften, unzähligen Abfahrtsmöglichkeiten bis mitten in die Orte und vielen urigen Hütten als eines der

Von den wunderschön eingedeckten Tischen genießt man eine unvergessliche Sicht auf die tief verschneite Winterlandschaft.
From the beautifully laid and decorated tables you enjoy an unforgettable view to the winter landscape covered by deep snow.

schönsten Skigebiete der Alpen und selbst für langjährige Zürs-Kenner gibt es immer wieder etwas Neues zu entdecken.

Neben dem traumhaften Skigebiet am Arlberg, dem luxuriös behaglichen Ambiente ist die hervorragende Gastronomie eines der zugkräftigsten Argumente, um Gäste hoch auf den Flexenpass zu locken. Unter der Leitung eines

the very personal service offered by the host family and their staff. The mountain location is peaceful and the skiing is marvellous. Zürs is one of the smartest and most beautiful skiing resorts in the world, and its first class ski runs lead right up to the front door of this charming five-star residence. An hotel which combines family tradition, luxury and an international ambience so harmoniously presents limitless possibilities for a unforgettable winter vacation. While each of the 40 luxuriously furnished rooms and suites – some have their own whirlpools and fireplaces – has a different décor, all are spacious and have delightful details. The hotel caters for all tastes, whether the preference is for simple elegance, a more romantic décor or Mediterranean style.

Winter holidaymakers who manage to reach the heights of the Flexen Pass in daylight, are rewarded by the amazing views of sparkling snowfields. Skiers are very well catered for. The hotel obtains the Ski Passes, and skis stored and looked after by the hotel are also available for the new skiing season. The ski lift is right beside the door so there are no queues. On the Arlberg lifts have been systematically developed so visitors reach the broad ski slopes in no time at all. You can go skiing on your own or set out with Roman, the hotel's very knowledgeable Activities' Assistant, to discover the 162 miles of superbly prepared pistes or the 112 miles of trackless ski slopes. There is also the Snowboard Fun Park. Arlberg's 88 funicular railways and ski lifts, the innumerable ski runs which lead right down into the villages and the many rustic mountain lodges, has earnt it a reputation of being one of the most beautiful skiing areas in the whole of the Alps. Even people who know Zürs well are always discovering something new. As well Arlberg's superb skiing and the luxurious ambience, gastronomy is one

Regionaler Touch: gebackene Riesengarnele auf Püree mit grünem Veltinerschaum.
Green Veltin froth lends a regional touch to the baked king prawns on pureé.

Ein Schuss Madeira ist das raffinierte Geheimnis der Kräuterkruste des Lammfilets.
The secret to the herb crust of the filets of lamb is a dash of Madeira.

HIDEAWAYS 181

of the main attractions for visitors to this corner of the Alps. Under the supervision of one of the best known chefs in Austria, a team of cooks serves up the finest cuisine. The morning starts with a breakfast buffet to delight the eyes of every gourmet. Breakfast fans can slaver over a massive spread of high quality sausage, ham, cheeses which can sliced on the spot, freshly-made egg dishes, exotic fruit, a variety of fruit juices, cakes from the hotel's own patisserie, bread and rolls of the highest quality and much else. Mediterranean influence is noticeable in the dinner menu, but its the chef's own creations and authentic Asian dishes which make the cuisine a memorable culinary experience. This is as true of the regular Sunday gala

der bekanntesten Küchenchefs Österreichs fährt das Küchenteam kreative Kulinarien vom Feinsten auf. Und das fängt schon am Morgen mit dem Gourmet-Frühstücksbuffet an, das seinen Zusatz „Gourmet" mit gutem Recht trägt, denn es glänzt mit einer Vielfalt an hochwertiger Wurst, Schinken- und Käsesorten, die vom Stück geschnitten werden, frisch zubereiteten Eierspeisen, exotischem Obstsalat, verschiedenen Fruchtsäften, Kuchen aus der hauseigenen Patisserie, Brot und Brötchen in allerbester Qualität und vielem mehr und bringt die Augen eingefleischter Frühstücksfans zum Leuchten.

Die abendlichen Speisenfolgen verleugnen den Hang zur feinen mediterranen Küche nicht, aber es sind gerade die individuellen Eigenkreationen oder die authentisch asiatisch servierten Zubereitungen, die den Erlebniswert der kulinarischen Genüsse ausmachen. Dies zeigt das sonntägliche Gala-Diner genauso wie der einmal in der Woche stattfindende original

In der Hotelboutique „Little Dream" findet man ein ausgesuchtes Angebot exklusiver Wohnaccessoires.
At the hotel-boutique "Little Dream" someone finds an assorted selection of exclusive home-accessories.

Nicht nur durchgefrorene Skifahrer lockt das Schwimmbad mit 30 Grad warmem Wasser und Gegenstromanlage.
Not only frozen skiers are drawn to the swimming pool with a counter-current and water at 30° centigrade.

österreichische Heurigenabend mit Livemusik. Die Weinkarte, die sich dazu aufblättert, zeigt ein Sortiment ausgesuchter Tropfen, unter denen es so manches Schätzchen zu entdecken gibt.

Die kompetente Weinberatung ist in Thurnhers Alpenhof genauso selbstverständlich wie tausend andere kleine Annehmlichkeiten, deren komplette Auflistung einfach den Rahmen sprengen würde.

dinners as it is for the weekly Heurigenabend, an evening when this year's wine is served to the sound of live music. Quite a number of little treasures can be found among the selected wines on the wine list. Informed advice on the wines is as much part of the service as are all the little luxuries at Thurnhers Alpenhof far too numerous to mention.

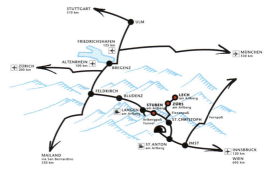

Die „guten Geister" des Hauses: Alois und Johann kümmern sich einfach um alles.
The moving spirits of the household – Alois and Johann see to everything.

HIDEAWAYS 183

Räumen Glanz und Klasse. Ob Prominenten, Golf- und Sportbegeisterten, Feinschmeckern oder Wellnessurlaubern – jedem Gast vermitteln die 71 großzügigen Zimmer und Suiten mit gemütlichem Mobiliar, antiken Charakterstücken und Marmorbädern Luxus und Behaglichkeit in höchstem Maße. Klimaanlage? Minibar? Sat-TV? Telefon, Fax- und Internetanschluss? Kein Thema. Wer gewohnt ist, Ansprüche zu stellen, der kommt im Schloss Seefels auf seine Kosten. Charmante Gastfreundschaft begleitet die Gäste jederzeit durch's Haus, das von Direktor Egon Haupt gut auf Kurs gehalten wird und nun entsprechend mit der begehrten „Moët & Chandon Welcome Trophy 2003" für unter anderem konstanten First-Class-Service ausgezeichnet wurde. Befragt nach den Annehmlichkeiten seiner Luxusherberge muss Egon Haupt nicht lange überlegen: „Es ist neben der Atmosphäre und Ausstattung, der einmaligen Lage, den luxuriösen Wellnesslandschaften und den erstklassigen Darbietungen aus Küche und Keller der Service als wichtigstes und persönlichstes Aushängeschild eines Hotels."

Einen entscheidenden Beitrag zum Rundum-wohl-Fühlen leistet auch die feine

The charming ambience of the interiors reveal a sound sense of colour and form, stylistic confidence, and an inherent ability to coordinate. Exquisite materials, quality fabrics, and the antiques and period furniture lend the place gloss and class. Whether you are a VIP, a golf or sports' fan, a bon viveur or a health & fitness enthusiast, the 71 generously appointed and comfortably furnished rooms and suites with antiques full of character and marble bathrooms, the guest is surrounded by the highest degree of luxury and comfort. Air-conditioning? Minibar? Sat TV? Telephone, fax and Internet access? No problem. Guests who are used to sophisticated living certainly get value for money here.
Charm and hospitality accompany the guest throughout the hotel. The steady course steered by General Manager Egon Haupt, has now been rewarded with "Moët & Chandon's Welcome Trophy 2003"

Die Zimmer und Suiten erhalten durch das geschmackvolle Design ihren ganz persönlichen Charme.

The tasteful décor lends the rooms and suites a very personal charm.

Herrlich geht der Blick vom Porto Bello auf den Wörthersee.
Wonderful views of Porto Bello beside Lake Wörther.

Topfendessert „Schloss Seefels".
"Schloss Seefels" quark dessert.

Chefkoch Hermann Andritsch steht für kulinarische Höhenflüge am Wörthersee.
Head chef Hermann Andritsch produces haute cuisine at Wörthersee.

for, among other things, a constantly first class service. Asked about the hotel's amenities Egon Haupt doesn't need much time to reply. "As well as the whole atmosphere, the equipment and the exclusive location, there is the luxurious health & beauty zone and a first class cuisine and wine list. The service is the most important and most personal aspect which advertises the hotel."

A considerable contribution to creating a general feeling of well-being is the attraction of the fine cuisine, an experience to relish for foodies. Only the very best ingredients are used when cooking, high-grade olive oil, fresh herbs and products from carefully selected producers. At the La Terrasse gourmet restaurant the chef, Hermann Andritsch, produces the finest cuisine evening after evening to delight his guests who sit in candlelight overlooking the Lake.

Cuisine, deren Zauber zu einem lustvollen Schlemmererlebnis für Genießer wird. Gekocht wird nur mit allerbesten Zutaten, hochwertigem Olivenöl, frischen Kräutern und Produkten von ausgesuchten Erzeugern. Im Gourmetrestaurant La Terrasse läuft Küchenmeister Hermann Andritsch allabendlich zur Höchstform auf, um seine Gäste bei Kerzenschein und Seeblick mit neuen lukullischen Hochgenüssen zu begeistern. Dazu empfiehlt Sommelier Johannes Doujak stets den passenden edlen Tropfen aus dem Weinkeller mit seinem außergewöhnlich exklusiven Angebot. Neben dem kulinarischen Herzstück mit 15 Gault-Millau-Punkten hat der Feinschmecker die Wahl zwischen den Restaurants Orangerie mit österreichischer und internationaler Küche und dem Strandrestaurant Porto Bello mit italienisch-mediterranen Zubereitungen und erstklassigen Fischgerichten als Spezialstrecke während der Saison. Als wunderbarer Ausklang des Abends und denkbar schöner Übergang zur Nacht bietet sich die Schlossbar an. Das Barteam verwöhnt mit phantasievollen Cocktails und einer großen Auswahl an internationalen Zigarren.

Am nächsten Tag entführt das neu gestaltete Seefels Felsen Spa dann in ein Wellnessreich des Wohlgefühls. In der 1000 Quadratmeter großen Oase rückt der Alltag rasch in weite Ferne. Nach einem erfrischenden Bad im Innen- und Außenpool oder im

einzigartigen beheizten 26 °C Grad warmen Seebad lädt die mit römischen Säulen verzierte und mit Luxusliegen ausgestattete Panoramaterrasse zur Erholung. Für absolutes Relaxen sorgen die großzügige Saunalandschaft mit Kräutersauna, Damensauna, gemischter Sauna und finnischer See-Sauna. Dampfbad und Laconium sowie Erlebnisduschen und Solarium sind weitere Highlights. Sportlich aktive Gäste können sich außerdem im Fitnessraum an den modernsten Life-Fitness-Geräten wieder in Form bringen. Wahrhaft entspannende Stunden erlebt man durch das professionell geschulte Massage- und Beautyteam des Seefels-Beauty-Vital-Centers. Zahlreiche Arrangements, wohltuende Massagen, Thalasso-Anwendungen, luxuriöse Bäder und „Beauty Permanent Make-up" nach der bekannten REZA-Methode kommen zur Anwendung. Neu und einzigartig für Südösterreich ist das ausgewogene Angebot von Anti-Aging-Therapien.

Wer Lust hat, beginnt einen sportlich geprägten Tag auf den Tennis-Sandplätzen oder relaxt am Privatstrand mit Liegewiese. Die Motorboote der Wasserskischule laden zu Touren über den Wörthersee, zu einer Runde Wasserski oder zum Paragliding ein. Nicht nur die hoteleigene Bootsmarina und die zahlreichen Freizeitmöglichkeiten machen das Hotel Schloss Seefels zu einer begehrten Adresse: Liebhaber des Golfsportes haben die Auswahl

To accompany the food, sommelier Johannes Doujak can always produce a suitable wine from the cellar where his exclusive wines are stored. As well as the haute cuisine restaurant awarded 15 Gault Millau points, gourmets have a choice of restaurants: the Orangerie which serves an Austrian and a global cuisine and the Porto Bello beach restaurant where you can get Italian-Mediterranean dishes and first class fish courses served as a speciality during the season. As a wonderful end to the evening the Schloss Bar serves nightcaps to bring the day to close. The bar staff pamper you with ingenious cocktails and a large selection of international cigars. The next day, the recently designed Seefels Felsen (rocks) Spa seduces you into realm of well-being. In the oasis occupying 10,764 sq. feet, you can leave the daily round far behind. After a refreshing swim in the indoor or outdoor pool, or in the unique seawater bath heated to 26 °C, you can relax on one of the luxurious loungers on the panorama terrace, which has decorative Roman pillars.

Gehobenes Ambiente im „La Terrasse".
Exclusive ambience on "La Terrasse".

Entspannung pur im Panorama- und Felsenruheraum.
Pure relaxation in the panorama rest room.

The spacious sauna area with a herbal sauna, a ladies' sauna, a mixed sauna and a Finnish lake sauna help you to relax completely. Other attractions are the steam bath and laconium, and the adventure showers and solarium. The more sport's minded can get back into shape in a gym equipped with state-of-the-art equipment. You can enjoy hours of real relaxation with the help of the professional staff of masseurs and beauticians at the Seefels "Beauty Vital Center". It provides numerous packages, feel-good massage, thalasso treatment, luxurious baths, beauty treatment and permanent make-up following the famous REZA method. An exciting innovation for southern Austria is the balanced range of anti-aging treatment. Those who fancy it can begin the

zwischen sieben hochklassigen Golfplätzen in unmittelbarer Umgebung.

Fünf Minuten dauert die Überfahrt mit dem Motorboot zum Golfplatz Dellach am Südufer des Wörthersees. Der 1927 von Graf Lato Hoyos und Major Foster gegründete KGC Dellach steht für Golfsport im klassischen Sinn und ist der älteste und traditionsreichste Club Kärntens. Die 18-Loch-Anlage bietet eine leicht gewellte Struktur mit mäßigen Steigungen sowie außergewöhnliche landschaftliche Reize. Blumenwiesen, Wald und See ergeben eine Naturkulisse, die ihresgleichen sucht. Herrliche Ausblicke und einsame, ruhige Spielbahnen laden zu einer der schönsten Runden in Österreich ein.

Nicht weniger attraktiv zeigt sich die drei Kilometer von Pörtschach entfernt liegende Golfanlage Moosburg-Pörtschach. Mit gut 6 000 Meter ist einer der längsten Plätze des Landes entstanden. Das Design im Einklang mit der Natur wurde von der „European Society of Golf Course Architects" mit dem

höchsten Preis, dem „Premier European Golf Course", ausgezeichnet. Die großzügige 18-Loch-Anlage mit Par 72 gibt dank recht breiter Fairways auch dem Durchschnittsspieler eine faire Chance, für Profis stellen die geschickt platzierten Hindernisse knifflige Aufgaben dar. Schafft ein Spieler bis zum neunten Loch ein „Eagle", so kann er an der hier befindlichen „Eagle-Bar" darauf anstoßen. Nach dem 18. Loch geht es einige Meter zurück, vorbei an der Zielgolfanlage mit acht verschiedenen Abschlägen und einem Pitching- und Putting-Green, zum Clubhaus mit Restaurant und wunderschöner Terrasse. Selbstverständlich erhalten die Seefels-Gäste auf allen benachbarten Plätzen „Preferred Tee-Times".

Gastgeber mit glänzender Crew: Direktor Egon Haupt.
Host with a brilliant staff:
General Manager Egon Haupt.

packages, feel-good massage, thalasso treatment, luxurious baths, beauty treatment and permanent make-up following the famous REZA method. An exciting innovation for southern Austria is the balanced range of anti-aging treatment. Those who fancy it can begin the day's activities on the sand tennis court, or relax on the hotel's private beach which has its on sunbathing lawn. The motorboats belonging to the water skiing school make it possible to tour Lake Wörthersee, go water skiing, or go paragliding. Yet, it is not only the hotel's own marina and the numerous leisure facilities which make the Hotel Schloss Seefels a popular address. Golf-lovers have a choice of seven superb golf courses in the vicinity. Crossing by motorboat to the Delach golf Course on the south bank. The KGC Dellach was founded in 1927 by Graf Lato Hoyos and Major Foster and on it a traditional game of golf is played. It is the oldest and most traditional Club in Carinthia. The 18-hole course has a gently undulating surface with moderate rises and unusually beautiful scenery. Flowery-strewn meadows, forests and lakes make for a

landscape unmatched elsewhere. The wonderful views and the empty peaceful fairways seem to invite you to play one of the most beautiful rounds in Austria. No less attractive is the Moosburg-Pörtschach course under two miles away. Its length, 6,561 yards makes it the longest in Austria. The design of the course, which flows easily into the surrounding countryside, has been awarded first prize by the European Society of Golf Course Architects which rated it "Premier European Golf Course".
The broad fairways of the generously-laid-out 18-hole course, Par 72, give the average player a fair chance. The cleverly placed obstacles pose tricky problems for the professionals. If a player manages the ninth hole with an eagle, he can drink to it at the "Eagle Bar" at this very spot.
After the 18th, a few yards past the practice range which has eight different tees and a pitching-and-putting green, is the clubhouse which has a restaurant and a wonderful terrace. It goes without saying that Seefels guests also enjoy "preferred tee times" at all the neighbouring courses.

Ganz bequem und exklusiv erreichen Golffreunde den Golfplatz Dellach mit dem hoteleigenen Motorboot.
Golf fans are transported to the Dellach Golf Course by exclusive and convenient means, the hotel's own motor boat.

Extraordinary!
SANDY LANE

Etwas abseits von den übrigen Antillenschwestern präsentiert sich das kleine Barbados als eine der schönsten und friedlichsten Inseln der Karibik. Die exklusivste und außergewöhnlichste Art, diese beschauliche Postkartenidylle in vollen Zügen zu genießen, ist das Preferred Hotel Sandy Lane am nahezu endlosen St. James Beach.

Slightly isolated from the rest of the Lesser Antilles is Barbados, one of the most beautiful and friendliest of the Caribbean islands. The most exclusive and unusual way to enjoy this peaceful postcard idyll to the full is to stay at the Preferred Hotel Sandy Lane near the virtually endless St. James Beach.

Text: Sabine Herder • Fotos: Stefan Fister

Spektakuläre Sonnenuntergänge und feinste Cuisine sind die Trümpfe des Gourmetrestaurants L'Acajou.

Spectacular sunsets and exquisite cuisine are the trump cards of the L'Acajou gourmet restaurant.

Für Nachtschwärmer: The Monkey Bar.

Popular with night birds – the Monkey Bar.

Eye-Catcher im neu gebauten Spa- und Shopping-Center: das herrschaftliche Treppenhaus.

The magnificent stairwell is an eye-catcher in the recently-built spa and shopping centre.

Die rund 260 000 Bajans, so nennen sich die Bewohner der kleinen Antilleninsel Barbados, können sich wirklich glücklich schätzen: Ihre Heimat – mit 34 km Länge und 22 km Breite nicht gerade ein Inselriese – verfügt über 110 km strahlendweiße Sandstrände. Das Meer zeigt sich auf der Atlantikseite tiefblau, auf der karibischen dagegen jadegrün. Die warmen Wassertemperaturen – immer über der 25-Grad-Grenze – haben farbenprächtige Korallenriffe hervorgebracht und animieren zu jeder Art Wassersport. Und die beständig wehenden Passatwinde sorgen das ganze Jahr für angenehme Abkühlung. Doch nicht nur die Natur meint es gut mit den immer lächelnden Bajans. Während andere Inseln über Jahrhunderte hinweg den Kolonialmächten als Spielball dienten, ist Barbados das einzige Eiland, das ausschließlich in der Hand einer Kolonialmacht, England, war. Das Bildungswesen und die Umgangsformen des unabhängigen Mitglieds des Commonwealth sind bis heute britisch geprägt. Und obwohl Barbados die dicht besiedelste Insel der Karibik ist, läuft das Leben in beschaulichen Bahnen und die Kriminalitätsrate ist nicht einmal erwähnenswert. An ihrem Glück lassen die liebenswerten Bajans jeden Besucher teilhaben und sie wirken mit ihrem „Don't-worry-be-happy"-Lebensgefühl einfach ansteckend.

Nördlich der Hauptstadt Bridgetown ist dieses Lebensgefühl zu Stein geworden. Im Resort Sandy Lane, das zu den Preferred Hotels gehört, erlebt man exklusive und unbeschwerte Urlaubsfreuden von der ersten bis zur letzten Minute. Am nahezu endlosen St. James Beach sammelt die Seele magische Momente wie seltene Muscheln: wenn die Sonne spektakulär im Meer versinkt; der Platinmond sein Licht über den mehlfeinen Strand legt und der Wassermann mit seinen Diamanten spielt; die

The roughly 260,000 Bajans, the inhabitants of the small island of Barbados in the Lesser Antilles, really can count themselves lucky. Their homeland – 21 miles long and 13 miles wide isn't exactly a huge place, but has over 68 miles of pure white sandy beaches. The sea on the Atlantic side is deep blue, yet on the Caribbean side it is jade green. The temperature of the warm water – always over 25 °C – has produced bright coral reefs and is ideal for all manner of water sports. The constantly blowing trade winds have a cooling effect all the year round. However, it isn't only nature which has been kind to the ever-smiling Bajans. While other islands changed

geschulten Hände der Wellness-Expertinnen die Energiezentren des Körpers öffnen und man in weichen Kissen auf Wolke 7 schwebt. Und spätestens wenn die fröhlichen Rhythmen erstklassiger Bands die sternenklare Nacht erfüllen, spürt man die besondere Aura der Hotellegende auf Barbados.

Schon seit den frühen sechziger Jahren machte das luxuriöse Domizil von sich reden und zog anspruchsvolle Reisende, darunter jede Menge Prominenz, in seinen Bann. Um den ständig steigenden Ansprüchen zu genügen, wurde die gesamte Anlage 1998 abgetragen und in drei Jahren nach den Originalplänen wieder neu aufgebaut. Die gelungene Architektur aus hellem Korallengestein duckt sich unter das grüne Dach der Tropenvegetation, das neue Gebäude wurde um die im Laufe der Jahrzehnte gewachsene Flora herumgebaut und empfängt seine Gäste mit zurückhaltender Eleganz und viel Raum für Privatsphäre. In der Lobby und den öffentlichen Bereichen ist der Blick auf das Farbenspiel der Karibischen See genauso allgegenwärtig wie in den 112 luxuriösen Zimmern und Suiten.

hands between the colonial powers like playthings for centuries, Barbados is the only island which was held by one power alone, England. The education system and social behaviour of the citizens of this independent member of the Commonwealth remain British to this day.
Although Barbados is the most densely populated of the Caribbean Islands, life is ordered and peaceful, and the crime figures are not even worth mentioning. The kindly Bajans draw everyone into their own happiness and their don't-worry-be-happy-philosophy is catching.
North of the capital, Bridgetown, this zest for life has been set in stone. At the Sandy Land resort which belongs to the Preferred Hotels, you experience what it is to

Schöner kann ein Tag nicht beginnen!
A day can't begin any better than this!

Abwechslungsreiche Frische-Küche und regionale Spezialitäten speist man im Restaurant Bajan Blue direkt am Strand.
The Bajan Blue Restaurant on the beach serves a variety of fresh dishes and regional specialities.

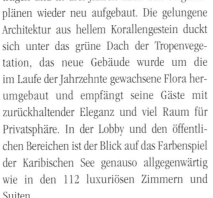

Nach Stationen in den besten Restaurants in Paris und London „verschlug" es Fredrick Forster nach Barbados.
Fredrick Forster moved to Barbados after posts at top restaurants in Paris and London.

Das gesamte Resort wurde nach Originalplänen aus den 60-er Jahren wieder aufgebaut.
The whole resort has undergone major reconstruction and rebuilt to the original 1960s footprint.

Direkt am Strand schmiegt sich das Preferred Hotel dezent unter das grüne Dach der tropischen Bäume.
This elegant hotel nestles beneath a green canopy of tropical treetops.

have an exclusive and untroubled holiday. On the virtually endless St. James Beach, the soul can revel in magic moments as one might in rare shells, such as when the sun sets spectacularly beneath the horizon and the platinum moon shines on the powdery fine sandy beach lying beneath a sky glittering with diamonds. Moments when experienced hands of a wellness expert seek the body's energy centres while one reclines on the soft cushions of cloud nine. At the very latest you experience the special atmosphere of this hotel legend

Nach genauer Besichtigung seiner ganz privaten Wohlfühlinsel fällt es einem fast schwer, die perfekt eingerichteten Wohnräume wieder zu verlassen. Die Architekten haben wirklich an alles gedacht. Große, einladende Betten mit unzähligen weichen Kissen sind genauso obligatorisch wie mondäne Bäder, edle Natursteinfußböden, die eigene Terrasse/Balkon und Hightech-Equipment. Die zentral installierten Panels – über die man vom Licht über das Airconditioning bis zu den Vorhängen fast alles steuern kann – bieten ein Höchstmaß an Bequemlichkeit. Ein riesiger Flachbildfernseher, DVD-Player (eine große Auswahl CDs und DVDs kann man kostenlos in der Bibliothek leihen), E-Mail und Internet-Anschluss, Fax und ISDN-Telefon versprechen Multimedia-Spaß und im Bad gehören Whirlpool, Wellnessdusche und ein zusätzliches Telefon zur Grundausstattung.

Don't worry be happy! Dieser Devise scheinen sich auch der persönliche Butler und die übrigen professionell geschulten Sandy-Lane-Service-Mitarbeiter verpflichtet zu fühlen. Mit einem Lächeln, das wirklich von Herzen kommt, übernehmen sie das Ein- und Auspacken des Gepäcks, bringen die gewünschte Tageszeitung, richten das Zimmer zweimal täglich, putzen Schuhe, servieren rund um die Uhr Getränke und Speisen und selbst ausgefallene Wünsche werden stets mit einem Lächeln erledigt. Ein Rundum-

Die warmen Wassertemperaturen animieren zu jeder Art von Wassersport.
The warmth of the water encourages every kind of water sport.

Verwöhnprogramm, an dem es wirklich nichts auszusetzen gibt und das deutlich macht: Dieses Resort glänzt mit mehr als fünf Sternen und macht dem erlauchten Kreis der Preferred Hotels alle Ehre. In einem der besten Hotels der Welt kommt natürlich auch jeder Feinschmecker auf seine Kosten. Küchenchef Fredrick Forster, den es nach Stationen in den besten Restaurants in Paris und London nach Barbados „verschlug", zelebriert in der eleganten Atmosphäre des Gourmetrestaurants L'Acajou kulinarische Kunst auf höchstem Niveau. Wer es lieber etwas ungezwungener mag, speist abwechslungsreiche Frische-Küche und regionale Spezialitäten im Restaurant Bajan Blue direkt am Strand.

on Barbados when the air is filled with the cheerful rhythms of first class bands.

Ever since the 1960s, this luxurious hotel has been a talking point and has been attracting distinguish visitors, including many celebrities. In order to meet increasing demands, the whole place was razed to the ground in 1998 and successfully rebuilt to the original architectural plans. The hotel is built of light coralstone and nestles beneath a canopy of tropical vegetation. The new building has been designed around the plants which have been flourishing for years, and welcomes its guests to understated elegance and private space. The lobby, the public areas, and the 112 luxurious rooms and suites all afford views of the kaleidoscope of colours that is the Caribbean. After close inspection of one's very private accommodation it isn't easy to venture out again. The architects really have thought of everything. Large, inviting beds with numerous soft pillows are as much of a fixture as the smart bathroom, the high-grade natural stone floors, your private terrace or balcony and the hi-tech equipment. The centrally-installed panel from which everything from lights and air-conditioning to the curtains can be remote-controlled, is the last word in convenience. A giant wide-screen DVD-player (the library has a large selection of CDs and DVDs for loan), E-mail and Internet connection, fax and ISDN telephone, are provided for your multi-media entertainment. In the bathroom the whirlpool, a wellness shower and an additional telephone are all part of the basic amenities. Don't worry, be happy! This appears to be the general attitude of the trained Sandy Lane staff. With a broad smile which really comes from the heart they unpack and pack the luggage, deliver your daily newspaper, see to your room twice a day, clean shoes, serve drinks and meals around the clock, and even fulfil the most unusual request with a smile. It's quite obvious that this is indeed an all-embracing pamper regime which lacks for nothing. The resort sparkles with more than five stars, and certainly does credit to that elite group of hotels which is a member of Preferred Hotels.

Der Blick über das Meer ist auf den drei Golfcourses allgegenwärtig.
The view across the sea is on to the three golf courses.

Die riesige Poolanlage lässt die Herzen eingefleischter Wasserratten höher schlagen.
The enormous pool area delights and excites all who are keen on the water.

Exklusive Materialien und dezente Farben prägen die Wohlfühlatmosphäre in den Suiten.

Exclusive fabrics and discreet colours are crucial elements of the feel-good atmosphere in the suites.

Obviously, bon vivants are also well served at one of the best hotels in the world. Chef Fredrick Forster who moved to Barbados after posts in top restaurants in Paris and London, celebrates a culinary art of the highest standard in the elegant atmosphere of the L'Acajou gourmet restaurant. Those favouring something lessformal can eat at the Bajan Blue restaurant on the beach which serves a variety of fish dishes

Doch es sind nicht nur die hervorragende Küche, der perfekte Service, die einmalige Lage und die wunderschöne Architektur, die den außergewöhnlichen Zauber des Sandy Lane ausmachen. Das breit gefächerte Angebot für sportlich aktive und wellnessorientierte Urlauber sucht in der Karibik seinesgleichen. Fünfundvierzig vom renommierten Golfplatzarchitekten Tom Fazio designte Löcher auf den drei (!) hoteleigenen Golfplätzen bieten Liebhabern des grünen Sports alle Möglichkeiten und selbst erfahre-

ne Spieler finden auf den sehr modern ausgestatteten Meisterschaftsplätzen ihre Herausforderung. Das professionell geführte Wassersportzentrum animiert zum Tauchen, Surfen, Segeln oder Wasserski. Und die riesige Poollandschaft mit großem Wasserfall und Poolbar entpuppt sich als ein wahres Paradies für Wasserratten.

Der Pool und das Spa-Center sind im Zuge des Wiederaufbaus des legendären Resorts neu hinzugekommen. Die Zahl der Superlative für das herrliche Gebäude und

Über die Panels lassen sich alle Hightech-Raffinessen fernsteuern.

All the hi-tech equipment can be remote-controlled from the panels.

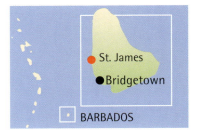

das Angebot der Treatments für Body & Soul ist schier unbegrenzt. Schon das herrschaftliche Treppenhaus, das den Spa und die exklusiven Ladengeschäfte miteinander verbindet, ist überwältigend. Die Treppen hinab lustwandelt man zu den verschiedenen Therapieräumen und den außergewöhnlichen Spa-Suiten, die zum Teil über einen eigenen Garten und Whirlpool verfügen. Unter der Leitung von Brigitte Laurayne spielt sich hier ein modernes Märchen ab – ausgerichtet auf Revitalisierung von Körper, Geist und Seele, abgestimmt auf Entspannung und luxuriöse Erholung.

Und so drehen sich allabendlich beim Cocktail in der Monkey Bar viele Gespräche um die exklusiven Treatments und die Wahl des ultimativen Entspannungkicks erhitzt die Gemüter.

Nur die Gäste, die am nächsten Tag abreisen müssen, halten sich zurück; ihnen schwant schon jetzt, dass erst viele Wochen ins Land gehen müssen, bis ihre Sandy-Lane-Sehnsucht wenigstens etwas abgeklungen sein wird.

Zwischen den Anwendungen relaxt man im eigenen Pool des Spa-Centers.
One can relax between treatment sessions beside the Spa Centre's own pool.

and local specialities. Yet, it isn't just the superb cuisine, the perfect service, the unique location and the wonderful architecture which make the magic of Sandy Lane. The broad range of activities for sports' and wellness enthusiasts has no parallel elsewhere in the Caribbean. Forty-five of the golf holes designed by the golf architect Tom Fazio, across the three golf courses owned by the hotel provide golf lovers with every opportunity. Even experienced players find the latest championship courses challenging.

The professionally managed water sports' centre makes one want to go diving, surfing, sailing and water-skiing. The huge pool area which has a big waterfall and pool bar is simply paradise for those who love the water.

The pool and the spa centre are new additions to this legendary resort, having been added during the hotel's major reconstruction programme. There is no limit to the superlatives needed to describe the beautiful building and the treatment it offers for body and spirit. Even the stairwell which links the spa and the exclusive shops is awesome. One glides down the stairs to the various therapy rooms and the outstanding amazing spa suites, some of which have their own garden and whirlpool. Under the management of Brigitte Laurayne, a modern fairy tale is taking place – focused on the revitalization of body, mind and spirit balanced with relaxation and recuperation.

Each evening over cocktails in the Monkey Bar, obviously the conversation often turns to the treatment, and the question of exactly which kind is the ultimate for relaxation often leads to a lively exchange of views.

Only the guests who have to leave the next day are a little subdued. They sense that once they are gone many weeks will have to pass before their yearnings for Sandy Lane begin to fade.

Direkt vor der eigenen Terrasse zeigt sich das Karibische Meer von seiner schönsten Seite.
Viewed from the terrace, the Caribbean at its most beautiful.

Choose your paradise!

MUSTIQUE

Wenn es auf dem Globus ein Fleckchen Erde gibt, das den Titel „tropisches Urlaubsparadies" verdient, dann das Inselchen Mustique. Obwohl schon der Name allein Bilder magischer Schönheit heraufbeschwört, wurde das karibische Eiland vor allem als Feriendomizil namhafter Persönlichkeiten bekannt. In ihren traumhaften Privatvillen können Luxustraveller die Karibik von ihrer exklusivsten Seite kennen lernen.

If there is a spot on the face of the globe which deserves to be called a tropical paradise, it is the tiny island of Mustique. Although the name itself conjures up images of magical beauty, this Caribbean island is known above all as the place where the rich and famous spend their vacations. In their fantastic private villas, luxury class travellers are only familiar with the island's most exclusive side.

Text: Sabine Herder
Fotos: Mustique Company

Villa Blue Moon

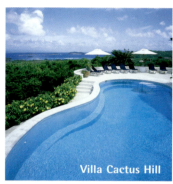

Villa Cactus Hill

Umsäumt von weißen Stränden, umgeben von türkisfarbenem Wasser – ein tropisches Urlaubsparadies.

Ringed by pure white beaches, set in turquoise water – a tropical paradise.

Villa Cactus Hill

Jeder, der sich die Zeit nimmt, einmal seine ganz geheimen Sehnsüchte zu erforschen, sieht sich durch ein türkisfarbenes Korallenmeer segeln. Es ist warm, aber eine leichte Brise sorgt für Abkühlung. Voran eine kleine Insel. Man watet durch badewannenwarmes Wasser an einen schneeweißen Strand, das Rauschen der Wellen und der Palmen im Ohr. Unter dem tropischen, sattgrünen Blätterdach eine Quelle, die der Seele „Willkommen daheim!" zuflüstert. Auf der Suche nach dem verlorenen Paradies weisen uns unsere Träume den Weg. Inseln symbolisieren den Gegenentwurf zum hektischen Alltag. Dabei hat jeder ein fest verankertes Insel-Idealbild vor Augen: Überschaubar ohne komplexe Infrastruktur; umsäumt von weißen Stränden; umgeben von türkisfarbenem Wasser; sich im Wind wiegende Palmen, viel Raum für Privatsphäre und freundliche, stets lächelnde Bewohner.

Wenn es auf dem Globus ein Fleckchen Erde gibt, das diesem Traumideal entspricht und verdient, als „tropisches Urlaubsparadies" betitelt zu werden, dann das Inselchen Mustique. Das gerade einmal zwölf Quadratkilometer große karibische Eiland gehört im Bereich der Kleinen Antillen zu den Grenadinen, an denen der Tourismus bisher weitgehend vorbeigegangen ist.

Obwohl schon allein der wohlklingende Name Bilder von magischer Schönheit heraufbeschwört, machte die Privatinsel vor allem als exklusiver Urlaubsort international

Anyone who ever took time to reflect on his most secret longings, sees himself sailing across the turquoise waters between coral islands. It is warm, but there is a light cooling breeze. Ahead, a small island. One is wading through the lukewarm water towards a snow-white beach and swaying palms to the sound of the surf. Beneath the lush green tropical canopy is a spring whispering "welcome home!" the soul. It is our dreams which show us the way in our search for paradise lost. Islands symbolize the very opposite of our hectic daily lives. Yet, each of us harbours a fixed notion of our ideal island. Set in turquoise water, it should have swaying palms and be ringed by pure white beaches. A manageable size with no complex infrastructure, the ideal island would offer plenty of privacy and have ever-smiling inhabitants.

If there is a spot on the face of the globe which perfectly fits this description, it is Mustique. This tiny tropical Caribbean island paradise which is only approx. 4,5 square miles in area, is in the South Grenadines.

bekannter Persönlichkeiten von sich reden. Für die gekrönten Häupter Europas ist Mustique ebenso ein Zufluchtsort wie für die großen Stars aus der Film- und Musikszene. Weit weg von Paparazzi und Autogrammjägern, können sie auf einer der schönsten und sichersten Inseln der Karibik unbeschwerte Tage verbringen.

Ihren Status als Privatinsel und Entwicklung zur Promi-Insel verdankt Mustique ursprünglich Colin Tennant. Der Spross einer schottischen Industriellendynastie, der die Insel 1958 käuflich erwarb, hatte die Vision, Mustique zu einem Feriendomizil für seine aristokratischen Freunde zu machen. Der Durchbruch kam, als er 1960 Prinzessin Margret von England zu ihrer Hochzeit ein großes Grundstück schenkte und sie darauf eine private Villa errichten ließ. Der Prinzessin folgten andere europäische Adlige, Modefürsten, jede Menge Stars, Politiker und Industrielle. Dem behutsamen Umgang mit der Natur und dem kontinuierlichen Ausbau der Infrastruktur – Flughafen, Wassersportzentrum, moderne Arztpraxis, ein erstklassiges Restaurant und die legendäre Bar Basil's sind genauso selbstverständlich wie ein breit gefächertes Sportangebot mit mehreren Tennisplätzen sowie Gestüt, Physiotherapeuten und ein professionelles Beautycenter – ist es zu verdanken, dass sich inzwischen 85 exklusive Villen über die Insel verteilen. 55 von ihnen werden heute über die Mustique Company, die die Insel heute verwaltet, an Luxustraveller vermietet. Jedes Anwesen ist von renommierten Architekten und Designern ganz nach dem Geschmack des jeweiligen Besitzers eingerichtet worden und entpuppt sich besonders für Liebhaber außergewöhnlicher Wohnträume als wahre Offenbarung. Das eigentliche Geheimnis der Legende Mustique liegt vor allem in den vielschichtigen Facetten der unterschiedlichen architektonischen Stilrichtungen, den tropischen Gärten, den riesigen Terrassen, den traumhaften Aussichten und der perfekten Gastfreundschaft. Egal wie groß, ob mit zwei Schlafzimmern oder mit sieben, jede Villa vermittelt das Gefühl, bei Freunden zu Gast zu sein und die fleißigen Hausangestellten, die seit eh und je ein fester Bestandteil der Mustique-Philosophie sind, sorgen sich rund um die Uhr um das Wohl der Gäste. Den unverwechselbaren Charakter und außergewöhnlichen Charme beweisen die neuen oder die in den letzten beiden Jahren renovierten Villen besonders eindrucksvoll.

Villa Clonsilla

Villa Clonsilla

Die Essenz der Mustique-Philosophie: Großzügigkeit und Exklusivität.

The essence of the Mustique philosophy: Spaciousness and hospitality.

Villa Clonsilla

Villa Hibiscus

Die Architektur der Villa Hibiscus erinnert an die Palazzi der Toskana.

The architecture of the Villa Hibiscus is reminiscent of the palaces Tuscany.

Even the lovely name of this private island conjures up images of enchanting beauty. It has gained its reputation primarily for providing an exclusive hideaway for world famous celebrities. But Mustique is also a place which attracts the crowned heads of Europe as well as stars from the worlds of music, film and entertainment. Far from the paparazzi and autograph-hunters, they find they really can relax on one of the safest and most beautiful islands in the Caribbean. Mustique's status as a private island developed for the rich and famous is entirely due to Colin Tennant. The son of an old Scottish industrialist family, he purchased the island in 1958 and developed it into a holiday refuge for his aristocratic friends. The breakthrough came in 1960 when he gave Princess

Villa Blue Moon

Die spektakuläre Aussicht über die Britannia Bay auf die Nord-Grenadinen ist nur einer der herausragenden Pluspunkte dieser luxuriösen Villa in prädestinierter Lage. Gebaut aus edlen Hölzern, glänzt das Interieur mit viel Holz, Natursteinen, antikem Marmor und venezianischem Stuck. Die vier überaus luxuriösen Schlafräume verfügen über romantische

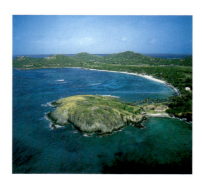

Schlafzimmer mit grandiosen Aussichten.
Bedroom with grandiose views.

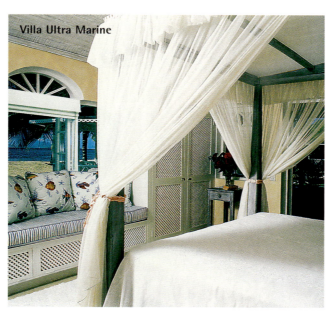

Villa Ultra Marine

Villa Ultra Marine

Himmelbetten aus Holz, privaten Balkon und je zwei Bäder. Der weitläufige Wohnraum mit einer interessant bestückten Bibliothek bietet Rückzugsmöglichkeiten und am großzügigen Pool finden acht Personen bequem Platz. Blue Moon reflektiert bis ins letzte Detail Raum und Luxus und ist perfekt für drei bis vier Paare.

Villa Hibiscus

Die in 80 Meter über dem Meeresspiegel gelegene Fünf-Schlafzimmer-Villa verfügt über eine der spektakulärsten Aussichten auf den Marcaroni Beach und einige der kleineren Grenadinen. Die Architektur und das Interieur erinnern an die herrschaftlichen Palazzi der Toskana. Die drei Wohnebenen öffnen sich zum Meer, und so prägt die grandiose Aussicht die Atmosphäre sowohl in den fünf Schlafzimmern, die jeweils über ein eigenes Bad und eine eigene Terrasse verfügen, als auch im Spiel- und Fernsehraum und im sehr weitläufigen Wohn- und Essbereich. Der Koch ist einer der besten der Insel, und so bietet ein Urlaub in der Villa Hibiscus jede Menge kulinarische Highlights, egal ob die Mahlzeiten am großen Pool, im windgeschützten Innenhof oder im Haus serviert werden. Die Besitzer haben selbst drei Kinder, deshalb eignet sich die Villa Hibiscus insbesondere für Familien, aber auch für einen Urlaub mit Freunden.

Villa Carissa

Ohne Frage eines der ungewöhnlichsten Anwesen der Insel. Createur Arne Hasselquist, der seit 1969 ein Großteil der Häuser auf Mustique entworfen hat, diente der französische Wohnstil des 18. Jahrhunderts als Inspirationsquelle. Wie in den Plantagenhäusern französischer Edelleute schmücken sich die

Margaret a large plot of land on the island as a wedding present, and she had a private villa built on it. The Princess was only following in the steps of other European aristocrats, top designers, a galaxy of stars, politicians and industrialists. As the island's infrastructure continued to develop, great attention was paid to the conservation of its natural environment. The island now has its own airport, a water sports' centre, a modern surgery, a first class restaurant, and the legendary Basil's Bar. Obviously, all the usual amenities are available, but there are also many sports facilities on offer, such as an equestrian centre and tennis courts, not to mention the physiotherapists and a professional beauty centre. The wide-ranging provision of excellent facilities account for the fact that there are now 85 exclusive, privately-owned villas scattered across the whole island, 55 of which are managed and let to luxury-class travellers by the Mustique Company which admin-isters the island.
All the villas have been designed by famous architects and designers to meet the requirements of their respective owners. They are a revelation for those who harbour

Mustique – Bilder von magischer Schönheit.
Mustique – images of enchating beauty.

Villa Alumbrera

Villa Callaloo

Villa Salamander

Villa Seabreeze

Jede Villa entpuppt sich als individueller Wohntraum.
Each Villa is a revelation of individual dreams.

unusual dreams about lifestyle. The real mystique of Mustique is found above all in the extremely different architectural styles, the tropical gardens, the vast terraces, the fantastic views, and the perfect hospitality. It doesn't matter how big or how small, each villa conveys the feeling that one is staying with friends. The hardworking domestic staff who have always been an integral part of the Mustique philosophy, provide an around-the-clock service for their guests. The new villas and the ones which have been renovated in the last two years have unmistakable character and unusual charm.

Blue Moon

The spectacular view over Britannia Bay in the north Grenadines is only one of the outstanding features of this luxurious villa set in a prime location. Built of precious woods, the interior décor also includes a lot of wood, natural stone, antique marble and Venetian stucco work. Each of the four super luxurious bedrooms is furnished with a romantic four poster bed made of wood, and a double-facility bathroom, and a private balcony. The large living room has a library well-stocked with interesting reading matter provides a space to withdraw. There is room beside the generous-sized pool to accommodate eight people comfortably. The Blue Moon villa is spacious and luxurious to the last detail, perfect for three to four couples.

Hibiscus

Standing 262 feet above sea level, this 5-bedroom villa offers one of the most spectacular views over Macaroni Beach and some of the smaller Grenadines. Its architecture and interior design is reminiscent of the grand palaces in Tuscany. The three levels of the living area are open to the sea, so one is always conscious of the grandiose view in the five bedrooms (each of which has its own bathroom and terrace), in the games and TV-room, and the very spacious living and eating area. The chef is one of the best on the island, so a holiday at Hibiscus Villa has many culinary highlights whether meals are served beside the large pool, in the shelter of the courtyard, or in the house. The Villa's owners have three children themselves, so the house is particularly suitable for a family, but also ideal for a vacation with friends.

Villa Sea Star

Räume mit antiken Familienporträts, wertvollen Gobelins und Antiquitäten. Mit den umlaufenden Veranden öffnet sich der Wohnbereich zum Meer und dem zwei Hektar großen Garten, in dem unzählige exotische Pflanzen und Blumen ihre Pracht entfalten. Die Wasserfläche des lang gestreckten Pools scheint mit der unendlichen Weite des Meeres zu verschmelzen und in den fünf Schlafzimmern, die selbstverständlich über Aircondition und geräumige Bäder verfügen, fühlt man sich wie ein König. In der Carissa verbindet sich der nostalgische Glanz vergangener Tage vorbildlich mit dem Komfort von heute.

Villa Les Jolies Eaux

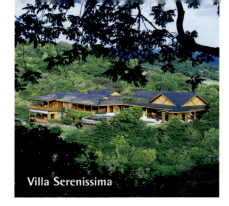
Villa Serenissima

Villa Serenissima

Villa Serenissima

Hommage an die Architektur Balis:
Villa Serenissima.

Homage to the architecture of Bali:
Villa Serenissima.

Villa Serenissima

Diese Vier-Schlafzimmer-Villa ist eine Hommage an die Architektur Balis. Oberhalb eines zauberhaften grünen Tales in der Nähe des Macaroni Beach genießt man traumhafte Ausblicke auf das Meer, umgeben von einem fernöstlichen Wohlfühlambiente. Die Zimmer gruppieren sich um einen lauschigen Fischteich und sind mit balinesischen Antiquitäten eingerichtet. Jedes Schlafzimmer verfügt über eine eigene Veranda, die den Blick auf das Meer und den tropischen Garten freigibt. Im eigenen Pavillon erlebt man den Sonnenuntergang besonders intensiv und der talentierte Koch versteht sich besonders gut auf die Zubereitung vegetarischer Köstlichkeiten.

Die Großzügigkeit und die Exklusivität der aufgeführten Villen spiegeln zwar die Essenz der Mustique-Philosophie wider, doch die Frage nach der ultimativ schönsten Villa muss einfach unbeantwortet bleiben. Auf Mustique kann sich jeder seinen ganz persönlichen Traum vom Paradies erfüllen!

Carissa

One of the most unusual houses on the island is without doubt Carissa. Its designer, Arne Hasselquist, who has designed most of the houses on Mustique since 1969, has drawn his inspiration from 18th century French style. As was usual in houses of the French nobility who were plantation owners, the rooms are full of old family portraits and valuable tapestries and antiques. The verandah encircling the house means that it has constant views of the sea and the 5-acre garden where innumerable exotic plants and flowers are in bloom. The surface of the water in the long narrow pool seems to merge with the infinite expanse of the sea beyond. It goes without saying that the five bedrooms are air-conditioned and have large bathrooms. The Carissa combines the nostalgic splendour of a past era with all the luxury of today.

Serenissima

This four-bedroom villa pays homage to the architecture of Bali. Overlooking an enchanting green valley near Macaroni Beach, the visitor can enjoy fantastic sea views while surrounded by the pleasant ambience of the Far East. The rooms, furnished with Balinese antiques, are grouped around a shady fishpond. Every bedroom has its own verandah overlooking the sea and the tropical garden. To watch the sun set from one's own pavilion is a particularly moving experience. The talented chef is very skilled at producing delicious vegetarian food. The spaciousness and hospitality of the villas listed reflect the essence of the Mustique philosophy, but the question about which villa is the loveliest remains open. On Mustique one really can fulfil one's own special dream.

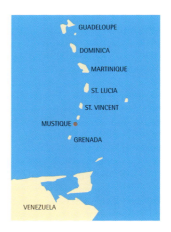

Basil's Bar

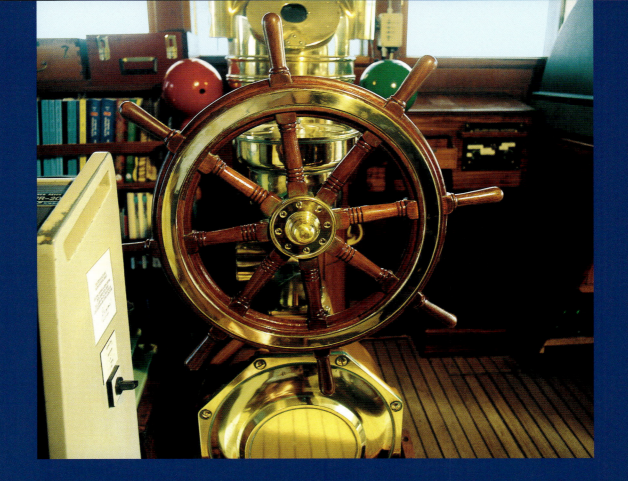

Die Legende unter weißen Segeln

SEA CLOUD

A Legend amongst Sailing Ships

Seit Anfang 2003 erstrahlt der schönste Windjammer der Welt, die SEA CLOUD, nach aufwändigen Renovierungsarbeiten in neuem Glanz. Obwohl sich nun hinter den Kulissen modernste Technik verbirgt, verzaubert die stolze Viermastbark wie eh und je mit nostalgischem Charme und Segelromantik pur. Abseits der viel befahrenen Big-Ships-Routen kreuzt das luxuriöse Fünf-Sterne-Schiff in den schönsten Segelrevieren und garantiert unvergessliche Erlebnisse unter 3 000 Quadratmetern weißen Segeln.

At the beginning of 2003, the most beautiful windjammer in the world, the SEA CLOUD, emerged clothed in fresh glory after costly refurbishment. Equipped with the latest hi-tech discreetly integrated out of sight, this proud four-masted barque has all the nostalgic charm and romance associated with life on the ocean wave. The five star ship cruises in the most beautiful sailing areas guaranteeing unforgettable experiences beneath nearly 33,000 sq. ft of sail-cloth.

Fotos: Hapag-Lloyd Kreuzfahrten
Text: Sabine Herder, Jürgen Gutowski

In the past few years an increasing number of travelers have been discovering the benefits of holidays on the high seas. The branch is booming, reflecting the increasing demand for ever more luxurious ships. However, the growing popularity of this fascinating way of travelling has its down side. Increasingly, ships are getting bigger and less personal, especially in America. There is no opportunity

In den letzten Jahren entdecken immer mehr Reisende die Vorzüge vom Urlaub auf hoher See. Die Branche boomt und entspricht der steigenden Nachfrage mit immer luxuriöseren Schiffen. Doch die wachsende Beliebtheit dieser faszinierenden Form des Reisens hat auch ihre Nachteile. Gerade in Amerika werden die Schiffe immer größer und immer unpersönlicher. Die Reisenden können keinerlei persönliche Verhältnisse mehr aufbauen – weder zu Mannschaft und Schiff noch zu Natur und fremden Kulturen. Oft sind sie nur noch Nummern, die an den beeindruckendsten Landschaften vorbeirauschen, ohne sie wirklich erfassen zu können.

Diesem Trend setzt das traditionsreiche Unternehmen Hapag-Lloyd Kreuzfahrten eine exklusive Flotte entgegen, die nur ein Ziel vor Augen hat: anspruchsvollen Kreuzfahrern unvergleichliche Reiseerlebnisse zu bieten.

Diesen Anspruch unterstreichen die umfangreichen Renovierungsarbeiten an dem legendären Großsegler SEA CLOUD auf besonders eindrucksvolle Art und Weise: Es dokumentiert sich Klasse statt Masse. Die stolze Viermastbark präsentiert sich nach einem längeren Werftaufenthalt schöner denn je und lässt schon beim bloßen Anblick die Herzen aller Segler höher schlagen. Auch wenn man den Blick nur schwer vom strahlend weißen Rumpf und den stolzgeblähten Segeln wenden kann, lohnt sich auf jeden Fall ein Blick hinter die Kulissen. Während der Liegezeit in der Victor Lenac Werft im kroatischen Rijeka wurde die „alte Dame", die 1931 in Kiel vom Stapel lief, nicht nur äußerlich für

ein weiteres Jahrzehnt auf den Weltmeeren gerüstet. Die bereits im Vorjahr begonnene Erneuerung der Hauptantriebsanlage wurde abgeschlossen. Pumpen, die Hilfsdieselmotoren und das gesamte Rigg wurden überholt, unzählige Meter Kabel verlegt und der Rumpf durch umfangreiche Stahlarbeiten stabilisiert. Für mehr Sicherheit und besseren Service sorgen nun modernste Sicherheits- und Kommunikationseinrichtungen sowie ein komplett neuer Küchenbereich.

Obwohl die SEA CLOUD nun mit modernster Technik glänzt, verzaubert die elegante Schönheit der Meere wie eh und je mit nostalgischer Atmosphäre der Belle Epoque. Denn das Meisterwerk der Schiffsbaukunst war einst vom Wallstreet-Tycoon Edward Hutton als äußerst großzügiges Geschenk für seine

for passengers to establish really personal relationships either with the crew and their ship or with the natural environment and other cultures. They are often only numbers who are rushed past the most stunning locations without having a chance to get to know them properly. The old-established Hapag-Lloyd cruise company is bucking this trend with an exclusive fleet of ships with one aim in view: to provide discriminating cruise passengers with unforgettable experiences. The extensive refurbishment of the legendary SEA CLOUD, impressively bears out that Hapag-Lloyd is focusing not on mass but on class. After

a long period at the shipyard, the proud four-master is now even more beautiful than before, an amazing sight to behold which makes the yachting heart beat faster. If one can drag one's eyes away from the gleaming white hull and the magnificent full-blown sails, it is well worth while taking a look behind the scenes. During its time at the Victor Lenac Shipyard in Rijeka in Croatia, the "Old Lady" - launched in Kiel in 1931 - underwent refurbishment to equip it for a further ten years on the oceans of the world - but not only externally. The renewal of the main propulsion plant which was started last year was accomplished and the pumps, the auxiliary engine, and the entire rigging were overhauled. Countless yards of cable have been laid, and the hull has been thoroughly stabilized with steel. There is a

Die SEA CLOUD ist eine elegante Schönheit der Meere. Sie wurde 1931 für die amerikanische Milliardärserbin Marjorie Merriweather Post-Hutton gebaut. Sie liegt meist abseits der Big-Ship-Routen vor Anker.
Links: Beliebter Treff am Heck: die so genannte Blaue Lagune.

The SEA CLOUD is an elegant ocean beauty. She was built in 1931 for Marjorie Merriweather Post-Hutton, an American billionaire. She casts anchor in places well off the main routes used by the big liners.
Left: Popular meeting place at the stern - the so-called Blue Lagoon.

Die Badezimmer der ehemaligen Eignersuiten glänzen mit Badewannen und goldenen Wasserhähnen. Extravagantes Wohnhighlight: die liebevoll restaurierte Eignersuite.

The bathrooms of the former Owners' Suites have an outstanding feature: baths with gold taps. Highlight: the lovingly restored Owner's Suite provides lavish accommodation.

completely new galley area and the very latest hi-tech safety equipment and communications' facilities ensuring increased safety and a better service. Although the SEA CLOUD is outstanding because of its state-of-the-art technology, this elegant ocean beauty still conjures up the nostalgic atmosphere of the Belle Époque. This masterpiece of shipbuilding was once an incredibly lavish present given by Wall Street tycoon Edward Hutton to his wife Marjorie Merriweather Post-Hutton. For this somewhat eccentric millionaire heiress, only the very best of fitments, fittings and furnishings were good enough for the ship, from the red cararra marble fireplace and the valuable antique furniture (which she collected from all over the world) to the gilded swan-shaped taps. In short, the American dollar princess created a floating palace. In fact, her palace soon became a society venue of the first order, where even crowned heads had to be seen. Following the Post-Hutton epoch the big ship managed to survive the turmoil of a particularly chequered history and very difficult circumstances. Today, the SEA CLOUD is one of the five largest sailing ships in the world but is the only one combining the

Frau Marjorie Merriweather Post-Hutton in Auftrag gegeben worden. Der etwas exzentrischen Milliardärserbin war für die Ausstattung ihres Seglers das Beste und das Schönste gerade gut genug: vom Kamin aus rotem Carrara über kostbare antike Möbel, die sie auf der ganzen Welt sammelte, bis hin zu vergoldeten Wasserspendern in Schwanenform. Kurz: Die amerikanische Dollarprinzessin schuf einen schwimmenden Palast. Einen Palast, der sehr schnell zu einem gesellschaftlichen Ereignis ersten Ranges avancierte und dem sich selbst gekrönte Häupter nicht entziehen konnten. Nach der Post-Hutton-Epoche durchlebte der Großsegler eine überaus wechselhafte Geschichte, deren Wirren er trotz widrigster Umstände überstand. Heute gehört die SEA CLOUD zu den fünf größten Segelschiffen der Welt und verbindet als einziges das Flair eines stolzen Windjammers mit dem Luxus eines Fünf-Sterne-Kreuzfahrtschiffes.

Besonders nach der aufwändigen Renovierung im Jahr 2002 präsentiert sich die SEA CLOUD als der konservierte Traum einer Epoche unvorstellbarer Lebenslust. Mit großer Detailversessenheit wurden die historischen Einrichtungen der zehn Originalkabinen, des Salons und des Dining Rooms restauriert. Umgeben von einem altweiß geschliffenen französischen Himmelbett, wallenden Gobelins, Marmorkamin, geschnörkelten Kronleuchtern an den stuckverzierten Decken und goldenen Wasserhähnen atmen vor allem die ehemaligen Eignergemächer, die Nummern 1 und 2, in denen in den 30er und 40er Jahren

Marjorie Merriweather Post-Hutton und ihr Mann residierten, das extravagante Flair vergangener Zeiten. Nicht minder elegant zeigen sich die zwei neu entstandenen Luxuskabinen und die übrigen modernen Kabinen, die mit viel Gefühl für die Seele der Viermastbark von hamburgischen und venezianischen Schiffsdesignern im SEA-CLOUD-Stil entworfen wurden. Ohne auf die Errungenschaften modernsten Komforts zu verzichten, residiert der Reisende in einer Welt, die einer anderen Zeit entsprungen zu sein scheint. Und da macht das Restaurant im ehemaligen Salon der Huttons keine Ausnahme. In diesem prachtvollen Rahmen wird jede Mahlzeit zu einem Fest – zumal die international erfahrene Küchencrew das Beste aus den Küchen der Welt serviert. (Bleibt die Atmosphäre unter Seglern normalerweise leger, kommt zum traditionellen Welcome und Farewell Dinner die festliche Garderobe zum Einsatz.) Der Service agiert mit der gleicher Leidenschaft wie die restliche Crew, die selbst bei härtesten Wetterbedingungen ihre gute Laune nicht verliert. Mit scheinbar spielerischer Leidenschaft meistert sie jedes Segelmanöver, jeder Handgriff sitzt und man spürt, dass jeder Einzelne eine tiefe Zuneigung mit „seinem" Windjammer verbindet. Und so wird es nie langweilig, die Mannschaft beim Segelsetzen zu beobachten: Geschickt balancieren die Männer in 40, 50 Meter Höhe über die Laufseile zu den noch aufgewickelten Segeln, Motorwinden spulen dicke Taue ab, eine Glocke ertönt, dann fallen 30 Segel gleichzeitig von den Rahen, flattern einen Augenblick unschlüssig in der Brise, bis sie den Wind gefunden haben und sich majestätisch in den Himmel blähen. Sanft neigt sich das Schiff, ist in seinem Element! Wie eine weiße Wolke zieht es über die See, jung und elegant, graziös und selbstbewusst – SEA CLOUD, nomen est omen. Mit 10 Knoten sticht sie in See, außer dem Schäumen der Wellen und dem Knarren der Taue liegt friedliche Stille über dem Windjammer. Man liest ein Buch, sonnt sich auf der „Blauen Lagune" am Heck des Schiffs, trinkt etwas Gutes an der Bar und genießt bis zu sechs Mahlzeiten am Tag. Die große Fahrt und das Leben auf See sind für die meisten Reisenden die eigentlichen Höhepunkte ihrer Traumreise. Ihre nostalgische Liebe gehört dem Wind und dem Meer, und ihr Faible für die älteste Art, mit Schiffen die Meere zu befahren, ist auf der SEA CLOUD eine besonders reizvolle und überaus luxuriöse

remarkable elegance of a proud windjammer with the luxury of a five-star cruise ship. Following its costly refurbishment in 2002, the SEA CLOUD has become the conserved dream of a past epoch of unimaginable joie de vivre, especially now. The historic furnishings and fittings of the original cabins, the lounge, and the dining room have been restored with an obsessive attention to detail. Surrounded by a polished antique white French four-poster, graceful tapestries, a marble fireplace, elaborate chandeliers hanging from stucco-ornamented ceilings and gilded taps, the former owner's suites Nos 1 and 2 in which Marjorie Merriweather Post-Hutton and her husband once lived in the 1930s and 1940s, breathe the atmosphere and style of the extravagant times gone by. No less elegant are the two newly created luxury cabins and the other modern cabins designed in SEA CLOUD style by Hamburg and Venetian ship designers with great sensitivity for the spirit of the four-masted barque. Without having to do without any of the very latest amenities or luxury, the passenger resides in a world which appears to have emerged from a past epoch, and the dining room in the Hutton's former lounge

is no exception. In these magnificent surroundings every mealtime is a festive occasion, especially since the international galley staff produces a global cuisine. While the general atmosphere on board is laid back, formal dress comes into its own for the traditional Welcome and Farewell Dinners. The ship's service staff works with as much fervour as the crew, who are always in a good mood, even in the worst possible weather conditions. They manage every sailing manoeuvre with the greatest of ease. Their grip is firm, and one senses each one of them has a deep and binding affinity with "his" windjammer. It is never boring watching the crew setting the sails. They balance deftly on the rigging at heights of over 130 to 165 feet up as they walk over to the furled sails. Motorized winches let down thick coils of rope, a bell tolls and 30 sails unfurl simultaneously from the yards, first to flap hesitating in the breeze, then to catch the wind as it blows the sails out to their full majesty. The SEA CLOUD leans gently to one side and is then in its element, sailing across the sea like a white cloud, young and elegant, gracious and self-confident. Nomen et omen. She slices through the sea at ten knots, and apart from the sound of the surf and the creaking of the ropes, there is peace and quiet on the windjammer. One can read a book, sunbathe in the Blue Lagoon at the stern of the ship, enjoy a tasty drink at the bar and enjoy the six meals a day. The voyage and life at sea are for most of the passengers the actual highlights of the dream journey. Their nostalgic love is for the wind and the water, and their fondness for sailing the high seas in the oldest kind of ship becomes an anachronism on the SEA CLOUD of a particularly luxurious kind. In 2004 the SEA CLOUD sets out for the Caribbean as well as the western and eastern Mediterranean where there are still mini paradises to be discovered well away from the major shipping routes.

Spielart des Anachronismus. 2004 nimmt die SEA CLOUD Kurs auf die Karibik sowie das westliche und östliche Mittelmeer, wo es abseits der viel befahrenen Big-Ship-Routen noch so manches paradiesische Fleckchen Erde zu entdecken gibt.

Im ehemaligen Salon der Huttons befindet sich heute das Restaurant.
The dining room is in the Hutton's old lounge.

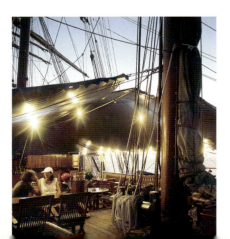

Seeluft macht Appetit. Der Tag auf der SEA CLOUD beginnt mit einem opulenten Frühstücksbuffet, das keine Wünsche unerfüllt lässt. Insgesamt werden sechs Mahlzeiten pro Tag angeboten. Selbst ein paar Stunden nach dem festlichen Dinner in dem mahagonivertäfelten Restaurant wird um Mitternacht noch einmal ein kleiner Imbiss bei besinnlicher Klaviermusik serviert.

Sea gives you an appetite. Each day on the SEA CLOUD begins with an opulent breakfast buffet which leaves no desire unfulfilled. All in all, six meals a day are on offer. Even at midnight, only a couple hours after the festive dinner in the mahogany-panelled restaurant, a small snack is served to the quiet accompaniment of the piano.

THE ROYAL PITA MAHA

The Royal Pita Maha wurde gebaut nach traditionellen balinesischen Entwürfen, und man nahm sensibel und umweltbewusst Rücksicht auf die Natur, was auch auf Bali leider nicht immer der Normalfall im Fünf-Sterne-Hotelbau ist. So sind die zwölf Hektar des Resorts, das in seinem Erscheinungsbild einem königlichen Dorf ähnelt, vollkommen integriert in die ländliche Umgebung mit ihren geschwungenen Reisterrassen, den Wildwasserschluchten und tropischen Wäldern. Diese Verschmelzung von Natur und Raum durchdringt das gesamte Anwesen mit einer überwältigenden Atmosphäre von Frieden und Harmonie und Einssein mit der Natur.

The Royal Pita Maha was built following traditional Balinese architectural designs, and great care has been paid to making it environmentally-friendly – sadly not always the case with five-star hotels in Bali. The resort's thirty acres which resemble a royal village, is perfectly integrated into its surroundings. It has sweeping rice terraces, ravines and tropical forest. This fusion of nature and space pervades the whole resort filling it with an overwhelming sense of peace and harmony.

Text: Jürgen Gutowski
Fotos: Jürgen & Martina Gutowski

Traditionelle balinesische Bauformen waren Vorbild für das neue „Royal Pita Maha", bei dem die Architekten gleichzeitig Rücksicht auf die Natur nahmen.
Traditional Balinese architecture provided the model for the new Royal Pita Maha. The architects have also taken account of the natural environment.

Laughing, the boys on the rice field pull on the long lines which stretch from one end of the flooded field to the other like washing lines. Tin cans and pennants on the lines bob up and down fluttering, sparrows and irritated herons flee into the air. "Living scarecrows" comments Pande, the imaginative faithful retainer of the Pita Maha. There are wood carvers at work on the edge of the road. We look at fearful demons and graceful dancers, wooden mobiles for the tourists and spirit houses for the locals. Long, thin switches adorned with colourful pieces of cloth and black-and-white flags form a kind of trellis along this tropical street high above the Ayung River near Ubud. Down below on the wild river, a few fearless wildwater rafters shrieking with delight struggle through the rapids in red rubber dinghies. On the side of the road people are enjoying a cockfight, and in the middle of one of the 80,000 temples people are gambling, smoking, laughing and chatting. Here, life and faith are not in opposition but united as nowhere else in Indonesia. "Indonesia?" asks Pande winking, "we're Balinese". Yes indeed, here in Bali, this religious state of emergency within the giant islands' state, women eschew wearing the veil worn in the rest of this Islamic country, and the

Die Jungs auf dem Reisfeld zerren lachend an den langen Schnüren, die wie Wäscheleinen von einem Ende des gefluteten Ackers zum anderen reichen. Blechdosen und Wimpel an den Leinen wippen scheppernd und flatternd auf und ab, verschreckte Spatzen und irritierte Reiher flüchten sich in die Lüfte. „Lebende Vogelscheuchen", erklärt Pande, der kreative Geist aus dem Hause Pita Maha. Am Straßenrand wird geschnitzt, wir sehen furchterregende Dämonen und liebreizende Tänzerinnen, Holzmobiles für die Touristen und Geisterhäuschen für die Einheimischen. Schlanke hohe Gerten, farbenfroh mit Tüchern und schwarz-weißen Fahnen umkleidet, bilden das Spalier des tropischen Sträßchens, hoch oben über dem Ayung River in der Nähe von Ubud. Dort unten auf dem wilden Fluss kämpfen sich einige unerschrockene Wild Water Rafters in roten Schlauchbooten juchzend durch die Stromschnellen. Am Straßenrand frönt man dem Hahnenkampf, mitten in einem der 80 000 Tempel wird gezockt und

geraucht, gelacht und geplaudert, Leben und Glaube sind hier eben kein Gegensatz, sondern eine Einheit, wie sonst nirgends in Indonesien. „Indonesien?", fragt Pande augenzwinkernd, „wir sind Balinesen!" Klar, hier auf Bali, diesem religiösen Ausnahmezustand innerhalb des riesigen Inselstaates, sind die Frauen nicht verschleiert wie im Rest des islamischen Landes, hier trinken die Männer Bier, und alle zünden sie Räucherkerzen zu Ehren Buddhas und der Hindugötter an, verehren, fürchten und besänftigen ohne Unterlass die allgegenwärtigen Geister.

Wir sind unterwegs zum jüngsten Hotelkind von Ubuds königlicher Familie: The Royal Pita Maha, das soeben seine Tore auf Bali geöffnet hat, und zwar an einem auserwählten Ort, wie Pande erzählt. Vor vielen Jahrhunderten nämlich, so erfahre ich von meinem Begleiter, machte sich ein heiliger Mann namens Maharsi mit seinen Schülern aus Java auf den Weg nach Bali. Nachdem er spirituelle Zeichen von den Göttern empfangen hatte, gelangte er an einen beein-

men drink beer. Everyone lights joss sticks in honour of Buddha and the Hindu gods, and worship the ever-present spirits without ceasing.

We're on our way to the latest hotel of Ubud's royal family, The Royal Pia Maha has just opened its doors in Bali in a very special place, according to Pande. My companion tells me that many hundreds of years ago, a holy man called Maharsi set off with his students from Java to Bali. After he had received spiritual messages from the gods he reached an imposing mountain encircled by the waters of two rivers. It was as if the mountain was being guarded by two dragons.

Maharsi and his disciples built a monastery in this place so vibrant with spirituality, and soon after farmers came to ask permission to take away some of this holy soil to spread on their own fields back home. The place became known as the "God Zone" due to its heavenly ambience, its spiritual significance, and its over-abundance.

There is a temple in "Kedewatan" where the people of Bali still pay homage to the gods, even today. This dragon's river still swirls around the beautiful hill and its "heavenly" slopes, and it is here that the sister hotel of the famous Pita Maha in Ubud is being built. It goes without saying that it

Die Maße der Wohnräume dürften auf Bali neue Maßstäbe setzen: die „kleinsten" Unterkünfte bieten 300 Quadratmeter zum Leben.
The living space sets new standards in Bali. Even the smallest accommodation has an area of 3,230 square feet.

druckenden Berg, um den herum sich zwei klare Flüsse schlängelten. „Ein Berg, bewacht von zwei Drachen", so könnte man meinen. Maharsi und seine Jünger bauten ein Kloster in dieser vor Spiritualität vibrierenden Gegend, und schon bald kamen Bauern, die darum baten, ein wenig gesegnete Erde von dieser heiligen Stätte davontragen zu dürfen und sie in die heimischen Äcker zu mischen. Man nannte das Gebiet „die Zone Gottes" wegen seines himmlischen Ambientes und seiner spirituellen Bedeutsamkeit und seiner überbordenden Fruchtbarkeit. Noch heute steht in „Kedewatan" ein Tempel, an dem die Menschen von Bali den Göttern huldigen, noch heute rauscht dieser Drachenfluss um den lieblichen Berg und an seinen „himmlischen" Hängen entstand das Schwesterhotel des berühmten Pita Maha in Ubud. Klar, dass es die Essenz von Bali widerspiegelt, denn es handelt sich schließlich um einen Ort, wie geschaffen dazu, sich verwöhnen zu lassen, zu genesen von den Krankheiten unserer Zivilisation, zu meditieren und zu entspannen.

The Royal Pita Maha wurde gebaut nach traditionellen balinesischen Entwürfen, und man nahm sensibel und umweltbewusst Rücksicht auf die Natur, was auch auf Bali leider nicht immer der Normalfall im Fünf-Sterne-Hotel-Bau ist. So sind die zwölf Hektar des Resorts, das in seinem Erscheinungsbild einem königlichen Dorf ähnelt, vollkommen integriert in die

reflects the very essence of Bali, after all this is a spot which appears to have been created for pampering and recuperation from the diseases of our civilization, a place for meditation and relaxation.
The Royal Pita Maha was built following traditional Balinese architectural designs, and great care has been paid to making it environmentally-friendly – sadly not always the case with five-star hotels in Bali. The resort's thirty

ländliche Umgebung mit ihren geschwungenen Reisterrassen, den Wildwasserschluchten und tropischen Wäldern. Diese Verschmelzung von Natur und Raum durchdringt das gesamte Anwesen mit einer überwältigenden Atmosphäre von Frieden und Harmonie und Einssein mit der Natur. Diese Stimmung setzt sich fort in den 74 Pool Villas, den elf Royal Villas sowie im Royal House.

Alle Villas stehen auf ihrem eigenen Grundstück, alle bieten einen atemberaubenden Panoramablick auf Schlucht und Fluss und Berge mit tropischem Grün, alle sind gesegnet mit einem privaten, sprießenden Garten, alle verfügen über einen Pool, der die Bezeichnung Pool tatsächlich verdient hat, weil man wegen seiner großzügigen Maße darin nämlich tatsächlich schwimmen kann. Aber auch die Maße des Wohnraums dürften auf Bali neue Maßstäbe setzen: Selbst die „kleinsten" Unterkünfte, die „Pool Villas", bieten 300 Quadratmeter zum Leben, die „Royal Villas" setzen noch einmal 100 Quadratmeter drauf, und das „Royal House" darf man angesichts von 800 Quadratmetern Auslauf samt zwei Schlafzimmern, Hof, Küche und Salon durchaus als Residenz bezeichnen! Duschen kann man wahlweise klimatisiert oder unter freiem Himmel, wobei man neugierige Blicke der Nachbarn nicht zu fürchten braucht, denn die Grundstücke sind absolut „blickdicht". Durch ein riesiges handgeschnitz-

acres which resemble a royal village, is perfectly integrated into its surroundings. It has sweeping rice terraces, ravines and tropical forest. This fusion of nature and space pervades the whole resort filling it with an overwhelming sense of peace and harmony. This atmosphere reaches into and permeates the 74 villas, 11 Royal Villas and the Royal House. All the villas stand on their own plots, and all have breathtaking panoramic views of the ravine, the river and the tropical green mountains. All are blessed with a private, luxuriant garden, and all have a swimming pool which really does live up to its name because it is actually big enough to swim in. The living rooms too set new standards for Bali, and even the smallest units, the "Pool Villas", have 3,230 square feet of floor space. The "Royal Villas" have 4,305 sq. ft, and the "Royal House" which ought to be described as a residence because it has 8,610 square feet of space. It has two bedrooms, a courtyard, a kitchen and a drawing room. One can either shower

air-conditioned or outside, albeit one needn't fear nosy neighbours because the grounds are secluded, away from public view. Through giant hand-carved doors surrounded by beautifully decorated walls, past the two-winged stone guards, I enter my Pool Suite. The air is cool and a light jasmine fragrance fans me. I take off my shoes straight away because it's only with bare feet than one can appreciate walking on the exquisite parquet and Italian marble floors. The ceiling-high windows

Das Bad der Pool-Villa mit edlem Parkett und italienischem Marmor.
The bathroom of the Pool Villas has high-grade parquet flooring and Italian marble.

Den Garten ziert ein großer, sanft gerundeter Privatpool.
The garden is enhanced by a gently curved pool.

Im Zentrum des Schlafzimmers thront ein extrem breites und bequemes Bett.
The bedroom is dominated by an extremely wide and comfortable bed in the centre.

Ingredienzien für die Anwendungen im größten Spa auf Bali.
Ingredients for treatment at the largest Spa in Bali.

are really sliding glass doors. I push them aside and immediately feel the breeze which carries the sound of the distant rushing of the bubbling river waters. In the centre of the bedroom is a mega-wide bed. I lie on it stretching out my legs and arms to all sides but they don't even reach the sides of this plush piece of furniture. Overhead is plenty of space owing to the typical pointed roof made of wood and reeds woven in typical Balinese style. The walls are adorned by Indonesian works of art, massive, glorious illustrations of Balinese mythology. Beside them orchids and fresh fruit. The state-of-the-art hi-tech equipment includes satellite TV and video, but there is also the obligatory mini-bar, telephone, safe, coffee machine and much else. To the left of the bedroom is the living room which is furnished with comfy sofas and large indoor plants. On the right is a bathroom with a jacuzzi and a separate shower. In front of the house – in the middle of the garden – is the large, gently curved private pool, real competition for the two "official" pools down in the valley. Every part of this villa overlooks the legendary Valley of Maharsi. There is no record of whether the valley's saintly conqueror of long ago was an ascetic or a bon vivant. Today, despite the presence of the largest and most exclusive spa and wellness centre (under Shiseido management) in Bali, there is no shortage of delights to indulge in at the Royal Pita Maha, which offers a wide variety indeed. The two terrace restaurants dramatically situated above the wildwater serve a colossal range of international dishes and local specialities – in line with the two other Pita Maha hotels. In keeping with the aesthetic philosophy of the Pita Maha concern, this hotel is distinct from the others in Bali

Wände und Anrichten schmücken indonesische Kunstwerke.
Indonesian works of art adorn the walls and sideboards.

tes Portal, eingefasst von ebenfalls fein gearbeitetem Mauerwerk, vorbei an zwei steinernen geflügelten Hauswachen, betrete ich meine Pool Suite. Die Luft ist kühl, ein leichtes Jasminaroma umfächelt mich. Ich ziehe sofort die Schuhe aus, denn nur barfuß geht sich's komfortabel auf edlem Parkett und italienischem Marmor. Die raumhohen Fenster sind eigentlich gläserne Schiebetüren, ich rolle sie ganz zur Seite und sofort trifft mich ein leichter Wind, der das entfernte Rauschen des brodelnden Flusses heraufträgt. Im Zentrum des Schlafzimmers thront ein megabreites Bett, ich

lege mich drauf, strecke meine Beine und Arme nach allen Seiten aus, aber den Rand dieses Feudallagers erreiche ich dennoch nicht. Auch nach oben hin ist viel Raum, typisch balinesisch aus Holz und Reet zusammengefügt, erblicke ich ein beschirmendes Spitzdach über mir. An den Wänden finden sich indonesische Kunstwerke, massive und erhabene Darstellungen der balinesischen Mythologie, daneben Orchideen und frische Früchte. *State of the art* präsentiert sich auch die High Tech, die neben Satelliten-TV und Video natürlich eine Minibar, Telefon, Safe, Kaffeemaschine und mehr beinhaltet. Links vom Schlafzimmer der Salon mit gemütlichen Sofas und großen Zimmerpflanzen, rechts das Bad mit Sprudelwanne und Extradusche, vor dem Haus „mitten im Garten" – der große, sanft gerundete Privatpool, der den beiden „offiziellen" Pools unten im Tal scharfe Konkurrenz machen dürfte. Und von jedem Punkt dieser Villa öffnet sich der Blick auf das legendäre Tal des Maharsi. Es ist nicht überliefert, ob der heilige Eroberer des Tales von einst eher Asket oder Gourmet war, aber vielgestaltiger Genuss kommt im Royal Pita Maha trotz des größten und exklusivsten Spa- und Wellness-Centers (managed by Shiseido), das Bali zu bieten hat, auf keinen Fall zu kurz. Die beiden Terrassenrestaurants, in dramatischer Lage oberhalb des Wildwassers platziert, garantieren eine kolossale Auswahl an internationalen und lokalen Spezialitäten, wie das bei den zwei anderen Hotels der Pita-Maha-Familie ja auch selbstverständlich ist.

Ganz im Sinne der künstlerischen Philosophie im Hause Pita Maha unterscheidet sich das Hotel von den anderen auf Bali durch sein ausgesuchtes kulturelles Programm, dargebracht von einheimischen Musikern mit teilweise sensationellen Performances, von Malern, die in der hoteleigenen Galerie ihre Werke präsentieren. Pita Maha, das bedeutet bereits seit Jahrzehnten die Förderung der Kunst und der Künstler in großzügiger Hinwendung an die Schöpfergeister. Noch vertreiben die Artisten von morgen vielleicht drüben auf dem Reisfeld die Vögel. Aber an langen Bändern lassen sich irgendwann auch Drachen in die Lüfte schwingen, aus Dosen werden mal Installationen und aus Wimpeln Tempelschmuck. Nur das Lachen, das wird sich nicht ändern hier im Tal.

owing to its cultural programme which involves native musicians, some of whom produce sensational performances, and painters whose work is exhibited in the hotel's own art gallery. Pita Maha is a term which has been associated for many years with the promotion of art and artists who dedicate their work to the spirits of creation. Maybe the artists of tomorrow will be scaring off the birds from the rice fields, but at some point they will still be flying kites on long lines. Maybe installations will be created from the tin cans, and pennants will decorate the temple. Yet, one thing that won't change here in this valley is the laughing.

Die Terrassenrestaurants garantieren eine kolossale Auswahl an internationalen und lokalen Spezialitäten.
The terrace restaurants provide a colossal choice of international dishes and local specialities.

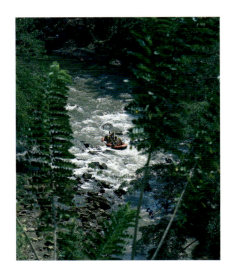

Auf dem Ayung River kämpfen sich einige Wild Water Rafters in Schlauchbooten durch die Stromschnellen.
Wildwater rafters in rubber dinghies battle against the rapids on the Ayung River.

ÜBERSICHT DER HOTELS

The Peninsula Hong Kong

Salisbury Road, Kowloon, Hong Kong
Telefon: 0 08 52 / 29 20 / 28 88
Telefax: 0 08 52 / 27 22 / 41 70
Internet: www.peninsula.com
Zimmerbuchungen auch
Leading Hotels of the World
Deutschland 08 00 / 8 52 11 00
Österreich 08 00 / 29 52 84
Schweiz 08 00 / 55 11 23

Direkt am Victoria-Hafen, mitten im Herzen des Shopping-, Geschäfts- und Unterhaltungsviertels Kowloon, nur wenige Fußminuten von den wichtigsten Sehenswürdigkeiten Hongkongs entfernt.

Home away from home, anders kann man die insgesamt 246 Zimmer und 54 Suiten nicht bezeichnen. 141 Superior-, Deluxe- und Harbour-View-Räume, die berühmte Marco-Polo-Suite, 26 Granddeluxe- und Junior-Suiten liegen im Hauptgebäude.
Zimmer von 3 000 bis 4900 Hongkong-Dollar, Suiten von 5 600 bis 32 000 Hongkong-Dollar, Peninsula Suite 39 000 Hongkong-Dollar (7 Hongkong-Dollar entsprechen ungefähr 1 Euro).

Auf über 1 600 qm präsentiert sich das Peninsula Spa mit einem Gesundheits-, Fitness- und Beautycenter der Extraklasse. Im Schwimmingpool und auf der Sonnenterrasse schwebt man praktisch über der Stadt.

Das gastronomische Angebot offeriert sieben verschiedene Restaurants. Absolutes Highlight: das von Philippe Starck designte Felix mit seinem atemberaubenden Panoramablick.

Die schillernde Weltmetropole ist ein Ganzjahresziel.

Air France fliegt täglich von acht deutschen Städten nach Hongkong.

Mitglied The Leading Hotels of the World.

The Oriental Bangkok

48 Oriental Avenue
Bangkok 10500, Thailand
Telefon: 00 66 / 26 59 90 00
Telefax: 00 66 / 26 59 00 00
E-Mail: reserve-orbkk@mohg.com
Internet: www.mandarinoriental.com
www.mandarinoriental.com
Reservierungsbüro Deutschland:
0 61 96 / 57 48 80

Umgeben von Terrassen und Gärten liegt das berühmte Hotel am Ufer des Chao Praya Rivers direkt im besten Shoppingviertel Bangkoks.

395 Zimmer davon 35 Suiten. Die außergewöhnlichsten Suiten befinden sich in der „Author Residence" und sind berühmten Schriftstellern gewidmet.
Preise: Zimmer von 300 bis 440 US$, Suiten von 440 bis 1 500 US$, Oriental-Suite 2 200 US$.

Zwei Außenpools, Tennis, Squash, Saunen, Fittnessraum und das luxuriöse Spa mit Spa-Suiten.

Das legendäre Hotel offeriert ein unvergleichliches gastronomisches Angebot. Das Restaurant The Normandie ist eine der besten kulinarischen Adressen Asiens.

Die schillernde Weltmetropole ist ein Ganzjahresziel.

Air France fliegt täglich von acht deutschen Städten nach Bangkok.

Mitglied The Leading Hotels of the World.

Banyan Tree Seychelles

Anse Intendance, Intendance Road
Mahé, Republic of Seychelles
Telefon: 0 02 48 / 3 83 / 5 00
Telefax: 0 02 48 / 3 83 / 6 00
E-Mail: seychelles@banyantree.com
Internet: www.banyantree.com

Völlig abgelegen an einer der schönsten Buchten im Südwesten Mahés, der Intendance Bay. 45 Autominuten bis zur Inselhauptstadt Victoria.

Exklusives Villenkonzept mit einzigartiger Privatsphäre. 20 Hillside-Pool-Villen mit je 104 qm, Aircondition, Deckenventilator, Fön, Bademantel, Minibar, Kaffeekocher, Sat-TV, DVD-Player, CD-Spieler, Safe (je nach Saison 750–1180 US$), 15 Beachfront-Pool-Villen mit 251 qm, Ausstattung wie oben, zusätzlich mit Dampfsauna, Outdoor-Jacuzzi, Massagepavillon (je nach Saison 950–1480 US$), eine Präsidentenvilla (2 800 US$).

Pool; Schnorcheln, Wasserski, Surfen, Hochsee- und Nachtfischen; Banyan Tree Spa mit einem Topangebot an Massagen, Körper- und Beautyanwendungen; Fitnesscenter.

Preisgekrönte Thai-Küche im Gourmetrestaurant „Saffron". Internationale und asiatische Küche im Restaurant „Au Jardin d'Epices" mit herrlichem Blick auf die Bucht.

Tropisch-äquatoriales Seeklima, bei Temperaturen zwischen 26–30 ºC. Hohe Luftfeuchtigkeit, ganzjähriges Reiseziel.

Ab Frankfurt mit Air Seychelles oder Condor nonstop nach Mahé. Abholservice durch das Hotel, ca. 30 Minuten Transferzeit.

Mitglied bei „The Leading Hotels of the World" und „Small Luxury Hotels of the World".

SUMMARY OF THE HOTELS

The Peninsula Hong Kong

Salisbury Road, Kowloon, Hong Kong
Telephone: 0 08 52 / 29 20 / 28 88
Telefax: 0 08 52 / 27 22 / 41 70
Internet: www.peninsula.com
Reservations too
Leading Hotels of the World
Germany 08 00 / 8 52 11 00
Austria 08 00 / 29 52 84
Switzerland 08 00 / 55 11 23

Hong Kong, right on the Victoria Harbour, in the heart of Kowloon's shopping, business and entertainment district. Only a few minutes' walk from the most important sights of Hong Kong.

A home from home – there's no other way of describing all 246 rooms and 54 suites. The main building houses 141 rooms of superior, deluxe and harbour-view class, the celebrated Marco Polo Suite, 26 grand-deluxe and junior suites. Prices: Rooms from 3,000 to 4,900 Hong Kong Dollar, Suites from 5,600 to 32,000 Hong Kong Dollar, Peninsula Suite 39,000 Hong Kong Dollar (7 Hong Kong Dollar are worth about one Euro).

One salient feature on more than 1,600 square metres is the Pensinsula Spa with a health-, fitness- and beauty centre of the select class. In the swimming pool and on the sun terrace you are practically floating above the city.

You have the gastronomic choice of seven different restaurants. The absolute highlight is Felix, designed by Philippe Starck, with its breathtaking panoramic view.

The shimmering world metropolis is an all-season destination.

Air France provides daily flights to Hong Kong from eight German cities.

Member of The Leading Hotels of the World.

The Oriental Bangkok

48 Oriental Avenue
Bangkok 10500, Thailand
Telephone: 00 66 / 26 59 90 00
Telefax: 00 66 / 26 59 00 00
E-mail: reserve-orbkk@mohg.com
Internet: www.mandarinoriental.com
www.mandarinoriental.com
Reservations in Germany:
0 61 96 / 57 48 80

Surrounded by terraces and gardens, the famous hotel is located on the banks of the River Chao Praya directly in Bangkok's best shopping district.
Rooms & Suites: Thirty-five of the 395 rooms are suites. The most extraordinary suites are in the "Author Residence" and are dedicated to famous writers.
Rooms from 300 to 440 US$, Suites from 440 to 1,500 US$, Oriental Suite 2,200 US$.

Two outdoor pools, tennis, squash, saunas, gym, and the luxurious spa with Spa Suites.

The legendary hotel offers an unparalleled gastronomic range. The Normandie restaurant is one of the best culinary destinations in Asia.

The shimmering world metropolis is an all-season destination.

Air France provides daily flights from eight German cities to Bangkok.

Member of The Leading Hotels of the World.

Banyan Tree Seychelles

Anse Intendance, Intendance Road
Mahé, Republic of Seychelles
Telephone: 0 02 48 / 3 83 / 5 00
Telefax: 0 02 48 / 3 83 / 6 00
E-mail: seychelles@banyantree.com
Internet: www.banyantree.com

Totally isolated beside Intendance Bay, one of the most beautiful bays in the south-west of Mahé, a 45-minute drive to Victoria, the island's capital.

Exclusive villa settlement enjoying great privacy. 20 Hillside Pool Villas, each with a floor area of approx. 1,120 square feet, air conditioning, ceiling fan, hair-dryer, bath robe, minibar, coffee machine, Sat-TV, DVD-player, safe (depending on season 750–1,180 US$. 15 Beachfront Pool Villas with an area of 2,700 sq. ft., same mod cons as above with the addition of a steam sauna, outdoor jacuzzi, massage pavilion (depending on season, 950–1,480 US$. President's Suite (2,800 US$).

Pool, snorkelling, water skiing, surfing, deep sea and night fishing, Banyan Tree Spa which offers exceptional massage, body treatment, beauty treatment. Fitness Centre.

Award-winning Thai cuisine served at the "Saffron" gourmet restaurant. International cuisine and Asian dishes served in the "Au Jardin d'Epices" restaurant which has heavenly views of the bay.

Tropical-equatorial marine climate, temperatures between 26–30 °C. High humidity, all-year destination.

Air Seychelles from Frankfurt or non-stop to Mahé with Condor. Hotel collection service, transfer approx. 30 minutes.

Member of "The Leading Hotels of the World" and "Small Luxury Hotels of the World".

ÜBERSICHT DER HOTELS

Sainte Anne Resort

P.O. Box 388, Victoria, Mahé / Seychelles
Telefon: 0 02 48 / 29 20 00
Telefax: 0 02 48 / 29 20 02
E-Mail: sainteanne@bchot.com
Internet: www.sainteanne-resort.com
Beachcomber Hotels, Repräsentanzbüro
Dianastraße 4, D-85521 Ottobrunn
Telefon: 00 49 / 89 / 6 29 84 90
Internet: www.beachcomber.de

Äquatornah als Teil des Inselarchipels Seychellen, 10 Bootsminuten von der Hauptinsel Mahé.

4 verschiedene Raumkonstellationen: 79 Villas „Providence" (ca. 100 qm Gesamtfläche) ab 720 Euro; 3 Villas „Bel Air" mit 1 Schlafzimmer (ca. 180 qm Gesamtfläche) ab 1400 Euro; 4 Villas „Belle Vue" mit 2 Schlafzimmern (ca. 270 qm Gesamtfläche) ab 2525 Euro; 1 „Villa Royal" mit 3 Schlafzimmern (ca. 500 qm Gesamtfläche) ab 3500 Euro. Alle Preise inkl. Frühstück und Steuern. Zuschlag für Halbpension 92 Euro p. P./Tag.

„Spa by Clarins": 2 Hamams, 2 Saunen, 3 Massageräume, 1 x Außen-Balneotherapie, Friseur, Maniküre, 2 Krafträume innen und außen mit Cardio-Equipment. 2 Flutlichttennisplätze, Mountainbikes für Erwachsene und Kinder. Wassersport: Segeln, Windsurfing, Kajak, Pedalo, Glasbodenboot, Tauchen, Schnorcheln.

Internationale, italienische und regionale Meisterleistungen in zwei Restaurants mit der Betonung auf Fisch, nahezu alle Lebensmittel werden frisch aus Paris und Singapur importiert.

Äquatorialklima bei Höchsttemperaturen um 30 °C das ganze Jahr hindurch.

Neben Thomas Cook fliegt auch Air Seychelles nonstop nach Mahé.

Hubschrauberlandeplatz für Helikoptertransfers oder private Exkursionen. Konferenzraum bis 30 Personen.

Soneva Gili Resort & Spa

Lankanfushi Island, North Male Atoll
Republic of Maldives
Telefon: 0 09 60 / 44 03 04
Telefax: 0 09 60 / 44 03 05
E-Mail: sonresa@sonevagili.com.mv
Internet: www.six-senses.com/sonevagili

Die Insel Lankanfushi befindet sich in Privatbesitz und liegt im Nord-Male-Atoll.

Insgesamt 44 Suiten und Residenzen in jeweils einer „Water Villa" auf Stelzen direkt ins Meer gesetzt, davon 7 „Crusoe Residences", die ausschließlich per Boot erreichbar sind. Zimmerpreise: Soneva Gili Suite ab 500 US$, Soneva Gili Residence ab 680 US$, Soneva Gili Crusoe Residence ab 780 US$, Mahlzeiten: Frühstück 25 US$, Lunch 30 US$, Dinner 55 US$ (p. P./Tag), Schnellboottransfer von/bis Airport Male: 70 US$ p. P.

Spa in Over Water Villas, Massagen: schwedisch, Thai, hawaiisch, holistisch, Aromatherapie, Akupressur, Shiatsu, Kopfhautmassage; Behandlungen: Milch- und Honigbäder, Rosenblätterbad, Entgiftungsbehandlungen, Stress-Management, diverse Schönheitsbehandlungen. Tennis, Tischtennis, PADI-Tauchschule, Segelyacht-Charter, Wassersport.

Open-Air-Restaurant mit internationalen Spezialitäten unter besonderer Berücksichtigung asiatischer und lokaler Rezepte mit Schwerpunkt auf Fisch und Meeresfrüchten.

Äquatorialklima bei Höchsttemperaturen um 30 °C das ganze Jahr hindurch.

Neben LTU wird Male von vielen Linien- und Charter-Airlines angeflogen, darunter Emirates, Austrian Airlines, Condor und Singapore Airlines.

„Small Luxury Hotel of the World".

Hilton Maldives Rangali Island

P.O. Box 2034
Male, Republic of Maldives
Telefon: 0 09 60 / 45 06 29
Telefax: 0 09 60 / 45 06 19
E-Mail: info@maldiveshilton.com.mv
www.hilton.com/worldwideresorts
Reservations: escape tours
Grandlstraße 26, D-81247 München
Telefon: 00 44 / 89 / 8 29 94 80
Telefax: 00 44 / 89 / 82 99 48 97
E-Mail: info@escape-tours.de

Die beiden Inseln Ranglifinolhu und Rangali liegen durch eine kleine Brücke verbunden im Süd-Ari-Atoll, 90 km südwestlich von Male und drei Grad nördlich des Äquators als Teil der Republik Malediven: *„A million miles from the nine to five!"*

Beach-Villa: 250–360 US$, Water-Villas 710 US$, Sunset-Villa 2500 US$, alle Raten & 10 % Tax & 6 US$ pro Tag Secondary Tax.

Spa in Over Water Villas, Massagen: schwedisch, Thai, holistisch, Aromatherapie, Akupressur, Shiatsu, Entgiftungsbehandlungen, Stress-Management, diverse Schönheitsbehandlungen u.v.m. Tennis, Tischtennis, Fitnessraum, Jogging-Track, Pool, PADI-Tauchschule, Segelyacht-Charter, alle Wassersportarten.

4 exquisite Open-Air-Restaurants mit internationalen Spezialitäten unter besonderer Berücksichtigung asiatischer und lokaler Rezepte mit Schwerpunkt auf Fisch und Meeresfrüchten.

Äquatorialklima bei Höchsttemperaturen um 30 °C das ganze Jahr hindurch.

Neben LTU wird Male von vielen Linien- und Charter Airlines angeflogen, darunter Emirates, Austrian Airlines, Thomas Cook und Singapore Airlines.

Bestbestückter Weinkeller der Malediven, 24 Stunden kostenloser Internet-Kiosk.

SUMMARY OF THE HOTELS

Sainte Anne Resort

P.O. Box 388, Victoria, Mahé / Seychelles
Telephone: 0 02 48 / 29 20 00
Telefax: 0 02 48 / 29 20 02
E-mail: sainteanne@bchot.com
Internet: www.sainteanne-resort.com
Beachcomber Hotels, Repräsentanzbüro
Dianastrasse 4, D-85521 Ottobrunn
Telephone: 00 49 / 89 / 6 29 84 90
Internet: www.beachcomber.de

Close to the equator. An offshore island in the Seychelles archipelago close to the main island of Mahé, 10 minutes by boat.

4 different types of accommodation: 79 "Providence" Villas (area approx. 1,076 sq. feet) from Euro 720; 3 "Bel Air" Villas with one bedroom (area approx. 1,937 sq. feet) from Euro 1,400; 4 "Belle Vue" Villas with 2 bedrooms (area approx. 2,906 sq. feet) from Euro 2,525; 1 "Royal Villa" with three bedrooms (area approx. 5,382 sq. feet) from Euro 3,500. All rates include breakfast and taxes. Half board surcharge of Euro 92 per person per day.

Clarins Spa: 2 Hamams, 2 saunas, 3 massage rooms, 1 x outside balneo-therapy, hairdressing, manicure, 2 inside gyms with power-training equipment, outside gym with cardio equipment. 2 floodlit tennis courts, mountain bikes for adults and children. Watersports: sailing, windsurfing, kayak, pedal, glass bottomed boat, scuba diving, snorkelling.

Superb international, Italian and regional dishes available in two restaurants. Focus on fish. Nearly all provisions are shipped in from Paris or Singapore.

Tropical equatorial climate, daily temperature about 30 °C throughout the year.

Thomas Cook and Air Seychelles fly non-stop to Mahé.

Helipad for helicopter transfers and private excursions. Conference facilities available for up to 30 persons.

Soneva Gili Resort & Spa

Lankanfushi Island, North Male Atoll
Republic of Maldives
Telephone: 0 09 60 / 44 03 04
Telefax: 0 09 60 / 44 03 05
E-mail: sonresa@sonevagili.com.mv
Internet: www.six-senses.com/sonevagili

The island Lankanfushi is privately owned and lies in the north atoll.

A total of 44 suites and residences, each in a Water Villa on stilts actually standing in the sea, of these 7 are the Crusoe residences which can only be reached by boat. Rates: Soneva Gili Suite from US$ 500, Soneva Gili Residence from US$ 680, Soneva Gili Crusoe Residence from US$ 780. Meals: Breakfast US$ 25, Lunch US$ 30, Dinner US$ 55 (per person per day). Transfer by speedboat to/from Male Airport US$ 70 per person.

Spa in Overwater Villas. Swedish, Thai, Hawaiian and holistic massage, aromatherapy, acupressure, Shiatsu, cranial massage. Treatment: milk and honey baths, rose petal bath, detoxifying and purifying treatment, stress management, diverse beauty treatments. Tennis, table tennis, PADI diving school, yacht charter, water sports.

Open-air restaurant serving international specialities including Asian and local dishes with particular emphasis on fish and seafood.

Tropical equatorial climate, maximum daytime temperatures throughout the year approx. 30 °C.

Male is served by LTU and many other main airlines and charter companies, including Emirates, Austrian Airlines, Condor and Singapore Airlines.

Soneva Gili is a member of the "Small Luxury Hotels of the World".

Hilton Maldives Rangali Island

P.O. Box 2034
Male, Republic of Maldives
Telephone: 0 09 60 / 45 06 29
Telefax: 0 09 60 / 45 06 19
E-mail: info@maldiveshilton.com.mv
www.hilton.com/worldwideresorts
Reservations: escape tours
Grandlstrasse 26, D-81247 Munich
Telephone: 00 44 / 89 / 8 29 94 80
Telefax: 00 44 / 89 / 82 99 48 97
E-mail: info@escape-tours.de

The two islands of Ranglifinolhu and Rangali in the South Ari Atoll in the Republic of Maldives are linked by a little footbridge. They lie 56 miles south west of Male and three degrees north of the equator, "a million miles from nine to five!"

Beach Villa 250–360 US$, Water Villas 710 US$, Sunset Villa 2,500 US$, all rates plus 10 % tax & 6 US$ per day Secondary Tax.

Spa in overwater villas. Swedish and Thai massage, holistic treatment, aromatherapy, acupressure, Shiatsu, detox treatment, stress management, diverse beauty treatments and much else. Tennis, table tennis, gym, jogging track, pool, PADI diving school, yacht hire, all water sports.

4 exquisite open-air restaurants serving international specialities with particular attention to Asian and local dishes, primarily fish and seafood.

Tropical, equatorial climate, highest daily temperatures throughout the year approx. 30 °C.

As well by LTU, many airlines and charter companies fly to Male, including Emirates, Austrian Airlines, Thomas Cook and Singapore Airlines.

The best stocked wine cellar in the Maldives, 24-hour Internet kiosk free of charge.

ÜBERSICHT DER HOTELS

The Oberoi, Mauritius

Baie aux Tortues, Ponte aux Piments
Mauritius / Indian Ocean
Telefon: 0 02 30 / 2 04 / 36 00
Telefax: 0 02 30 / 2 04 / 36 25
reservations@oberoi-mauritius.com
Internet: www.oberoihotels.com

An der Nordwestküste von Mauritius, am feinen Sandstrand der Baie aux Tortues, ca. 20 Autominuten von Port Louis.

Vier luxuriöse Zimmerkategorien: Luxus-Terrassen-Pavillons (70 qm), großer Wohn-/Schlafraum, begehbarer Schrank, Air-Con, Safe, Minibar, Marmorbad mit im Boden eingelassener Wanne und Pflanzenatrium, Terrasse je nach Saison 700–850 Euro; Luxus Villa (325 qm), Ausstattung wie oben, jedoch mit privatem Garten und Speisepavillon, 950–1 300 Euro; Luxus Villa mit Pool, Ausstattung wie oben, jedoch mit eigenem Swimmingpool, 1 250–1 750 Euro; Royal Villa (650 qm), getrennte Wohn- und Schlafhäuser, größerer Pool, direkt am Wasser, 2 100–2 600 Euro.

Zwei Poolanlagen, Wassersportbasis für Wasserski, Surfen, Pedalos, Kayaks, Schnorcheln, Hobby-Cats (alles inklusive), Hochseeangeln, Tauchen, Parasailing, Katamaran- und Speedboot-Exkursionen (gegen Aufpreis), eigene Tennisplätze; Fitness-Center, Sauna, Dampfbad, exklusives Spa.

„The Restaurant" mit Gourmetküche der Stilrichtungen international, orientalisch und kreolisch. Köstliche Pasta- und Snackküche serviert das legere „The Lagoon Pool Restaurant".

Ganzjähriges Reiseziel. Von Januar bis April (ca. 30 °C), Juli und September ca. 18–23 °C.

Rund 12-stündige Flugreise. Flüge ab Frankfurt gehen mehrmals wöchentlich nonstop. Abholung durch das Hotel.

Mitglied bei The Leading Small Hotels of the World.

Kurland Country Hotel

P.O. Box 209
The Crags 6602, South Africa
Telefon: 00 27 / 44 / 5 34 80 82
Telefax: 00 27 / 44 / 5 34 86 99
E-Mail: info@kurland.co.za
Internet: www.kurland.co.za
Reservierungen:
escape tours
Telefon: 0 89 / 8 29 94 80
Telefax: 0 89 / 82 99 48 97
E-Mail: info@escape-tours.de

An der südafrikanischen Garden Route nahe dem Städtchen Plettenberg Bay am Indischen Ozean gelegen.

Insgesamt 12 individuell gestaltete Gästezimmer. Zimmerpreis: 2 200 Rand (ca. 220 Euro) p. P. im DZ, inkl. Frühstück und Abendessen, Steuern, lokale Getränke und Hauswein.

4 Polofelder, 1 Polo Arena (50 x 100 m), 1 Übungssandplatz von einem Kilometer Länge, kleiner Health Spa mit voll eingerichtetem Kraftraum, Sauna, Dampfbad und Jacuzzi. Schönheitsbehandlungen auf Anfrage, Massagen täglich von 9–17 Uhr.

Einfache, rustikal-wertvolle Küche mit südafrikanischen und europäischen Gerichten.

Heiße Sommer (Weihnachten) und milde Winter, ausgeglichenes klares „kanarisches" Klima das ganze Jahr hindurch. Durchschnittliche Tageshöchsttemperaturen: Juli 15–20 °C, Dezember 25–30 °C.

Außer South African Airways fliegen u. a. auch Lufthansa, British Airways, KLM und LTU Südafrika an.

The Collection by Liz McGrath

The Plettenberg
The Marine
The Cellars-Hohenort
The Collection Johannesburg Office:
Telefon: 00 27 / 11 / 8 83 50 20
Telefax: 00 27 / 11 / 7 83 66 30
E-Mail: collection@icon.co.za
Internet: www.collectionmcgrath.com

Nahe Kapstadt und an der südafrikanischen Garden Route am Indischen Ozean gelegen.

Drei kleine Hotels aus der „Collection" der Südafrikanerin Liz McGrath, die sich alle durch eine virtuose und kreative Vielfalt der Raumgestaltung auszeichnen.

Plettenberg und Marine: Massagen und Schönheitsbehandlungen auf Anfrage durch externe Fachkräfte. Cellars-Hohenort: Golf Putting Green, kleiner Health Spa mit Beauty Salon, Tennis. Elf ausgezeichnete Golfplätze in der Nähe.

Kontinentale sowie einheimische Küche mit Akzent auf frischen Meeresfrüchten sowie malaysische Gerichte (Cellars-Hohenort).

Heiße Sommer (Weihnachten) und milde Winter, ausgeglichenes klares „kanarisches" Klima das ganze Jahr hindurch. Durchschnittliche Tageshöchsttemperaturen: Juli 15–20 °C, Dezember 25–30 °C.

Außer South African Airways fliegen u. a. auch Lufthansa, British Airways, KLM und LTU Südafrika an.

Alle Hotels sind Mitglied der renommierten Gruppe „Relais & Châteaux".

SUMMARY OF THE HOTELS

The Oberoi, Mauritius

Baie aux Tortues, Ponte aux Piments
Mauritius / Indian Ocean
Telephone: 0 02 30 / 2 04 / 36 00
Telefax: 0 02 30 / 2 04 / 36 25
reservations@oberoi-mauritius.com
Internet: www.oberoihotels.com

On the northwest coast of Mauritius, on the fine sandy beach of the Baie aux Tortues, about 20 minutes' drive from Port Louis.

Four luxury room categories: Luxury Terrace Pavilions (approx. 754 square feet), spacious living and sleeping quarters, walk-in cupboard, air conditioning, safe, minibar, marble bath with floor-inlaid tub and plant atrium, terrace 700–850 Euro chargeable according to season; luxury villa (approx 3,500 sq. feet), equipped as above, though with private garden and dining pavilion, 950–1,300 Euro; luxury villa with pool, equipped as above, though with private swimming pool, 1,250–1,750 Euro; Royal Villa (6,996 sq. feet), separate living and sleeping quarters, larger pool, directly on the waterfront, 2,100–2,600 Euro.

Two swimming pools, water-sports base for water skiing, surfing, pedalos etc., private tennis courts, gym, sauna, steam bath, exclusive spa.

"The Restaurant": gourmet cuisine with an international slant, oriental and Creole. Informal "Lagoon Pool Restaurant".

All-season destination. The Mauritian summer lasts from January to April (approx. 30 °C). The winter lasts from July to September, with temperatures of approx. 18–23 °C.

About twelve hours' flight. A number of non-stop flights leave Frankfurt every week. Hotel shuttle service.

Member of The Leading Small Hotels of the World.

Kurland Country Hotel

P.O. Box 209
The Crags 6602, South Africa
Telephone: 00 27 / 44 / 5 34 80 82
Telefax: 00 27 / 44 / 5 34 86 99
E-mail: info@kurland.co.za
Internet: www.kurland.co.za
Reservations:
escape tours
Telephone: 0 89 / 8 29 94 80
Telefax: 0 89 / 82 99 48 97
E-mail: info@escape-tours.de

On South Africa's Garden Route near the little town of Plettenberg Bay on the Indian Ocean.

12 guest rooms furnished with a personal note. Rates: 2,200 Rand (approx. Euro 220) p.p. sharing a double room. The price includes breakfast and an evening meal, tax, local drinks and house wine.

4 polo playing fields, 1 polo arena (50 x 100 metres), 1 kilometre long sandy practice area, small health spa with fully equipped power-training gym, sauna, steam bath and jacuzzi. Beauty treatment on request, massage daily from 9 a.m.–5 p.m.

Simple nourishing country food and South African and European dishes.

Hot summers (Christmas) and mild winters, moderate, mild, clear "Canaries" climate throughout the year. Highest average daytime temperatures: July 15–20 °C, December 25–30 °C.

Apart from South African Airways, Lufthansa, British Airways, KLM and LTU also fly to South Africa.

The Collection by Liz McGrath

The Plettenberg
The Marine
The Cellars-Hohenort
The Collection Johannesburg Office:
Telephone: 00 27 / 11 / 8 83 50 20
Telefax: 00 27 / 11 / 7 83 66 30
E-mail: collection@icon.co.za
Internet: www.collectionmcgrath.com

Near Cape Town on the South African Garden Route beside the Indian Ocean.

Rooms and Suites: Three small hotels from the "Collection" of the South African Liz McGrath, all of which have a distinctive character owing to their creative design and use of space.

Plettenberg and Marine: Massage and beauty treatment on request provided by external beauticians.
Cellars-Hohenort: Golf, putting green, mini-health spa and beauty salon, tennis. Eleven excellent golf courses in the vicinity.

Continental and local cuisine with emphasis on fresh seafood and Malayan dishes (Cellars-Hohenort).

Hot summers (Christmas) and mild winters, temperate, clear "Canaries" climate the whole year. Average daily temperatures: July 15–20 °C, December 25–30 °C.

As well as South African Airways, Lufthansa, British Airways, KLM and LTU also fly to South Africa.

All hotels are members of the renowned "Relais & Châteaux".

ÜBERSICHT DER HOTELS

One & Only Royal Mirage

Telefon: 0 09 71 / 4 / 3 99 99 99
Telefax: 0 09 71 / 4 / 3 99 99 98
www.oneandonlyroyalmirage.com
Kerzner International
Deutschland GmbH
Feldbergstraße 8b, D-61440 Oberursel
Telefon: 0 61 71 / 63 60-0
Telefax: 0 61 71 / 63 60 90
E-Mail: info@kerznerint.de
Internet: kerzner.com

Das Resort One & Only Royal Mirage mit den Luxus-Hideaways The Palace, Arabian Court und Residence & Spa liegt in Dubai, einem der sieben Vereinigten Arabischen Emirate.

The Palace of the One & Only Royal Mirage: 250 elegant im arabischen Stil gestylte Zimmer und Suiten mit allem Komfort. Preise: Palace Deluxe bis Gold Club Suite von 104 bis 560 Euro. The Arabian Court: 172 Zimmer und Suiten. Preise: Arabian Court Deluxe bis Arabian Court Prince Suite von 114 bis 715 Euro. The Residence & Spa: 53 intime Wohnoasen. Preise: Prestige bis Junior Suite von 164 bis 558 Euro.

600 Quadratmeter großer Swimmingpool, Wasserski, Windsurfen, Hochseefischen, Angeln, Tennis, Volleyball. Fünf 18-Loch-Golfplätze in unmittelbarer Nähe, Health-&-Beauty-Center.

Gourmetrestaurant Celebrities: Feinschmeckerküche, Olives: „Cuisine du soleil", Tagine: marokkanische Küche, The Beach: Meeresspezialitäten, Pool Bar: leichte Snacks.

Subtropisches Klima mit Sonne und wolkenlosem Himmel übers ganze Jahr. Nur wenige Tage Regen. Beste Reisezeit im Winter, von Oktober bis Mai.

Emirates fliegt täglich von Frankfurt und München nonstop nach Dubai.

The Royal Coco Palm

2/1 Moo 8 Tumbon bang Muang
Amphur Takua Pa
Phang Nga 82192, Thailand
Telefon: ++66 (0) 76 59 21 00
Telefax: ++66 (0)76 59 21 10
E-Mail: info@cocopalm.co.th
www.theroyalcocopalmresortandspa.com
In Deutschland buchbar über:
Paradise Consult
Ballhof/Kreuzstr. 1, D-30159 Hannover
Telefon: 05 11 / 32 79 37
Telefax: 05 11 / 3 00 45 12
E-Mail: paradise-consult@t-online.de
Internet: www.paradise-consult.de

Die 44 palmstrohgedeckten Deluxe Villen verteilen sich locker über das Grundstück und bieten Aussicht auf das Meer die Poolanlage oder den See. Mit einer Grundfläche von 80 m inkl. Terrasse sind sie mit allen erdenklichen Luxus ausgestattet. Die wunderschönen Bäder verfügen über eine Open-air Dusche. Die sieben luxuriösen 150 m großen Pool Villen bieten zur Ausstattung der Deluxe Villen einen kleinen, abgeschlossenen Garten mit privatem Pool. Preise je nach Saison pro Person und Tag inkl. Frühstück: Deluxe Villa von 146–295 US$, Pool-Villa von 244–392 US$.

Sportbegeisterte finden Fitnessraum, Wassersportzentrum, Tennis, Tischtennis, Dart, und Beach Volleyball. darüber hinaus bietet die nähere Umgebung ein breites Angebot von Golf über Tauchen bis zum Rafting. Erfahrene Spezialistinnen wirken im The Royal Coco Palm Spa.

Drei Restaurants: „Palm Grove Restaurant" mit regionalen und internationalen Spezialitäten, Restaurant „Ruam Jai Thai" mit authentisch thailändischer Küche. „The Mariner Bar & Grill" liegt direkt am Strand.

Die günstigste Reisezeit für den Süden Thailands beginnt nach dem Ende des Monsuns um November und dauert bis Ende März.

Elounda Mare Hotel

GR-72053 Elounda, Crete
Telefon: 00 30 / 84 10 / 4 11 02
Telefax: 00 30 / 84 10 / 4 13 07
E-Mail: mare@elounda-sa.com
Internet: www.elounda-sa.com

In unmittelbarer Meeresnähe nahe dem Ort Elounda im Norden Kretas.

Insgesamt 82 Zimmer und Suiten, davon 38 im Haupthaus und 44 in Bungalows verteilt über das 30 000 Quadratmeter große Gelände. Preisbeispiele Haupthaus: Superior-Doppelzimmer 210–350 Euro, Suite 240–390 Euro, Zweibett-Superior-Suite 450–749 Euro; Bungalows Shared Pool: Standard 235–410 Euro, Suite 280–470 Euro; Bungalows Private Pool: Einbett-Suite (2 Personen) 590–1 000 Euro, Prince Katreas (4 Personen) 880–1440 Euro, Princess Ariadni (4 Personen) 1030–1 615 Euro, King Minos (4 Personen) 1 230–1 910 Euro. Alle Preise je nach Saison inkl. Frühstück und Steuern.

Massage, Sauna, Türkisches Bad, Golf auf 9-Loch-Par-3-Golfplatz im Schwesterhotel Port Elounda, 2 Kunstgras-Tennisplätze, Tischtennis, Tauchschule, Segelyacht-Charter, Wassersport.

Drei Restaurants mit internationalen Spezialitäten unter Berücksichtigung mediterraner und lokaler Rezepte.

Mediterranes Klima mit milden Wintern und trockenen, warmen Sommern. Starke Hitze ist wegen des ständigen Nordwindes selten. Hochsommerliche Höchsttemperaturen um 27 ºC, winterliche Tiefstwerte bei 14 ºC.

Neben LTU wird Kreta von mehreren Charter-Airlines wie Condor oder Hapag-Lloyd angeflogen. Weitere tägliche Linienverbindungen via Athen. In der Hochsaison Fährschiffe von Ancona und Piräus nach Heraklion und Agios Nikolaos.

Moderne Konferenzräume für maximal 150 Personen.

SUMMARY OF THE HOTELS

One & Only Royal Mirage

Telephone: 0 09 71 / 4 / 3 99 99 99
Telefax: 0 0971 / 4 / 3 99 99 98
www.oneandonlyroyalmirage.com
Kerzner International
Deutschland GmbH
Feldbergstrasse 8 b, D-61440 Oberursel
Telephone: 0 61 71 / 63 60-0
Telefax: 0 61 71 / 63 60 90
E-mail: info@kerznerint.de
Internet: kerzner.com

The One and Only Royal Mirage Resort which comprises the luxury hideaways The Palace, The Arabian Court, and The Residence and Spa, is in Dubai, one of the seven emirates of the United Arab Emirates.

The Palace of The One and Only Royal Mirage: 250 elegant rooms and suites in Arab style with every amenity. Rates for the Palace Deluxe to the Gold Club Suite range from Euro 104.- to 560.-.
The Arabian Court: 172 rooms and suites. Rates for the Arabian Court Deluxe to the Arabian Court Prince Suite range from Euro 114.- to 715.-. The Residence and Spa: 52 intimate living oases. Rates for the Prestige Suite to the Junior Suites range from Euro 164.- to 558.-.

Large swimming pool (600 sq. metres), water skiing, windsurfing, deep sea fishing, angling, tennis, volleyball. Five 18-hole golf courses in the immediate vicinity, Health & Beauty Centre.

"Celebrities" gourmet restaurant serves haute cuisine; "Olives": "cuisine du soleil"; Tagine: Moroccan dishes; "The Beach": specializes in sea food; the Pool Bar: light snacks.

Subtropical climate – sun and cloudless skies throught the year. Rainfall is limited to a few days only. The best time to travel is in the winter, i.e. from October to May.

Emirates operates daily non-stop flights from Frankfurt and Munich.

The Royal Coco Palm

2/1 Moo 8 Tumbon bang Muang
Amphur Takua Pa
Phang Nga 82192, Thailand
Telephone: ++66 (0) 76 59 21 00
Telefax: ++66 (0) 76 59 21 10
www.theroyalcocopalmresortandspa.com
E-mail: info@cocopalm.co.th
In Germany reservations can be made by contacting: Paradise Consult
Ballhof/Kreuzstr. 1, D-30159 Hannover
Telephone: 00 49 (0) 5 11 / 32 79 37
Telefax: 00 49 (0) 5 11 / 3 00 45 12
Internet: www.paradise-consult.de
E-mail: paradise-consult@t-online.de

The 44 palm-thatched villas are scattered across the grounds and afford views of the sea, the pool area or the lake. Each has an area of over 860 sq. feet, and includes a terrace and every conceivable luxury. The wonderful bathrooms have an open-air shower. Each of the seven luxury Pool Villas (1,614 sq. ft.) has in addition to the de luxe furnishings and fitting an enclosed garden and a private pool. Rates per person depending on season including breakfast: Deluxe Villa from 146–295 US$, Pool Villa from 244–392 US$.

For sports enthusiasts there is a gym, a water sports centre, and tennis. Table tennis, darts and beach volley ball. In addition the area provides a wide choice of activities such as golf, diving and rafting. Experienced specialists work at the Royal Coco Palm Spa.

The three restaurants of the resort look after the culinary welfare of its guests. The Palm Grove Restaurant serves regional and international dishes; the Ruam Jai Thai Restaurant provides authentic Thai cuisine, and The Mariner Bar & Grill is down at the beach.

The most favourable time to travel to South Thailand begins around November after the end of the monsoon and lasts until the end of March.

Elounda Mare Hotel

GR-72053 Elounda, Crete
Telephone: 00 30 / 84 10 / 4 11 02
Telefax: 00 30 / 84 10 / 4 13 07
E-mail: mare@elounda-sa.com
Internet: www.elounda-sa.com

Close to the sea near Elounda in the north of Crete.

All in all 82 rooms and suites of which 38 in the main house and 44 in bungalows distributed across 7½ acres of grounds. Example of rates for accommodation in the main house: Superior double room Euro 210–350, Suite Euro 240–390, 2-bedroom Superior Suite Euro 450–749. Bungalows with shared pool: Standard Euro 235–410, Suite Euro 280–470. Bungalows with private pool: 1-bedroom suite (2 persons), Euro 590–1000; Prince Katreas (4 persons) Euro 880–1,440; Princess Ariadne (4 persons) Euro 1,030–1,615; King Minos (4 persons) Euro 1,230–1,910. All rates depending on season include breakfast and taxes.

Massage, sauna, Turkish bath, golf on 9-hole Par 3 course at the sister hotel of Port Elounda close by, 2 artificial grass tennis courts, table tennis, diving school, yacht charter, water sports.

Three restaurants serving international specialities including Mediterranean and local dishes.

Mediterranean climate, mild winters and warm dry summers. Owing to the constant north wind it never gets very hot. Maximum temperature in high summer, about 27 °C, lowest winter temperature around 14 °C.

LTU flies to Crete but also several charter airlines such as Condor, and Hapag-Lloyd. Other flights via Athens. In high season there are also ferries from Ancona and Piräus to Heraclion and Agios Nikolaos.

Modern conference rooms for a maximum of 150 people.

ÜBERSICHT DER HOTELS

Porto Elounda de Luxe

Crete GR-72053, Greece
Telefon: 00 30 / 2 84 10 / 4 19 03
Telefax: 00 30 / 2 84 10 / 4 18 89
Internet: www.porteelounda.com
E-mail: porto@elounda.com

Elounda liegt im Norden Kretas an der wunderschönen Mirabello-Bucht. Das Fünf-Sterne Hotel liegt auf einer winzigen Halbinsel.

23 zweigeschossige Superior-Suiten mit Meerblick (100 qm), sieben Präsidentensuiten (150 qm) mit eigenem Garten und Pool, Grande Suite (250 qm) mit 1 000 qm Privatgrundstück und eigenem Pool.

Großes Angebot an Wassersportmöglichkeiten wie Jet-Skiing, Schnorcheln, Tauchen, Surfen. Innen- und Außenpoolanlage, Tennis und Golf.

Das Panoramarestaurant Calypso bietet exquisite internationale und griechische Küche und eine exzellente Weinauswahl.

Für Ferien sind vor allem die Monate von April bis Oktober geeignet. Der Mai ist die schönste Reisezeit, da Kreta dann am grünsten ist und viel Blumen blühen.

LTU fliegt nonstop in drei Stunden von Köln, Düsseldorf, Frankfurt, Hamburg, München und Stuttgart. Das Resort liegt 70 Kilometer vom internationalen Flughafen Heraklion entfernt. Auf Wunsch Limousinenservice.

Grecotel Mykonos Blu

Psarou Beach Platys Gialos
Platis Yalos
GR-84600, Mykonos
Telefon: 00 30 / 2 28 90 / 2 79 00
Telefax: 00 30 / 2 28 90 / 2 77 83
E-Mail: hideaways@grecotel.gr
Internet: www.grecotel.gr

In bester Strandlage an der Psarou-Bucht vier Kilometer von Mykonos-Stadt sowie Airport entfernt.

102 Zimmer und Suiten mit 204 Betten, aufgeteilt in 4 Kategorien. Preisbeispiele: DZ mit Gartenblick ab 195 Euro, Island-Bungalow Deluxe mit Meerblick ab 280 Euro, Junior Suite mit privatem Pool ab 475 Euro. Alle Preise pro Raum inkl. Frühstück.

Fitness-Galerie mit Kraftraum, Sauna, Massagen. Ein großer Außenpool, ein kleinerer beheizbarer Innenpool.

Restaurant „Poets of Aegean": internationale und lokale Spezialitäten à la carte; „L'Archipel": Brasserie mit überwiegend einheimischen Snacks und leichten internationalen Gerichten.

Mediterranes Klima mit milden Wintern und trockenen, warmen Sommern. Starke Hitze ist wegen des ständigen Nordwindes selten. Hochsommerliche Höchsttemperaturen um 27 °C, winterliche Tiefstwerte bei 12 °C.

Neben Olympic Airways wird Mykonos von mehreren Charter-Airlines wie Thomas Cook oder Hapag-Lloyd direkt angeflogen.

Konferenzräume bis 200 Personen, *state of the art equipment.* Das Hotel ist geöffnet von April bis Oktober.

Hotel Romazzino

I-07020 Porto Cervo (SS)
Costa Smeralda / Italien
Telefon: +39 / 07 89 / 97 71 11
Telefax: +39 / 07 89 / 97 76 14
res067.romazzino@starwoodhotels.com
www.luxurycollection.com/romazzino

Das Hotel Romazzino liegt an Sardiniens berühmter Costa Smeralda und verfügt über den längsten Privatstrand dieses begehrten Küstenabschnitts.

94 luxuriöse Zimmer und Suiten mit privater Terrasse sowie Meer- oder Gartenblick. Alle Interieurs im typisch sardischen Stil, individuell regelbare Air-Con, Minibar, Direktwahltelefon, Sat-TV, Safe, Fön. Präsidenten-Suite mit eigenem Fitness-Studio. Je nach Saison DZ 500–870 Euro p.P. inkl HP. Suiten von 200–1320 Euro p.P.

Eigener Privatstrand, Meerwasser-Swimmingpool, Wassersportbasis mit vielseitigem Angebot, Tennisanlage mit Flutlicht, Mountainbiking, Fitness-Center, Health-Center, Pevero Golf Club, Cervo Tennis Club, Reiten, Hochseefischen, Wandern u.v.m.

Gourmetrestaurant „Romazzino" mit erstklassiger sardischer wie internationaler Cuisine. „Barbecue Restaurant" am Strand, leger, mit großer Antipastiauswahl und Grillspezialitäten. Zwei Bars.

Das Hotel ist von Mai bis Oktober geöffnet, was auch der besten Reisezeit für einen Sardinienaufenthalt entspricht.

Linienflug mit Lufthansa nach Mailand oder Rom. Von dort aus mit einer regionalen Fluggesellschaft zum internationalen Costa Smeralda Airport im sardischen Olbia. 30 Minuten Limousinen-Transfer zum Hotel.

The Luxury Collection Starwood Hotels & Resorts. Geöffnet von Mai bis Oktober.

SUMMARY OF THE HOTELS

Porto Elounda de Luxe

Crete GR-72053, Greece
Telephone: 00 30 / 2 84 10 / 4 19 03
Telefax: 00 30 / 2 84 10 / 4 18 89
Internet: www.porteelounda.com
E-mail: porto@elounda.com

Elounda is in northern Crete in the delightful Mirabello bay. The five-star hotel stands on a minute peninsula.

There are 23 two-storey Superior Suites with a view over the sea (1,076 square . feet), seven Presidential Suites (1,614 square. feet) with private garden and pool, the Grand Suite (2,691 square feet) with 10,764 square feet of private terrain and private pool.

An abundance of water sports is on offer, such as jet skiing, snorkelling, diving and surfing. Indoor and outdoor pool, tennis and golf.

The Calypso panoramic restaurant offers exquisite international and Greek cuisine and an excellent wine selection.

April to October is best time to go on holiday. May is the loveliest time to travel, as Crete is then at its greenest and in full bloom.

LTU provides nonstop three-hour flights from Cologne, Düsseldorf, Frankfurt, Hamburg, Munich und Stuttgart. The resort is 44 miles from Heraklion International Airport. Limousine service is available if require.

Grecotel Mykonos Blu

Psarou Beach Platys Gialos
Platis Yalos
GR-84600, Mykonos
Telephone: 00 30 / 2 28 90 / 2 79 00
Telefax: 00 30 / 2 28 90 / 2 77 83
E-mail: hideaways@grecotel.gr
Internet: www.grecotel.gr

Located beside the finest beach of the Psarou Bay, $3^1/_2$ miles from the town of Mykonos and the airport.

102 rooms and suites with 204 beds. Accommodation 4 categories. Examples of rates: Garden view double room from Euro 195; Island Bungalow Deluxe with sea views from Euro 280; Junior Suite with private pool from Euro 475. All rates apply per room and include breakfast.

Fitness gallery with power training gym, sauna, massage. Large open air pool and a smaller indoor pool which can be heated.

"Poets of Ægean" restaurant serves an international cuisine and local specialities à la carte; the "L'Archipel" brasserie serves mainly local snacks and light international dishes.

Mediterranean climate with mild winters and dry warm summers. It seldom gets very hot owing to the constant north wind. Highest summer temperature 27 °C, lowest winter temperature 12 °C.

As well as Olympic Airways Mykonos a number of other charter airlines operate flights to Mykonos, including Thomas Cook and Hapag-Lloyd.

Conference rooms with state of the art equipment accommodating up to 200 persons. The hotel is open from April to October.

Hotel Romazzino

I-07020 Porto Cervo (SS)
Costa Smeralda / Italy
Telephone: 00 39 / 07 89 / 97 71 11
Telefax: 00 39 / 07 89 / 97 76 14
res067.romazzino@starwoodhotels.com
www.luxurycollection.com/romazzino

The Romazzino Hotel is on Sardinia's famous Costa Smeralda and has the longest private beach on this particularly sought-after part of the coast.

94 luxurious rooms and suites with private terrace and views of either the sea or the garden. All interiors are in typical Sardinian style, and have adjustable air-conditioning, minibar, DDI telephone, Sat TV, a safe and a hairdryer. The Presidential Suite has its own fitness studio. Depending on season rates for a double room half board range from Euro 500.– to 870.– per person, Suites are from Euro 200 – 1,320.–. p.p.

Private beach, seawater swimming pool, water sports' centre offering a wide range on activities, floodlit tennis courts; mountain biking, Fitness Centre, Health Centre Pervero Gold Club, Cervo Tennis Club, riding, deep sea fishing, rambling and much else.

"Romazzino" gourmet restaurant serving first class Sardinian and global cuisine. Informal "Barbecue Restaurant" on the beach offering a large selection of antipasta and grill specialities. Two bars.

The hotel is open from May to October, the best time to visit Sardinia.

Scheduled Lufthansa flights to Milan and Rome. Connecting flight with a regional airline to the international Costa Smeralda Airport in Olbia, Sardinia. 30 minute limousine transfer to the hotel.

The Luxury Collection Starwood Hotels & Resorts. Open from May to October.

ÜBERSICHT DER HOTELS

Son Net

E-07194 Puigpunyent
Mallorca
Telefon: 00 34 / 9 71 / 14 70 00
Telefax: 00 34 / 9 71 / 14 70 01
E-Mail: recepcion@sonnet.es
Internet: www.sonnet.es

Son Net liegt auf der Baleareninsel Mallorca, am Hügel über dem Bergdorf Puigpunyent, ca. 12 Autominuten von Palma de Mallorca.

Zwei Gran Suiten, eine Suite mit eigenem Swimmingpool, vier Royal Suiten – sie bieten mit 130 bis 150 qm das größte Logis, 25 Zimmer und Suiten. Die restaurierte Architektur des alten mallorquinischen Herrenhauses verschmilzt mit edlem heutigen Interior Design. Zimmer von 255–390 Euro, Gran Suite 810 Euro, Royal Suite 956 Euro.

30 m langer Außenpool, Harttennisplatz, Fitnessraum mit Sauna und Jacuzzi, 5 Golfplätze etwa eine halbe Stunde entfernt; Beauty-Spa.

Grill-Restaurant Gazebo unter freiem Himmel mit tagesfrischem Fisch, Fleisch, Salat und Gemüse. Im Gourmetrestaurant L'Orangerie bietet Küchenchef Francisco Martorell aus Sóller stilvolle, anregend kreative, perfekt zubereitete Mittelmeer-Cuisine mit vielen Produkten von der Insel.

Mediterranes Klima mit trockenen heißen Sommern und milden Wintern. Ganzjahresziel.

Internationaler Flughafen von Palma. Auf Wunsch Transfer durch das Hotel.

Mitglied der Stein Group.

Schlosshotel Burg Schlitz

D-17166 Hohen Demzin
Mecklenburg-Vorpommern
Telefon: 0 39 96 / 1 27 00
Telefax: 0 39 96 / 12 70 70
E-Mail: burg-schlitz@t-online.de
Internet: www.Burg-Schlitz.de

Das Schlosshotel Burg Schlitz liegt im deutschen Bundesland Mecklenburg-Vorpommern, im Herzen der Mecklenburgischen Schweiz, etwas außerhalb des Ortes Hohen Demzin, ca. 50 km südlich von Rostock.

14 Einzel- und Doppelzimmer, 6 Suiten. Luxuriöser Komfort, Interieurs mit Antiquitäten und maßgefertigten Möbeln aus den Deutschen Werkstätten Hellerau. Man genießt die restaurierte klassizistische Architektur. Zimmer und Suiten von 160 bis 750 Euro.

Ginkgo-Spa, unter anderem mit den Kosmetikprogrammen von Kanebo. Reiten, jagen, Bogenschießen, angeln, wandern, Mountainbike, Bootsfahrten.

Schlosscafé mit pfiffiger Bistroküche, Schlossrestaurant mit mediterraner, regionaler und euro-asiatischer Gourmetcuisine.

Von der See beeinflusstes mildes Klima mit viel Sonne rund ums Jahr. Ganzjahresziel.

Flughafen Rostock 47 km. Flughafen Berlin-Tegel 170 km. Auf Wunsch Limousinenservice für die Transfers.

Seit 2002 Mitglied bei „Relais & Châteaux".

Fährhaus Munkmarsch

Heefwai 1
D-25980 Munkmarsch / Sylt
Telefon: 0 46 51 / 93 97-0
Telefax: 0 46 51 / 93 97-10
E-Mail: info@faehrhaus-sylt.de
Internet: www.faehrhaus-sylt.de

Das stattliche Fährhaus liegt am Munkmarscher Hafen mit Blick auf Yachthafen und Wattenmeer.

14 elegant, modern gestylte Zimmer und sechs Suiten mit allem Komfort zeugen von kultivierter Wohnkultur. Preise je nach Kategorie zwischen 150 und 295 Euro.

Großzügige Badelandschaft, Erlebnisduschen, Whirlpool, Dampfbad, Sauna, Solarium, Fitnessraum mit modernsten Geräten, Beautyfarm mit hochwertigen Produkten von LIGNE ST. BARTH, Golf und Radwanderungen.

Feine Sterne-Cuisine im Gourmetrestaurant und regionale Zubereitungen in der Käpt'n Selmer Stube.

Westwinde sorgen auf Sylt für angenehme Sommer und Winter. Die Luft ist dann besonders heilkräftig. Hauptferienzeit: Juni bis September.

Sylt wird von allen großen Flughäfen mit kleinen Maschinen angeflogen. Mit dem Autozug von Niebüll nach Westerland, weiter Richtung Sylt-Ost/Munkmarsch

Kultivierte Wohnoase am Wattenmeer fernab der Touristenhochburgen.

SUMMARY OF THE HOTELS

Son Net

E-07194 Puigpunyent
Mallorca
Telephone: 00 34 / 9 71 / 14 70 00
Telefax: 00 34 / 9 71 / 14 70 01
E-mail: recepcion@sonnet.es
Internet: www.sonnet.es

Son Net is on the Balearic island of Majorca situated on a hill overlooking the mountain village of Puigpunyent, about 12 minutes drive away from Palma de Mallorca.

Two Gran Suites, one suite with a swimming pool, four Royal Suites each with an area of 1,400 to 1,615 square feet, 25 rooms and suites. The restored architecture of this old Majorcan mansion blends with the fine contemporary interior design. Room rates from Euro 255,- to 390,-, Gran Suite Euro 810,-, Royal Suite Euro 956,-.

30 metre outdoor pool, hard tennis court, gym with sauna and jacuzzi, 5 golf courses about half an hour away; beauty spa.

Gazabo outdoor grill restaurant serving fresh fish daily, meat, salads and vegetables. At the L'Orangerie gourmet restaurant the chef, Francisco Martorell from Sóller, serves stylish, imaginative Mediterranean cuisine which has been superbly prepared. Many of his ingredients are island products.

Mediterranean climate with dry hot summers and mild winters. All year destination. Palma International Airport. Hotel transfer on request.

Member of the Stein Group.

Schlosshotel Burg Schlitz

D-17166 Hohen Demzin
Mecklenburg-Vorpommern
Telephone: 0 39 96 / 1 27 00
Telefax: 0 39 96 / 12 70 70
E-mail: burg-schlitz@t-online.de
Internet: www.Burg-Schlitz.de

The Schlosshotel Burg Schlitz is in the German State of Mecklenburg-Vorpommern at the heart of "Mecklenburg's Switzerland" just outside Hohen Demzin, about 31 miles south of Rostock.

14 single rooms, 6 suites. Luxurious accommodation, interiors furnished with antiques and made-to-measure furniture from the German Hellerau workshops. Restored classical architecture. Rates for rooms and suites from Euro 160 to 750.

Ginkgo Spa providing inter alia Kanebo cosmetics programme. Riding, hunting, archery, angling, rambling, mountain biking, boat trips.

Schlosscafé serving smart bistro food. Schlossrestaurant serving Mediterranean, regional and Euro-Asian gourmet cuisine.

Temperate marine climate with plenty of sunshine all the year round. All-year destination.

Rostock Airport approx. 30 miles away. Berlin-Tegel Airport 105 miles. Limousine transfer service on request.

Member of "Relais & Châteaux" since 2002.

Fährhaus Munkmarsch

Heefwai 1
D-25980 Munkmarsch / Sylt
Telephone: 0 46 51 / 93 97-0
Telefax: 0 46 51 / 93 97-10
E-mail: info@faehrhaus-sylt.de
Internet: www.faehrhaus-sylt.de

The impressive ferry house is in Munkmarsch Harbour overlooking the marina and the mud flats.

Fourteen elegant rooms and six suites with a contemporary design and every amenity provide stylish environment for sophisticated living. Rates depending on category: Euro 150.- to 295.

Spacious spa area, adventure showers, whirlpool, steam bath, sauna, solarium, gym with the very latest equipment, beauty farm using the exclusive products of LIGNE ST BARTH, golf and cycling.

Excellent "star" cuisine in the gourmet restaurant. Regional food in "Captain Selmer's Parlour".

The prevailing westerly winds ensure a temperate climate throughout the year. The air is particularly beneficial in the main holiday season from June to September.

Sylt is accessible from all major airports by small planes. The Autorail from Niebüll to Westerland, then onwards to Sylt-Ost / Munkmarsch.

Oasis offering a sophisticated lifestyle on the mud flats, far from the popular tourist resorts.

ÜBERSICHT DER HOTELS

Thurnhers Alpenhof

A-6763 Zürs / Arlberg
Telefon: 00 43 / 55 83 / 21 91
Telefax: 00 43 / 55 83 / 33 30
E-Mail: mail@thurnhers-alpenhof.at
Internet: www.thurnhers-alpenhof.at

Zürs liegt in 1720 Metern Höhe am österreichischen Arlberg. Direkt im Ort, nur ein paar Schritte vom Lift und der örtlichen Skischule entfernt.

17 großzügige Suiten teilweise mit Whirlpoolwanne und offenem Kamin, 9 Juniorsuiten, 12 individuell eingerichtete Doppelzimmer und 3 Einzelzimmer, Preis pro Zimmer je nach Saison von 240,– bis 532,– Euro, Suiten von 584,– bis 1 366,– Euro.

Ski total von November bis April, 220 Kilometer präparierte Piste und 180 Kilometer Tiefschnee-Abfahrten. Hallenbad, Sauna, Dampfbad, Tischtennis, Billard und Fitnessbereich im Haus.

Moderne, leichte Gourmetküche, mediterran, aber auch mal asiatisch inspiriert.

Mit einer Höhe von 1720 Metern ist Zürs von November bis Ostern absolut schneesicher. Das Hotel ist nur vom 12. Dezember bis Ostermontag geöffnet.

Flughäfen Innsbruck 150 Kilometer, Zürich 200 Kilometer, München 250 Kilometer, Friedrichshafen 100 Kilometer. Mit dem Zug fährt man bis zum Bahnhof Langen am Arlberg.

Mitglied der Leading Small Hotels of the World.

Hotel Schloss Seefels

Töschling 1
A-9210 Pörtschach / Wörthersee
Telefon: 00 43 / 42 72 / 23 77
Telefax: 00 43 / 42 72 / 37 04
E-Mail: office@seefels.com
Internet: www.seefels.com

Eingebettet in einen herrschaftlichen Schlosspark liegt das Hotel Schloss Seefels direkt am malerischen Wörthersee, 23 Kilometer von Klagenfurt entfernt.

Die 37 Deluxe-Zimmer, 20 Deluxe-Suiten und 14 exklusive Owners-Suiten bieten Luxus und Behaglichkeit. Alle mit luxuriösen Interieurs, Klimaanlage, Sat-TV, Radio, Minibar, Telefon, Fax- und Internetanschluss, teilweise mit Balkon und Seeblick.

Die Umgebung bietet vielerlei Aktivitäten. 7 Golfplätze befinden sich in unmittelbarer Nähe, eigenes Wassersportzentrum mit Bootsmarina, 1000 Quadratmeter Felsen Spa mit Innen- und Außenpool und einer großzügigen Saunalandschaft. Die Kosmetik- und Massagekabinen liegen direkt am See.

Gourmetrestaurant La Terrasse: Zwei-Hauben-Küche, Orangerie: 5-gängige Wahlmenüs oder Abendbuffet für die Hotelgäste, Porto Bello: A-la-carte-Strandrestaurant direkt am See.

Beste Reisezeit: ab 19. Dezember bis 31. Oktober

Bis zum Flughafen Klagenfurt sind es 23 Kilometer.

Kinderbetreuung, medizinische Anti-Aging-Therapien.

Sandy Lane

St. James
Barbados / West Indies
Telefon: 0 01 / 2 46 / 4 44 20 00
Telefax: 0 01 / 2 46 / 4 44 22 22
E-Mail: mail@sandylane.com
Internet: www.sandylane.com

Nördlich von Bridgedown, der Hauptstadt der Antilleninsel Barbados, liegt das Resort am nahezu endlosen St. James Beach.

Exklusive Materialien, dezente Farben, eigene Balkone/Terrassen und Hightech-Equipment prägen die Wohlfühl-Atmosphäre in den 112 luxuriösen Zimmer und Suiten. Strohbeck Reisen Stuttgart bietet interessant geschnürte Packages: z. B. 10 Tage inkl. Flug und tägliches Greenfee ab 3190 Euro pro Person, Übernachtung mit Frühstück.

Drei hoteleigene Golfplätze, Wassersportzentrum und ein Spa-Center der Superlative.

Das Gourmetrestaurant L'Acajou verwöhnt mit internationalen Spezialitäten. Abwechslungsreiche Frische-Küche und regionale Spezialitäten speist man im Restaurant Banjan Blue direkt am Strand.

Barbados ist fast das ganze Jahr mit Sonne gesegnet, Winde sorgen für eine angenehme Brise. Das ganze Jahr sind Luft und Wasser wunderbar warm, selbst in der Regenzeit von Juni bis Dezember regnet es immer nur kurz.

Thomas Cook fliegt von Frankfurt/Main direkt nach Bridgetown, der Hauptstadt von Barbados.

Kontakt in Deutschland
Strohbeck Reisen Stuttgart
Telefon: 07 11 / 46 85 18
Telefax: 07 11 / 48 77 68
E-Mail: info@strohbeckreisen.de
Internet: www.strohbeckreisen.de

SUMMARY OF THE HOTELS

Thurnhers Alpenhof

A-6763 Zürs / Arlberg
Telephone: 00 43 / 55 83 / 21 91
Telefax: 00 43 / 55 83 / 33 30
E-mail: mail@thurnhers-alpenhof.at
Internet: www.thurnhers-alpenhof.at

Zürs is located 1720 Meters high up on the austrian Arlberg. Central in the town, only a few steps away from the Ski lift and the austrian Ski academy.

17 spacoius Suits partly with Whirlpool bathtubs and open Fireplaces, 9 Juniorsuites, 12 individual furnished Doublerooms and 3 Singelrooms, Prices per person depending on season from 240,- to 532,- Euro, Suites from 584,- to 1366,- Euro.

Ski from November to April, 220 km prepared slopes and 180 km deepsnowslopes. Hotel own Indoorpool, Sauna, steamsauna, tabletennis, Pool und Fitnessarea.

Modern light Gourmet Cuisine, mediterrain as well as asiatic flavoured cuisine.

With a hight of 1720 Metern Zürs is snow guaranteed from November till the Easter holidays. The Hotel is open from December 9th to Eastermonday.

Airports Innsbruck 150 km, Zürich 200 km, München 250 km, Friedrichshafen 100 km. By train to Railwaystation Langen to Arlberg.

Member of The Leading Small Hotels of the World.

Hotel Schloss Seefels

Töschling 1
A-9210 Pörtschach / Wörthersee
Telephone: 00 43 / 42 72 / 23 77
Telefax: 00 43 / 42 72 / 37 04
E-mail: office@seefels.com
Internet: www.seefels.com

Set in heavenly castle grounds, the Hotel Schloss Seefels is situated right beside the picturesque Lake Wörthersee, about 14 miles from Klagenfurt.

The 37 Deluxe rooms, 20 Deluxe suites and 14 exclusive Owners' Suites provide both luxury and homeliness. All have luxurious interiors, air-conditioning, Sat TV, radio, minibar, a telephone, a fax and modem connection. Some have a balcony with sea views.

Plenty of opportunities for leisure activities are close at hand. 7 golf courses are nearby; the hotel has its own water sports' centre and marina, a of rock-based spa (10,764 sq. feet) with an indoor and outdoor pools and a spacious sauna area. The beauty treatment and massage cubicles are on the shore.

La Terrasse gourmet restaurant: two toque chefs. The Orangery: selection of 5-course menus or evening buffet for hotel guests. The Porto Bello: lakeside à la carte restaurant.

Climate, best time to travel: from 19th December to 31 October.

Approx. 14 miles to Klagenfurt Airport.

Child care, medical anti-aging therapies.

Sandy Lane

St. James
Barbados / West Indies
Telephone: 0 01 / 2 46 / 4 44 20 00
Telefax: 0 01 / 2 46 / 4 44 22 22
E-mail: mail@sandylane.com
Internet: www.sandylane.com

North of Bridgetown, the capitel of the caribbean island Barbados, on the virtually endless St. James Beach.

Exclusive fabrics, discret colours, private terrace/balcony and hightech-equipment are crucial elements of the feel-good atmosphere in the suite 112 luxurios rooms and suites. Strohbeck Reisen Stuttgart offers interesting packages deals: e.g. 10-day packages including flights, daily green fee and bed & breakfast, 3,190 Euro per person.

Three golf courses owned by the hotel, professionally managed water sports' centre and a Spa centre with many superlatives.

The L'Acajou gourmet restaurant offers exquisite cuisine. The Banjan Blue restaurant on the beach serves a variety of fresh dishes and regional specialities.

Barbados are sunny nearly all the year round. There is always a breeze so it never gets too hot. The air and the water are wonderfully warm throughout the year. Even in the rainy season from June to December, it never rains for very long.

Thomas Cook flies direct from Frankfurt/Main to Bridgetown in Barbados.

Contact in Germany:
Strohbeck Reisen Stuttgart
Telephone: 07 11 / 46 85 18
Telefax: 07 11 / 48 77 68
E-mail: info@strohbeckreisen.de
Internet: www.strohbeckreisen.de

ÜBERSICHT DER HOTELS

Mustique Villa Rentals

P.O. Box 349
St.Vincent & the Grenadines / West Indies
Telefon: 0 01 / 7 84 / 4 88-80 00
Telefax: 0 01 / 7 84 / 4 88-90 00
villarentals@mustique-islands.com
www.mustique-island.com

Die 12 Quadratkilometer große Insel gehört im Bereich der Kleinen Antillen zu den Grenadinen.

Die 55 exklusiven Villen sind ganz nach dem Geschmack der jeweiligen Besitzer eingerichtet und entpuppen sich besonders für Liebhaber außergewöhnlicher Wohnträume als wahre Offenbarung. Preise: pro Woche je nach Anzahl der Schlafzimmer, Größe und Saison von 3 500 (2 Schlafzimmer) bis 40 000 US$ (7 Schlafzimmer) inkl. Inselflughafen-Transfer, ein Mini-Van, Hauspersonal Koch, Gärtner und Haushälterin).

Das Sportangebot ist breit gefächert mit Tennisplätzen sowie Gestüt, Physiotherapeuten, professionelles Beautycenter und Wassersportzentrum.

Jede Villa verfügt über einen eigenen Koch, der von der internationalen Küche bis zu lokalen Spezialitäten allen Ansprüchen gerecht wird. Ein ausgezeichnetes Restaurant und die legendäre Bar Basil's ergänzen das Angebot.

Die Grenadinen sind fast das ganze Jahr mit Sonne gesegnet, Winde sorgen für eine angenehme Brise. Das ganze Jahr sind Luft und Wasser wunderbar warm, selbst in der Regenzeit von Juni bis Dezember regnet es immer nur kurz.

Die großen Flughäfen der Antillen-Inseln werden von vielen internationalen Fluglinien angeflogen. Von dort weiter mit Mustique Airways.

Kontakt in Deutschland:
Gerlinde Hofbauer
Telefon: 00 49 / (0) 89 / 5 43 95 04
Telefax: 00 49 / (0) 89 / 5 43 97 65
E-Mail: mustiquevillas@freenet.de

Sea Cloud

Buchungen im Reisebüro oder direkt bei:
Hapag-Lloyd Kreuzfahrten GmbH
Ballindamm 25
D-20095 Hamburg
Telefon: 0 40 / 30 01 46 00
Telefax: 0 40 / 30 01 46 01
Internet: www.hapag-lloyd.de

Die legendäre Segelyacht kreuzt in den schönsten Segelrevieren der Welt. Im Winter natürlich in der Karibik und von Mai bis Oktober im westlichen und östlichen Mittelmeerraum.

22 Außenkabinen von 9,5 bis 13,5 qm und 10 Originalkabinen von 18 bis 80 qm. Alle Kabinen sind mit Marmorbad mit Dusche (die Originalkabinen mit Badewanne, Ausnahmen Nr. 6 und 10), WC, Bademantel, Föhn, Badeaccessoires, individuell regelbarer Klimaanlage, Telefon, Kleiderschrank und Safe ausgestattet. Wohnhighlights sind die beiden originalgetreuen Eignerkabinen.

Die Sea Cloud verfügt über Schnorchel-, Wasserski- und Windsurfausrüstungen, die je nach Wetterlage und in Absprache mit der Schiffsleitung kostenlos genutzt werden kann.

Zum Lunch und Dinner verwöhnen die Köche im wunderschönen Restaurant mit erlesenen, internationalen Spezialitäten, mit edlen Weinen oder Barbecue an Deck.

Die Sea Cloud folgt ganzjährig der Sonne.

Linienflüge zu und von den Ausgangs- bzw. Zielflughäfen werden von Hapag-Lloyd organisiert. Tickets in der First- und Business-Class sind gegen Aufpreis – vorbehaltlich der Verfügbarkeit – buchbar.

Ein modern ausgestattetes kleines Hospital und Schiffsarzt.

Pita Maha Resort & Spa

P.O. Box 198
Ubud 80571, Bali / Indonesia
Telefon: 00 62 / 3 61 / 97 43 30
Telefax: 00 62 / 3 61 / 97 43 29
pitamaha@dps.mega.net.id
www.beauty-hotels.com/pita-maha

Wenige Kilometer außerhalb von Ubud, dem künstlerischen Zentrums Balis, in der Mitte der Insel.

86 private Villas mit 300 bis 800 Quadratmetern Wohnfläche, alle mit privatem Garten, Pool, getrennten Wohn-/ Schlafbereichen. Preisbeispiele: Pool Villa: 400 US$, Royal Villa 550 US$, Royal House 1 500 US$. Alle Preise inkl. Frühstück zzgl. 21 % Tax & Service Charge.

Größter und exklusivster Spa Balis, im Besitz und Management von Shiseido Co. Ltd. of Japan. 15 luxuriöse private Behandlungs-Villas, Spa-Garten mit Swimmingpools, Jacuzzis und Saunen.

Internationale und regionale Spezialitäten in 2 Restaurants in teils spektakulärer Lage.

Aufgrund der Äquatornähe ganzjährig um 30 ºC.

Von mehreren europäischen Flughäfen (zum Beispiel Frankfurt, London, Paris) wird Denpasar mit Garuda Indonesia via Singapur angeflogen. Ebenfalls mit Zwischenstop bedienen auch Lufthansa, Air France oder British Airways von Europa aus die indonesische Insel.

SUMMARY OF THE HOTELS

Mustique Villa Rentals

P.O. Box 349
St. Vincent & the Grenadines, West Indies
Telephone: 0 01 / 7 84 / 4 88-80 00
Telefax: 0 01 / 7 84 / 4 88-90 00
villarentals@mustique-islands.com
www.mustique-island.com

The 4,5 square miles in area Caribbean island is located in the South Grenadines.

55 exclusive villas have been designed by famous architects to meet the requirements of their owners. They are revelation for those who harbour unusual dreams about lifestyle. Rates: depending on the number of bedrooms, size and season, rates change from: 3,500 (2 bedrooms) to 40,000 US Dollar (7 bedrooms) and included transfer from the island's airport, a minivan and domestic staff (cook, gardener and housekeeper)

There are many sports facilities on offer, such as an equestrian centre, tennis courts, physiotherapists, professional beauty-centre and a a water sports' centre.

Every Villa has an own talented chef, who offers a spectrum of cooking to suite every palate, from international cuisine to local specialities.

The Grenadines Islands are sunny nearly all the year round. There is always a breeze so it never gets too hot. The air and the water are wonderfully warm throughout the year. Even in the rainy season from June to December, it never rains for very long.

The surrounding airports of the Windward Islands are served by many international airlines. The shuttle from there to mustique is served by Mustique Airways.

Contact in Germany:
Gerlinde Hofbauer
Telephone: 00 49 / (0) 89 / 5 43 95 04
Telefax: 00 49 / (0) 89 / 5 43 97 65
E-mail: mustiquevillas@freenet.de

Sea Cloud

Reservations can be made through a travel agent or direct at
Hapag-Lloyd Kreuzfahrten GmbH
Ballindamm 25
D-20095 Hamburg
Telephone: 00 44 (0) 40 / 30 01 46 00
Telefax: 00 44 (0) 40 / 30 01 46 01
Internet: www.hapag-lloyd.de

The legendary yacht sails the most beautiful cruise areas in the world. Obviously, in the winter it is in the Caribbean, and between May to October in the western and eastern Mediterranean.

22 outside cabins (102.25–145.3 sq. ft) and 10 original cabins (193–861 sq. ft.). All cabins have a marble bathroom with a shower (the original cabins have baths except Nos. 6 and 10), WC, bath robes, hairdryer, toiletries, adjustable air-conditioning, telephone, wardrobe and safe. Particular highlights are the two original Owners' Suite, which have been faithfully restored true to the original. The Sea Cloud provides equipment for snorkelling, water skiing and windsurfing which, depending on the weather, can be used with the agreement of the ship's management.

At lunch and dinner which are taken in the wonderful restaurant, the chefs pamper guests with the finest international cuisine, superb wines, and barbeques on deck.

The Sea Cloud follows the sun throughout the year.

Scheduled flights to and from departure airports are organized by Hapag-Lloyd. Tickets for First or Business Class – provided they are available – carry a surcharge.

The ship has a small, modern, well-equipped hospital and a Ship's Doctor.

Pita Maha Resort & Spa

P.O. Box 198
Ubud 80571, Bali / Indonesia
Telephone: 00 62 / 3 61 / 97 43 30
Telefax: 00 62 / 3 61 / 97 43 29
E-mail: pitamaha@dps.mega.net.id
www.beauty-hotels.com/pita-maha

A few miles outside Ubud, Bali's artists' quarter in the middle of the island.

86 private villas with floor space ranging from 3,230 - 8,610 square feet. All have a private garden, a pool and separate living and sleeping areas. Examples of prices: Pool Villa US$ 400, Royal Villa US$ 550, Royal House US$ 1,500. All rates include breakfast plus 21 % tax and service charge.

Largest and most expensive spa in Bali. Owned and managed by the Shiseido Co. Ltd. of Japan. 15 luxurious private treatment villas, Spa Garden with swimming pools, jacuzzis and saunas.

International cuisine and regional specialities served in 2 restaurants partly in a spectacular position.

Being close to the equator, the temperature is about 30 °C all the year round.

Garuda Indonesia operates flights to Denpasar from several European airports, e.g. Frankfurt, London and Paris. Lufthansa, Air France and British Airways also fly from Europe to the Indonesian islands, but flights include a stopover.